New Perspectives on Sport and 'Deviance'

The everyday makeup of contemporary sport is increasingly characterised by a perceived explosion of 'deviance' – violence, drug taking, racism, homophobia, misogyny, corruption, excess – associated with sport stars, spectators and institutions as represented by the mass media. Whereas once these behaviours may have been subject to the moral judgements of authority, in the face of dramatic socio-cultural change they become more a matter of populist consumer gaze.

In addressing these developments the book provides a new and insightful approach towards the study of 'deviance' in the realm of sport, including:

- a critique of the sociology of sport and deviance
- an exploration of consumptive 'deviance' as the concept that best describes rule breaking in contemporary social formations
- a 're-imagining' of 'deviance' through the metaphor of performativity
- an examination of the uses of the categorisation of 'deviance' for the forces of power and social control

New Perspectives on Sport and 'Deviance' awakens the sociology of sport to the possibilities of re-imagining 'deviance' and in so doing offers a compelling defence of its title. It will appeal both to academics and students of sport, sociology and cultural studies.

Tony Blackshaw is a Senior Lecturer in Social and Cultural Studies in Sport at Sheffield Hallam University. **Tim Crabbe** is a Reader in Social and Cultural Studies in Sport at Sheffield Hallam University.

New Perspectives on Sport and 'Deviance'

Consumption, performativity and social control

Tony Blackshaw and Tim Crabbe

Routledge
Taylor & Francis Group

LONDON AND NEW YORK

First published 2004
by Routledge
2 Park Square, Milton Park, Abingdon, Oxfordshire OX14 4RN

Simultaneously published in the USA and Canada
by Routledge
270 Madison Avenue, New York, NY 10016

Routledge is an imprint of the Taylor & Francis Group

© 2004 Tony Blackshaw and Tim Crabbe

Typeset in Goudy by
Keystroke, Jacaranda Lodge, Wolverhampton
Printed and bound in Great Britain by
TJ International Ltd, Padstow, Cornwall

Every effort has been made to ensure that the advice and information
in this book is true and accurate at the time of going to press. However,
neither the publisher nor the authors can accept any legal responsibility
or liability for any errors or omissions that may be made. In the case
of drug administration, any medical procedure or the use of technical
equipment mentioned within this book, you are strongly advised to
consult the manufacturer's guidelines.

British Library Cataloguing in Publication Data
A catalogue record for this book is available from the British Library

Library of Congress Cataloging in Publication Data
A catalog record for this book has been requested

ISBN 0–415–28884–3 (hbk)
ISBN 0–415–28885–1 (pbk)

For Fiona, Louis, Nick, Sarah and Siobhan

Contents

Preface   ix

PART I
Reviewing perspectives on sport and 'deviance'   **1**

1 Introduction: endings or new beginnings?   3

2 Gladiatorial sociology: grand narratives, deviancy theory and sport   18

3 Beyond grand narratives: poststructuralism, new directions and
   functionalist legacies   42

PART II
Re-imagining theory and 'method'   **61**

4 Understanding sport and 'deviance' in liquid modernity:
   a conceptual 'toolkit'   63

5 'Talking tactics': representing 'deviance' in sport   88

PART III
'Watching the game': evoking the new aesthetics of sport and
'deviance'   **107**

6 *The Premiership*: sporting soap opera and consumptive 'deviance'   109

7 Cruising and the performativity of consumptive 'deviance'   134

8 'Jumpers for goalposts': the community sports agenda and the search
   for effective social control   153

9   Conclusion: they call it 'roasting'   176

    Notes   184
    Bibliography   186
    Index   203

Preface

It is more than four years since the initial idea for this book was conceived. We found ourselves in the middle of writing the material for a new course on sport and 'deviance' with little published help to go on. For the reader, this situation might seem more than a little strange because sociology's enchantment with 'deviance' is of course time-honoured; it is a field of academic study – books, journals and conferences – that has always received a good deal of attention by sociologists, chiefly because of the 'juicy' disposition of the topic area. The difficulty was that although a large amount of literature was there, our preparation was hindered because what there was available paid little attention to sport. This problem was exacerbated by the fact that the theories and concepts available didn't always seem to work very well for explaining the world of sport we wanted to explore – that is the activities, players, institutions and audiences who are both at once haunted and fascinated by 'deviance'. This sense of a 'lack' led us to decide that we really had to develop some of our own theories and concepts in order to add something to the impressive body of work on the sociology of deviance already established, but in a way that would serve as a critical toolkit for other academics and students who are specifically interested in 'deviance' and sport. This book is the published outcome of the work which came as a result of that decision.

This book is then a sociological analysis of the relationship between sport and 'deviance'. However, the book is not about 'deviance' as it is often perceived in the sociology of sport literature, where all too often analyses are sullied by the lingering shadow of structure functionalism,[1] to the extent that the evidence of the belief in 'deviance' ends up being one of an ambivalent kind of cultural force in sport – with its attendant dysfunctions and functions – which turns up time and again.[2] Today we live in a world where much of the behaviour we once called 'deviance' in sport is not merely functional or dysfunctional, it is by definition necessarily and inevitably consumptive and performative – so much of a roller-coaster ride that not only do you not know whether it is the sport itself or the spectacle of 'deviance' that is the main attraction, but also whether or not the 'deviance' being played out is 'real' or 'illusory'. This is the case because much of the time 'deviant' behaviours in sport today manifest themselves less the works of monsters, or statements of 'deviant' identities, than instead ways in which individuals choose to accessorise themselves.

For all these shape-shifting changes we acknowledge that the relationship between power, knowledge and social control should continue to inform the major thrust of contemporary sociologising about 'deviance' in sport. With this in mind this book is both at once a conventional sociology that deals with 'deviance' in the form of the ritualised rule-breaking activities, such as football violence, to the more abhorrent forms of crime against the vulnerable, such as sexual abuse. It is also a sociology that pays respect to the ordinary and the overlooked – what Richard Rorty has described as the 'voices from the far off' – and in doing so it challenges its readers to imagine themselves as the 'deviant' other – in order to better understand the lived reality of that other. Indeed, by dramatising the harsh realities involved in the process of identifying the relations between 'deviance', power, knowledge and social control, this book will attempt to involve the reader by being confrontational – a compelling challenge in itself.

If this book can be read on the one hand as a conventional sociological account, it recognises too that just as the world of sport and 'deviance' has changed, the usefulness of some of the still dominant theories and concepts in the sociology of sport have deteriorated to such an extent that they no longer work as well as they once did. It is simply too often the case that orthodox sociology of sport is over-preoccupied with explaining, accounting for and providing political solutions for 'deviance' as the negative binary opposition of conformity in sport. Indeed, it is as if in relation to understanding 'deviance' in sport, sociology too often merely rolls out some old footage of theory from the past, whence all its old underground and conceptual tricks are reprised: the repeat footage with different soundtracks, new ideas that once trembled on the cusp of unintelligibility, but which now represent nothing more than paeans to a worn-out sociological hegemony. It is the contention of this book that in attempting to understand and explain 'deviance' in sport, sociology has become a bit like an ageing boxer who still knows the right punches and combinations, but can't seem to string them together with any sense of purpose or direction and as a consequence its analyses tend to be more illusion than hit.

One of the major reasons for writing this book then was that we felt the time was right for a reassessment of 'deviance' in the sociology of sport and it is with this task that the book is in the main concerned. We want to argue that in marked contrast to more conventional sociologies in this field of study our approach is more alert to the decline of the modernist project, with its certitudes about the past, the present and the future, along with the rise of 'postmodern' sensibilities, with their deconstruction of what was once understood as the dominant hegemony for an alternative narrative anti-structure, which encompasses a range of alternative discourses. We demonstrate in this book that with its ceaseless omnipotent ability to molest, change and displace our memories, identities and communities, using anxiety, risk, uncertainty and illusion as its essential weapons, capitalism in its liquid modern stage (Bauman, 2000) adopts an array of commodity forms of which 'deviance' is but an important one among many others.

The very term can sound like a perversion, but 'deviance' in sport is of special interest to us because the appetite for it – in the forms of scandals, sex, drugs, choreographed violence and the rest – has never been as keenly evidenced as it is today. Correspondingly, two other major themes loom large in the book. As the reader will discern from engaging with the following analysis, we argue that much 'deviance' surrounding sport today is often less about danger and more about its consumption and performativity: the ersatz corruption of a safe and clean life – 'deviance' without the sleaze, the filth and the sanctions. We argue that 'deviance' in sport is both consumed and performed quite simply because it makes the heart beat faster, and in this book we attempt to capture the central characteristics of the importance of this for the sociology of sport.

One of the most important functions of sociology is its nuisance factor and this book continues with Colin Sumner's (1994) philosophy that all truths concerning 'deviance' are relative. However, its foremost objective is a demand for responsibility in sociology. This is because dealing with the complex ethical dilemmas surrounding what is 'deviance' in sport is made possible only by embracing and dealing with the complexity of the world of sport and the world that chooses to describe it. Accordingly, our approach is invigorated with a sociology that believes that what it accomplishes should be able to tell our 'truths' more convincingly than we are capable of in 'real life'.

Indeed, this book works on the tacit assumption that just as sport is 'real life' driven by an energising imagination, so is sociology. One of the central aims of the book is to make sociology more cultural and as such this study might be called a sociological hermeneutic enquiry; and following the sociology of Zygmunt Bauman we take up the challenge of making hermeneutics more *sociological* by extending the sociological imagination. Our approach also follows Paul Ricoeur's (1991) understanding of hermeneutics, which recognises the inexorable circularity of interpretation: preconceived notions *always* guide explanations and determine interpretive understandings, which in turn define preconceived notions all over again. In trying to knit together a dense array of ideas, themes and concepts, our approach to understanding 'deviance' in sport assumes that every understanding and observation is theory-laden. It also recognises its own limitations.

At the same time the book is a work of the sociological imagination that always engages with both theory and the quotidian of sport. Accordingly, the book turns away from the 'universal' to deal with the 'specific'. The analysis places a premium on the contextuality and contingency of the local and historically specific social practices. However, it recognises too that in developing its own empirically grounded analyses, that what is written in the following pages is not about what 'really' happens in 'real' life, it is about what *we* as sociologists tell *you* the reader happened – often, as Clifford Geertz (1973) once observed, through first-, second-, third-, fourth-order narratives – our own observations, and what *we* make of all of these as interpreters.

That sociology is empirical does not ensure that it must be 'true'. But it is 'true' that all research involves an *invested* kind of performativity (Jones and Stephenson, 1997). The implication that runs as a thread throughout this self-reflexive project is not merely the recognition of the techniques of power and knowledge that underpin the research enterprise, but the idea of the aesthetic of the performativity of the research process and the ways this is connected to much wider cultural tendencies, such as the researchers' own fetishisms and voyeuristic pleasures in researching 'deviance' in sport.

Finally, the reader will see that in the performativity of the writing of our own ethnographic fictions (Rinehart, 1998a), in the final part of the book we are not afraid to borrow from popular culture and we try to be self-consciously cinematic writers. For some stretches of the analysis will seem closer to 'fiction' than to 'fact', but the reader should take care not to confuse the otherworldliness of our writing about 'deviance' in sport through this spurious dichotomy. Ethnographic fiction is not sociology's cheating lover but, more precisely, sociology itself looking in the mirror and recognising that it can still do everything it used to be able to do *and* much more. The trick of ethnographic fiction is that it is able to tell the 'truth' about the social world while not being exactly deceitful, but embellishing that 'truth'. Our point is that sociology shows its magic when it really counts for the reader and it was this that was foremost in our minds when we wrote this book.

Tony Blackshaw and Tim Crabbe

Part I

Reviewing perspectives on sport and 'deviance'

1 Introduction

Endings or new beginnings?

No-one can make sense of the notion of a last commentary, a last discussion note, a good piece of writing which is more than the occasion for a better piece
(Richard Rorty)

It perhaps seems incongruous to be confronted with a book about the sociology of deviance in sport when in the wider realm of orthodox sociology the subject area was pronounced dead a decade ago. Indeed, invoking a Barthesian interpretation, Colin Sumner (1994) in announcing the death of the sociology of deviance set about writing the obituary of the field of study. Sumner is the most important chronicler of the sociology of deviance and his eschatological account suggested that the academy no longer had a part and purpose for the sociology of deviance as its utility had been exhausted (Downes and Rock, 1998). In pronouncing this 'death', the central premise underpinning Sumner's argument was that it had become increasingly impossible to justify the existence of the *concept* of 'social deviance' – whereby what he meant was 'that which is censured as deviant from the standpoint of the norms of the dominant culture' (Sumner, 2001: 89). What *is* could no longer be conceived as either 'good' or 'bad', 'normal' or 'deviant' – it had become merely *is*. The crux of Sumner's argument was that even before the 1990s it had become increasingly impossible to justify the existence of the concept of 'deviance' in a plural world in which no one distinctive meaning of what was supposed to be 'deviant' should be allowed to gain ascendancy. Since no social group should be able to dominate, no person was being dominated in any singular sense, and no ground existed for any one principle of what could or should be constituted as 'deviant'.

As far as Sumner was concerned the efficacy of the sociology of deviance was exhausted once it had been established that there could no longer be any satisfactory or general agreed definition of what 'deviance' is – and therefore no way of being certain we could ever distinguish it. Sumner's conclusion was that human action *only* becomes 'good' or 'bad', 'normal' or 'deviant' when looked at and interpreted from the point of view of some alternative ideological position. Another way of thinking about Sumner's invocation of the 'death of deviance' then was his idea that the ideological constitution of what was tacitly understood as 'deviance' had actually outstripped the theory used to describe it.

If we cast our critical gaze on sport it would appear to do justice to much of Sumner's critique, because 'deviance' seems to reflect an ideologically laden force of its own in sport. Indeed, the popularity of 'deviance' in sport at the level of the popular imagination is certainly undiminished and it continues to keep exploding on the front as well as the back pages. From day to day, television, newspapers and magazines shower us with new stories, facts and figures, views and opinions. In relation to media representations of sport stars, for example, mention the concept of 'deviance' in sport today and any number of visual images spring to mind. Thirty years after the publication of Cohen's (1972) seminal critique, confirmation of the ways in which the mass media construct 'folk devils' and 'moral panics' in sport is still plain to see. For instance, the 'evidence' of the English professional footballer Lee Bowyer's culpability in beating up a young 'Asian' man was, at the time of his court appearances in relation to the matter, unequivocal. The conventional picture painted of Bowyer was that of some sort of monster and depraved maniac: 'a boozing, pot-smoking, violent, racist, cowardly, unapologetic, odious transfer-listed scumbag' to quote one journalistic commentary (Jones, 2003). More severe than even Bowyer's representation in the mass media has been Mike Tyson's metamorphosis from being the 'baddest' to the 'maddest' man on the planet, particularly in the wake of his biting off part of Evander Holyfield's ear.

Of course much of what is understood through these representations is merely posturing, which blurs the distinction between the real and the illusory, but the mass media still hold a powerful ideological significance. Indeed, in the light of what we have learned from the sociology of deviance, such images inevitably lead to certain assumptions about groups and individuals even though they are in reality contested terrain and are in effect discourses which must be understood in the context of the ideological power possessed by the mass media and the exhaustive penetration of media technology into both public places and spaces and individual's personal lives.

It is not merely in the mass media that this continued interest in 'deviance' in sport lies. Undeterred, sociologists too have continued to explore the problematic of both understanding and conceptualising the many practices, activities, situations, performances and problems which abound in sport. Indeed, whatever its public and moral hegemony, sociologists in our field of study have shown that sport has always offered spaces for the pursuit of the 'deviant', from the ritualised rule-breaking activities, such as football violence (see, for example, Dunning *et al.*, 1988; Armstrong, 1998), to the more abhorrent forms of crime against the vulnerable, such as sexual abuse (Brackenridge, 2001). Moreover, whatever we want to call these different forms of 'rule-breaking' behaviour, the sociology of sport has always tried to show that 'deviance' against others always has been and still is evidenced and experienced as 'real' in its consequences for those at its receiving end.

Yet in terms of Sumner's critique, those who continue to invoke the sociology of deviance are not only naïve, but also misconceived. For following the social constructionist logic of Sumner's position, even the most pernicious forms of so-called 'deviance' are inescapably vulnerable to ideological misrepresentation.

Sumner suggested that, for some in the field, there was a need for a neo-marxian recasting of the sociology of deviance, which would rewrite the field anew with its missing hybrid model of praxis and critique based on an egalitarian epistemology. But Sumner was having none of this and he wanted it to be recognised that faced with the realisation of the contingency of *all* ideological representations it had become pointless even to contemplate reconceptualising 'deviance' in sociology. He was unequivocal about this and in the concluding chapter of his book reconfirmed the prognosis by suggesting that:

> the sociology of deviance died in the mid-Atlantic returning home after its disastrous European tour. Its ghost lives on in American sociology courses, but that is none of our business. It is a mere appearance. Its life-force has actually expired. It is an irrelevance how many scholars continue to use it as opposed to how many do not – popularity or unpopularity should never be taken as a test of genuine conceptual vitality. In this case, the decline in the significance of the sociology of deviance is an effect of its conceptual bankruptcy. It no longer reflects the dynamics of our lived history.
>
> (Sumner, 1994: 309)

What we have here then is not simply a critique of the sociology of deviance, but the unequivocal disavowal of a whole subject area which had essentially become, in Sumner's eyes, domesticated because of the realisation that it was no longer possible to immunise even the most reasonable and ethical of perspectives against their own ideologies.

With due respect to Sumner we want to argue in this book that the view that 'deviance' is merely ideology – and everything that implies from a marxian perspective – offers very little else in terms of the justification for abandoning this subject area in sociology other than the conclusion that there really is no such thing as 'deviance', only the vested interests and the beliefs of the powerful. In a nutshell we want to suggest that Sumner's view that the sociology of deviance as ideology led to its final collapse was premature. We are not suggesting that the sociology of deviance is anything but a 'disunited enterprise', to use Downes and Rock's (1998: 21) apt expression, but we want to argue the case for a reflexive sociology which takes into account how the world has changed around it and what implications this has for a sociology of 'deviance' made to the measure of understanding the complex and often ambivalent nature of sport in contemporary times.

As the reader will see from our own account, while following a similar trajectory to Sumner's understanding of 'deviance', it nevertheless has an emphasis on beginnings rather than endings. In order that we can embark on this beginning exercise we first of all need to take a step back from the detailed consideration of our own position in order to provide a thoroughgoing critique of Sumner. This also involves a full consideration of the central tenets of Sumner's justification for 'killing' the sociology of deviance.

The 'end' of deviance thesis

Our first criticism of Sumner's thesis is that it falls for Barthes' (1968) invocation like a lover, most intensely and profoundly. And following Barthes, it seems to us that Sumner misses the point that, very much like the topic of his book, he is himself a concept, the creation of a particular epistemological position rather than the provision of an alternative paradigm for exploring the topic of 'deviance' post-the sociology of deviance. Indeed, it needs to be grasped at the outset that Sumner's thesis must be understood in the context of the time when it was written. In the early 1990s it had become fashionable in sociology to declare the death of anything and everything.

Another major criticism of Sumner's thesis is that he provides merely a top-down theoretical interpretation which understands social 'deviance' as an *object* of enquiry rather than a lived *subjective* experience. While we may live in a society in which Foucault's (1977) panoptical moralising gaze has all but disappeared, people's contingent and subjective lived experiences often mean that they are confronted by the reality and consequences of the pain and suffering which constitute 'deviant' acts and behaviour. It is our argument then, that any rigorous study of 'deviance' needs to begin and end with people's bottom-up, contingent and subjective experiences.

Sumner also has the theoretician's appetite for certainty – that is of a sureness that the sociology of deviance is dead – which is to all intents and purposes at odds with empirical understandings of 'deviance'. Basically, he seeks to kill off the sociology of deviance through a thoroughgoing theoretical approach, but because it is *merely* theoretical his project is inevitably unsatisfactory. There are always issues that seem to evade his grasp, issues which he sees but does not grapple with satisfactorily because they are contingent on times and on places and on those people involved.

These criticisms notwithstanding, Sumner the theoretician makes it very clear that he understood that the sociology of deviance had reached a point in its history when it needed another kind of theoretical understanding, which could only be written successfully through a quite different language. And he assumed that, because of the thoroughly ideological terrain within which he was operating – empirical data were more often than not insufficient to persuade otherwise – only a paradigm change would suffice. So Sumner makes a persuasive case *against* the sociology of deviance, largely on the grounds that it has become increasingly untenable to justify the case *for* the sociology of deviance.

In doing so Sumner invokes the ideas of Foucault to substantiate his case and it would have been more convincing had he enlarged his discussion of Foucault's ideas of discourse and discursive formation to accommodate the weaknesses inherent to the marxian approaches he identified. However, he was not looking to provide some new and authentic position; he realised from Foucault that all positions are 'ideological' and 'subjective'. Sumner set himself the task of reinterpreting 'deviance' in a different way, through a new language: the sociology of censures, which would be used to 'describe a set of negative ideological categories or condensations – a set of social censures which were rooted in everyday social practice and were tied to the processes of regulation within social practice' (Sumner, 1994: 302). This was his vision, which he thought would present his contemporaries with a new and more politically correct language and sociology, which would always be grounded in the quotidian to understand and make sense of what had previously been understood as 'deviance'.

Sumner (1994) offers little else beyond this thumbnail sketch, however, and he never at this point fully explicates what he means by a sociology of censures. He was much more intent on laying to rest the sociology of deviance. And at this juncture Sumner's major justification for the end of deviance thesis was the point that the consensus against which 'deviance' was established and understood had never actually materialised. As he points out, this meant that at all times through the history of sociology the question always remained: deviant, but 'deviant from what?'

The major problem with this aspect of Sumner's thesis is his reliance on hindsight. Essentially, Sumner's argument is present-centred and relies too heavily on retrospective wisdom. As Bauman's (2000) sociology shows, even if modern society in 'its solid and managed phase' never was completely successful in universalising its doctrine, the meta-discourse underpinning the modern project did a pretty good job of inculcating the 'truth' of what Bourdieu (2000) calls the *illusio* and the *lusiones* that there actually was a consensus against which all 'nonstandards' could be measured and understood. Sumner is right in suggesting that there never was such a consensus but what he underestimates is the extent to which people were caught up in and by the modernising game of consensus-making and believing that that game was the *only* game worth playing.

Sumner also underplays the fact that sociology itself was heavily implicated in this process, and as such played a key role in promoting the *illusio* and *lusiones* which maintained the opposition between majority consensus and minority 'deviance'. Indeed, the preservation and perpetuation of capitalism, as conflict theorists from Marx to Bourdieu have demonstrated, has always been and still is reliant on this sort of immoral code of duplicity. And as Bauman (2000) makes clear, the fact was that maintaining this opposition was not only the goal of the powerful but also, ironically, the *raison d'être* of sociology itself.

What is more, and for the purpose of our own analysis of 'deviance' in sport, this 'will to a consensus', despite the contingency and plurality of contemporary social life, still remains a highly significant one to this day. As Webb *et al.* (2002: 26–8) show, the process of maintaining the *illusio* and *lusiones* that sport is 'pure' is often still very much part of both official and non-official discourses which vie to represent the 'truth' about sport, as they attempt to maintain its '"lily-white" values as the only true manifestations of [sport's] undiluted essence'. The major difference now of course is that, as we will illustrate later, it is the discourses of *interpreters* rather than the *legislators* (Bauman, 1987) whose ideas compete to hold sway in the debates about what is 'right' and 'wrong', what is the consensus and what is 'deviant' in sport.

While remaining firmly in the orbit of marxian understandings of 'deviance' Sumner's suggestion of an alternative vocabulary does, none the less, have a difference of emphasis which, while recognising that any 'will' to 'deviance' is an ideological practice, focuses on social censures (Sumner, 1994: 308); since in Sumner's view the only alternatives to a sociology of censures are sterility or the endless repetition of old interpretations which no longer work as well as they once did. In a later publication he explains that the sociology of censures deals with two interrelated issues (Sumner, 2001: 90):

1   to locate, understand and create areas of social agreement which might constitute the basis of a social censure and control for a more healthy, secure and peaceful society, and

2   to expose, criticize and explain social norms and systems of social control which are discriminatory, hypocritical and oppressive in order to enable society where its members are allowed to develop their positive capacities to the full.

On the face of it Sumner successfully breaks away from the limitations of such orthodox marxian thought, most notably in his discussion of the responsibilities implied by a sociology of censures. Yet as will be shown in the following section of this critique, the efficacy of understanding 'deviance' changed with the language employed to describe it. It is our argument that with this sociology of censures the study of 'deviance' became part of a new vocabulary which could not deal with the complexity of an emerging and dominating consumer culture. As we show, once the 'reality principle' and the 'pleasure principle' (Bauman, 2002a: 187) imploded into each other, the firm divisions between 'normalcy' and 'deviance' shattered along with the illusion that 'rule-breaking' behaviour could be understood through a sociology of censures.

The limitations of a sociology of censures in the age of consumerism

From our perspective understandings of what constitutes 'deviance' are complicated all the more once we begin to recognise that today, in many ways, what we often perceive to be 'deviant' is nothing more than a reified commodity form. It is inconceivable that 'deviance' in sport could have found such an excess of commercial favour in the period before the 1980s, but particularly in the years since Sumner wrote his book the demarcation between 'real' 'deviance' and that which has been produced for consumption has blurred the line between 'fact' and 'fiction' as 'deviance' has turned into yet another marketable commodity. Indeed, our own analysis recognises that much so-called criminal activity and so-called 'deviant' behaviour in sport is now just that: all surface, flow and performance without the exit wounds.

Another striking difference between what Sumner understands as the high point of 'deviance' in the 1970s and today is not just the way 'deviance' is staged for consumption and the sense of the spectacular that is often involved, but the mass and the calibre of the audience for it. Since, as the reader will see, it is through marketised images, 'confessionals' and rumours of celebrity 'deviance' in sport that our desires for the 'deviant' other tend more and more to be fulfilled. In a culture in which consumption is paramount, consuming 'deviance' becomes yet another lifestyle choice. The consumption of 'deviance' seeks to capture a sense of the phantasmagoric nature of existence which eludes people in the mundane quotidian of their everyday lives. These phantasmagoria become part of the high altar of consumer capitalism which recall Baudelaire's reflection that consumers are like his children who see everything in a state of newness – they are always drunk.

For us, capitalism now 'needs' irrationality, acts of 'deviance' and impulse and as such the concept of 'deviance' as it is today conceived in the world of sport *does* reflect the dynamics of our contemporary lived condition. Today the 'solid' conventions associated with Freud's concept of the 'reality principle' (1920), which involved forsaking the irrational and postponing pleasure through the constant suppression of the desire for the transgressive and the 'deviant', might be considered to have been replaced by a 'precarised' hybrid existence which is both more intense but at the same time much less sure, lacking a distinctive singular feel. Since while the label of 'deviance' was easily applied in the producer-based capitalism of 'solid modernity' (Bauman, 2000) – with its requirement for self-discipline through the values of asceticism, hard work, thrift and frugality – in the era of 'liquid' consumer capitalism the ideal consumer is not a coherent and self-disciplined individual with a fixed identity, but somebody who can identify with an endless supply of commodity goods; somebody who is always open to new desires and new fantasies including the seductive allure of 'deviance' in sport which nourishes the desiring and fantasising impulses which are both acknowledged and necessary to sustain the mediated capitalist consumer-based economy.

Rather than censuring then, what might be considered as the 'deviance' in, and of sport, provides consumers with a passport, which allows them relatively safely to transgress the boundaries of the permissible, allowing unmitigated access to what is conventionally repressed or forbidden. Through sport it is possible to pursue the different and the 'deviant', from the ritualised and largely socially acceptable extremes of base jumping, white-water rafting and sky diving, through the legitimised violence of the rugby field, boxing ring and ice-hockey arena, and ultimately to the more pernicious forms of crime against the vulnerable, such as sexual abuse.

The sociology of 'deviance' reconfirmed

Part one: the emergence of queer theory

It is ironic that at the very moment Sumner was charting the eclipse of the sociology of deviance, the majority of the so-called 'deviant' theoretical positions in the wider realm of critical theory were shaping a collective political response to the 'normalising gaze' of the consensus under the critical perspective of queer theory. Queer theory was to become the political destiny of all minority studies and not just those relating to gays and lesbians. It emerged from Foucauldian, feminist, gay and lesbian studies' attention to the social construction of categories of, on the one hand, 'normative' and, on the other, 'deviant' sexual behaviour, and in this sense can be understood as a political response to the very same issues which were concerning Sumner in the sociology of deviance.

Indeed, while gay and lesbian studies had emerged in the 1970s and 1980s and had focused largely on questions of homosexuality and heterosexuality, queer theory expanded its critical gaze to focus on anything that fell into 'normative' and self-identified 'deviant' categories, particularly, although not necessarily, sexual activities and identities. Queer theory began to concern itself with any and all forms of practices, activities, situations, performances, behaviours and 'problems' which were considered to be 'deviant', that is, 'queer' and with 'normal' behaviours, identities and the like which define what is 'queer' (by being their binary opposites). Consequently, queer theory expanded the scope of its analysis to all kinds of behaviours, including those that involved 'gender-bending' – as represented by the American basketball player Dennis Rodman – as well as those involving 'queer' forms of sexuality (see for example, Butler, 1990) which were considered to deny the 'norm'.

The major success of queer theory was in shifting the emphasis from the labellers of 'queers', 'deviants' and 'deviance' to the 'queers' and 'deviants' themselves and their own self-identified understandings of what it was about them that was 'queer'. Yet, if this movement, with its Foucauldian epistemology, recognised and rightly challenged the processes of power-knowledge associated with normalising dominant categories, what it also showed us was that self-identified 'queer' or 'deviant' behaviour and identities cannot only be highly desirable but that they often also involve risky behaviours and identities worth pursuing to make life more exciting, worth living.

Part two: the power of the 'name'

Taking a different focus on what has already been discussed, what Sumner's analysis also suggests is that the 'naming' of deviance is not merely a reflection of some reality or an arbitrary label with no relation to that reality, it is rather always an ideological concept that tends to 'fix' different and diverse practices, activities, situations and performances as problems which come to be understood as a 'deviant' reality in a cultural world where there really is a multitude of possible meanings, beliefs and understandings.

As such, what his book is suggesting is that a key problem of the concept of 'deviance' is the power which is invoked in the *naming* of 'deviance' and the inevitability that certain behaviours and practices 'out there' will remain absent from the gaze of the sociology of deviance because they are not recognised as 'deviant' as such. The crimes of the powerful (Box, 1971, 1986) and the decentred nature of much institutional 'deviance' in sport (see, for example, Sugden and Tomlinson, 2003) come to mind here. Sumner does not himself put it this way, but essentially the crux of the problem is that the invocation of the name 'deviance' invariably leads to what Düttman (2002 in Jarvis, 2003) terms 'a theory of illusory concretion', which is the necessary partner of the 'empty proceduralism' surrounding the sociology of deviance. In a nutshell: 'naming' something deviant is not evidence that something *is* deviant or of a consensus that holds good, but invariably it is often an act of 'thinking-without-knowing [which] *decides*, precisely, that it is going to know after all in any case. So it *pronounces*, about various matters of which it is ignorant' (Jarvis, 2003: 45). Sumner's own analysis suggests that the name 'deviance' marks not only a negative dialectics in the marxian meaning, but also as a direct consequence, a massive distortion of the sociological project. This is because the concept too often tends to be *named* rather than explained.

Yet different to Sumner, Düttman is offering a decentred notion of power-knowledge which is concerned with 'the name' and as a logical consequence of this his analysis sets out to demonstrate the impossibility of escaping the power of 'the name'. As we have seen already Sumner's own approach can be seen as an attempt to deal with the 'limited and limiting character of the name' and his solution is to announce 'the death' of the name 'deviance'. What Sumner is not prepared to admit is Düttman's point about the impossibility of escaping 'the name'.

The evidence suggests then that, while Sumner himself has not baulked one bit at bidding an irrevocable farewell to 'the name' deviance, most other sociologists, queer theorists and lay interpreters continue to use the concept. Düttman's point about the impossibility of escaping 'the name' is confirmed further when one considers that Sumner's own attempt to establish a sociology of censures in the place of the sociology of deviance has hardly been a success. As Downes and Rock (1998: 367) point out, the concept of 'deviance' quite simply has not been superseded by 'events, fresh theories, or new ideas'. We should like to argue that what this body of evidence suggests is the key lesson to be learned from Düttman's analysis. Despite Sumner's promulgations there has been no end to the sociology of deviance. There can be no end because the concept of 'deviance' is indelibly part of the sociological imagination.

Quite simply, 'deviance' is a significant concept beside itself. It acts as a vehicle which transmits the fears, fetishisms and fantasies of the individualised society (Bauman, 2001): the uneasy fascination with the irrational, our obsessions and morbid interests with violence, the confessional and all the other desires and activities which make life worth living – all of those things which reveal the immoral and aesthetic thrill of wrongdoing at the moment of their revelation. And what is more, 'deviance' also provides us with a distorting lens of the gaze through which we can look at others and ourselves, scopophilic, warped and kinky, hardly recognisable.

Reconceiving the relativist challenge to the sociology of deviance

In this sense a further key problem with Sumner's thesis is that his understanding of the relativist position is never explicated in sufficient detail. We are not suggesting that following Coakley (1998) he makes the tacit assumption that in our contemporary plural society there are just too many truths. However, because

Sumner never really deals with this issue there are a number of implications for the sociology of deviance.

To begin at the beginning, the major issue is this: interpreters of the relativist position, such as Coakley, mistakenly imply that relativists perceive that there are many truths; that they tend to hold their own definitions of truth; and that they are content with those truths. Jenkins (1995) calls these 'truths without reasons'. Yet this interpretation is misconceived, because following Rorty, truth-making tends in the real world to be a culturally grounded conceptualisation of truth, 'that proves itself to be good in the way of belief, *and good, too, for definite, assignable reasons*' (Rorty in Jenkins, 1995: 125). Today we may carve up the world in different ways and in many respects we live in different worlds, but few of us are naïve relativists as implied by Coakley. In terms of 'real' world understandings of what constitutes 'deviance' in sport what we tend to get are culturally grounded conceptualisations, which consider behaviours, actions, individuals or institutions 'deviant' for explicit and assignable reasons. The 'reality' of 'deviance' is much more complex than we once imagined. What is naïvely understood as the relativist position has been more accurately described as anti-anti relativistic (Bauman, 1999) rather than relativistic. This position is relativist in the sense that it does not rely on universally accepted canons and formalised institutions for debate, but it both accepts and promotes the ideas that 'a never ending conversation' is played out in the arena of culture, where humankind has created its own polity, 'little by little, through ever larger and richer "compounds of opposed values"' (Rorty, 1985 in Connor, 1989: 38).

This position does not deny that in the sociology of sport a number of interpreters are still preoccupied with explaining, accounting for and providing political solutions for 'deviance' as the negative binary opposition of conformity in sport. However, in this book we want to suggest that the study of 'deviance' in sport defies easy categorisation but also that the over-convenient and naïve relativisation of this field of study is to say the least unhelpful. Indeed, beyond this over-simplistic interpretation of 'deviance' lies something more useful to the critically inclined interpreter. And the view that we develop in this book suggests that, if we are properly to understand the contingently constituted nature of 'deviance' in sport, we must also be able to see the 'world as it is' from the context in which this 'deviance' takes place. Indeed, the numerous and different forms of 'deviation' may no longer be understood as 'universal', but they can be considered as both more or less contingent, depending on how the individuals and groups involved navigate between the contingency of their own world and the wider polity we confusingly tend to understand as the world in itself. In Rorty's sense (1986), this entails the ability to recognise the point that ethnocentric 'communities' continually compete for time, space and partnership in what Sumner describes as the 'multi-cultural plurality' in which we live today.

It is too often the case, however, that, in the sociological literature, these 'communities' are in Rorty's (1986) meaning, 'treated just like the rest of us'. Our approach follows Rorty, then, in insisting that 'there are people out there whom society has failed to notice', or in our own terms, has failed to try to empathise with in order to understand where they are coming from. Rorty takes Wittgenstein's linguistic turn one step further to show that both irony and metaphoricity are of vital importance for 'carrying on the conversation' by providing the basis for 'new language games' (Jenkins, 1995: 108). In Rorty's (1991) schema, irony and metaphors are much more than simply explanatory devices, however, they provide the means for the voices from the far off (the 'deviants', the marginal, the outsiders and the strangers) to deconstruct and transcend the 'dominant discourses' of the powerful. Rorty's position is also indicative of the praxiological capabilities of 'continuing the conversation', in the sense that, as discourses brush, collide and intersect with each other, *new* truths emerge from those contingent worlds.

The world of sport itself can also be understood as a wholeheartedly contingent set of worlds. Not *a* world somehow separate from the rest of society, but a meta-discursive world and a series of postulated worlds in which taken-for-granted assumptions about *the* world we over simply tend to understand as 'reality' – with its prevailing norms, values, beliefs, behaviours and actions – are often subverted, changed or distorted.

Adopting Rorty's position for the sociology of deviance then does not mean accepting that 'anything goes'. On the contrary, it means that without the obligation of having to make their work take on an essentialist position, sociologists of sport can get on with the task of constructing their own narratives about the world of sport. For Richard Rorty ethical questions – including questions of what is or is not 'deviance' – must be dealt with in the untidy realm of human interaction rather than in the tidy transcendental realm of universal reason. And it is precisely because the sociologist is now in a stronger position to recognise and make explicit the ideological, the subjective, and the fictive elements in their writings that our understanding of 'deviance' in the social world of sport can be advanced. In Rorty's sense, the challenge is to construct narratives surrounding 'deviance' in sport that work, but which do not claim rights to *the* truth in the essentialist sense; *real theories* that are 'true enough', but which recognise 'that there will never be a final resting-place for thought' (Rorty, 1991: 19). Indeed, contrary to the postulations of some (Gane, 2001), a sociology of deviance made to the measure of our contemporary plural world always refutes the 'legislative moment', as it recognises that there is always something more that can be said. However, it does recognise that we should never shirk from the challenge of holding individuals or institutions responsible for 'deviance' if we have explicit and assignable reasons for doing so.

Our own analyses, as the reader will see in the subsequent chapters, provide interpretive bare bones sketches, rather than a legislative and fully delineated 'truth' about 'deviance', which none the less imply by their very nature an in-built responsibility. The contingent and peripheral nature of this interpretive sensibility is precisely its point: for interpretations are 'truths' which attempt to make meaning of the actions and behaviours of which they can have no definitive understanding. Interpreting a disordered and often bewildering world of sport, but attempting in so doing to muddle through in order to develop sociology as a responsible vocation. It is this sense of partiality which marks the success of a sociology of 'deviance'.

Recasting the sociology of deviance as the sociology of 'deviance'

In is our contention then that we must continue to draw on the concept of 'deviance' in order to keep the conversation going rather than allowing naming-without-knowing to decide and thereafter to arrive at a point of illusory concretion *vis-à-vis* Sumner. Following Düttman's lesson for understanding the story of 'deviance', we recognise that it is not some final resting place or a return to a general concept that should hold sway. Rather what we are suggesting is a revised interpretation of the sociology of deviance as the sociology of 'deviance'. An interpretation that is better suited to understanding the complexity that is the contemporary social world of sport and which recognises none the less that understandings of 'deviance' will always be both contested and tempered by contingency.

Our answer to this predicament is much more challenging than Sumner's argument suggests. For us, it is a waste of time debating whether or not the sociology of deviance is alive or dead. Following Ulrich Beck (2002) it would be perhaps more useful to suggest that the sociology of 'deviance' should better be perceived as a death-in-life zombie category: both alive and yet lifeless, at the same time living and dead. The social world around us has been transformed yet the sociology of deviance has not yet been able to adjust itself to those changes. As such our point is simply this: during the last 20 years or so, just as both the labellers and protagonists of 'deviance' – both individual and institutional – became different creatures, living in a different world, so did the sociology of deviance. And if we wish to carry on trying to understand something about 'deviance', 'deviants' and their motivations, fetishisms, wishes and desires, we need to develop a better understanding of the milieu in which it, they, and us, the sociologists who create it and them, currently operate.

While Sumner combined some excellent historical scholarship with a sociological imagination in order to contemplate the historical trajectory of a doomed concept, the problem is that he never really stopped to consider what the implications of this 'passing away' was for sociology, more generally, and what it might imply for researching and theorising patterns of 'rule-breaking' behaviour in turn of the twenty-first-century western societies.

It is in this context that we have argued in this chapter that the recognition of the problems of ideology need not lead the sociology of deviance to either a theoretical or an empirical impasse. We recognise that the fundamental lesson of marxism for the sociology of deviance was just the point Sumner made in his book: that *every* position is unavoidably ideological. Indeed, Sumner's critique was well attuned to the perils of ideology; that is of taking positions with regard to what is or is not considered to be 'deviant'. The point is that if Sumner recognised that the certitudes we once took for granted in both sociology and the 'world out there' had gradually been eroded and that we have come to admit that 'deviance' was always an ideologically driven social construct, he underestimated the capacity of sociology to unsettle taken-for-granted expectations and assumptions. While

Sumner argued that the sociology of deviance was no longer in a position to give us any answers to the ethical dilemmas associated with 'rule-breaking' activity in the contemporary world where 'anything goes', we want to argue that a sociology of 'deviance' reconceived as a beginning enterprise not only addresses the ethical dilemmas posed by such a situation but also puts some flesh on those questions.

However, what we most opposed with Sumner's approach was his inattention and imperceptiveness to the moral and political problems implied by the position he took. Sumner's eschatological position called our attention to the possibility of an ethical sociology of 'deviance'. But as a result of his conclusions it would seem we are left with two courses of action: to follow his own invocation to 'end' the sociology of deviance and reconceptualise the sociology of deviance as the sociology of censures, or to rethink the sociology of 'deviance' as a beginning enterprise. We are not for the moment suggesting that this is going to be plain sailing, but the one sure thing about this journey is going to be the potency of its intellectual, theoretical and empirical challenge. It is with this in mind that we place inverted commas around the concept of 'deviance', not only to remind the reader of its 'undecidability', its shape-shifting quality, but also to reflect the contested nature of its use value as it is contingently stressed in our writings.

In short, Sumner's is an erudite analysis, but he wears his learning too lightly and we believe that he shirked from re-imagining the sociology of deviance at a time when it demanded to be challenged, stretched and redefined; and he left this task to others. Our task, in this book then is to reconceive the sociology of 'deviance' as a beginning enterprise (Said, 1975) which not only enables us to consider that what it means to hold values is always open to question, but which also suggests that answering ethical dilemmas surrounding what is 'deviance' in sport is made possible only by embracing and dealing with the complexity of the world of sport and the world that chooses to describe it. As Bauman's (2000: 213) critical project shows, if sociology in its twentieth-century form was too preoccupied with the circumstances of conformity, obedience and consensus-making, the challenge facing sociology today is the matter of choice between taking *responsibility* as its focus or *bystanding* and 'taking shelter where responsibility for one's action need not be taken by the actors'. The aim of our approach then is to create a disorderly inquietude out of what has already been written about the sociology of deviance; and a new beginning rather than an end fulfils this task.

Yet in resurrecting the sociology of 'deviance' in sport we do so acknowledging that our work will always itself be in effect incomplete. The combination of this requirement with the responsibilities of 'never ending conversation' suggested by Rorty (1979) and the challenge of Bauman's (1987) hermeneutics presents a reinvigorated discourse for the sociology of 'deviance', which derives its strength from its essential incompleteness. Our approach, then, confronts pell-mell the substantive problems of the sociology of deviance highlighted by Sumner but with a commitment to a responsible sociology, which exposes itself to a vulnerability that we believe should be the mark of all meaningful theorising. Within our scheme of thought, then, instances which constitute our interpretations of 'deviance' are justified empirically, theoretically and ethically.

We move in our intellectual constructions from a beginning which always resolves to be responsible, and this book is an indictment of individuals, systems of power-knowledge and bystanders whose actions and complicity perpetuate oppression and exploitation within and without sport. It is also a demand for a never-ending dialogue between those who promulgate seemingly the most irreconcilable interpretations of 'deviance' as well as a constant questioning of ourselves, our tacitly accepted assumptions and the institutions that surround us. What is perhaps the most important conclusion to be drawn from this reinventing of the sociology of 'deviance' as a beginning enterprise, then, is in refusing the more comfortable role as bystander to take the active responsibility of engaging in unearthing and understanding even the most fiercely contested understandings of what is or is not 'deviance' in sport. Sociology will for sure never be value-free, but then again neither will it have become valueless.

Framework for the book

The book itself is divided into three parts. The first, entitled, *Reviewing perspectives on sport and 'deviance'* examines the range of literature which has engaged with the concept of 'deviance' and particularly those texts which have given attention to the sphere of sport and leisure. Our intention is to provide the reader with a comprehensive tour through the available scholarly work in this field while offering our own critical insights into the limitations of what has come before. We begin with a review of the relationships between the study of 'deviance' in sport and the key competing theoretical blocks associated with conventional sociology. In this review we develop the argument that much of the work in this field has been heavily influenced by a functionalist paradigm which has intruded into both conventional understandings of 'deviance' and the social 'functions' of sport itself. From here we move on to discuss some of the more recent and insightful developments associated with poststructuralist thought, beginning with the work of Michel Foucault before reviewing the contribution of the concepts of 'liminality', 'edgework' and 'abnormal' or 'wild' leisure which have derived from leisure studies and which provide a basis for consideration of the individualised pursuit of the 'risky' and the 'dangerous' which underpins our own analysis.

The second part of the book, entitled *Re-imagining theory and 'method'* provides the reader with an insight into our own theoretical and methodological orientation. Through an invocation, principally, of the work of Zygmunt Bauman and Jean Baudrillard we develop a range of concepts, which we have already alluded to in this chapter and which underpins our later analysis. We introduce the notion of liquid modernity and the significance of concepts such as individualism, 'the into', consumer culture and celebrity before evincing the usefulness of the notions of consumptive 'deviance', performativity and seduction for the task at hand. In Chapter 5 we then consider the methodological issues associated with researching the contemporary manifestations of sporting 'deviance' in liquid modernity through a critical consideration of Sugden and Tomlinson's (1999b) engagement with 'gonzo' techniques and our understanding of their efficacy for our own project.

In the last part of the book entitled '*Watching the game*': *evoking the new aesthetics of sport and 'deviance'* we present our own empirical findings and interpretive analysis relating to the three key concepts of consumptive 'deviance', performativity and social control developed in Part II. The first of the three chapters deals with consumptive 'deviance' in relation to the leading English football competition, *The Premiership*, through the metaphor of the soap opera. The second chapter takes us inside and reveals the verisimilitude of the performative social world of street 'cruising'. The final chapter in this section considers the shifting basis for the social control functions of sport in the context of the consumerist trends associated with the movement from 'solid' to 'liquid' modernity. We then seek to draw together our concluding thoughts in the final chapter of the book.

2 Gladiatorial sociology
Grand narratives, deviancy theory and sport

The benefits of athletic and other manly (sic) exercises, from an educational as well as a recreative point of view, are now very generally recognised. There is no better means of promoting a healthy action of the body or of bidding defiance to the doctor than a moderate indulgence in sports and pastimes. But not only are these exercises of supreme importance in maintaining a vigorous state of health in our boys, they have also a peculiar and decided value in what may be called a moral sense. . . . 'A boy', says Mr. Lyttelton, 'is disciplined by athletics in two ways: by being forced to put the welfare of the common cause before selfish interests, to obey implicitly the word of command, and act in concert with the heterogeneous elements of the company he belongs to; and secondly, should it so turn out, he is disciplined by being raised to a post of command, where he feels the gravity of responsible office and the difficulty of making prompt decisions and securing a willing obedience'.

(Cassell, not dated: iii)

Introduction

Despite the antiquity and inherent sexism of the language in this passage from a late nineteenth-century edition of *Cassell's Book of Sports and Pastimes* it is clear that its sentiments still resonate with much of the thinking about the role of sport within contemporary western social formations. Without necessarily seeking to do so, social considerations of sport have tended to be framed by structure functionalist narratives such as this which emphasise what sport does *to* people and *for* 'society'. In this sense we want to argue that the sociology of sport is heavily implicated in the reification of the kinds of social distinctions and judgements which underpin our present day 'understandings' of what it is to be 'deviant' in sport.

To a large extent the lack of maturity which has blighted much of the sociology of sport as a sub-discipline has meant that studies have tended to be framed by dominant popular and moral discourses, which emphasise the status of sport as an antidote to 'deviance', or which rely on theoretical frameworks developed outside the study of sport itself. In many respects academic enquiries into sports-related 'deviance' have been forced to hang on to the coat tails of wider theoretical considerations of 'deviance', power and social control. So in a situation where Downes and Rock (1998), whose book *Understanding Deviance* is widely regarded as a key text for the study of deviance, declare that 'functional analysis refuses to be struck from the sociological canon' (p. 94) it is not surprising that functionalist assumptions often lurk within those approaches favoured by theorists of sport, even where they are not acknowledged. Indeed, given that the sociology of deviance itself emerged out of the functionalist-inspired dichotomisation of the 'normal' and the 'abnormal', this is a legacy that may be inextricably bound to the very terminology of 'deviance' itself.

As such there is a functionalist legacy which extends across the theoretical boundaries established within the field of sociology and more particularly the sociology of sport which provides the focus for this chapter. In Chapter 3 we go on to consider the contribution of poststructuralist perspectives and the wider challenge to the grand narratives or theoretical blocks of sociological thinking considered here. In doing so, we remain attentive to the continuing discursive power of functionalist assumptions in underpinning the emergence of both modern sport and conventional theories of 'deviance'.

Foundation stones: Durkheim, structure functionalism and 'anomie'

In the period immediately before, during and after the Second World War functionalist perspectives could be considered as almost paradigmatic of the field of sociology. The paradox associated with its former domination of the discipline is that in the period since, functionalism has been subjected to almost universal critique and ridicule whilst simultaneously retaining a tacit, if concealed, presence within more recent theoretical developments, particularly in relation to the study of 'deviance' and within the realm of sport. The ubiquitous 'presence' of functionalist thought is principally related to the status of its leading exponent, Emile Durkheim, as one of the founders of modern sociology and his assertion that crime and 'deviance' are inevitable, normal and indeed healthy (or 'functional') for society (1964 [1895]).

For Downes and Rock (1998) the main tenets of functionalism are uncontentious. Namely, that societies can be understood as systems whose parts should be examined in terms of their interrelationships and contribution to society as a whole. In his classical sociology, *The Division of Labour in Society* (1938 [1893]), Durkheim argued that modern societies evolved from their simple, non-specialised largely agrarian form, which he called mechanical, towards a more highly complex, specialised industrial form, called organic. For Durkheim, in the former kind of society people tended to behave and think comparatively alike, perform more or less the same work tasks and have the same group-oriented goals. However, he stressed that in organic modern societies, people are no longer tied to one another to the same extent and that social bonds tend to be more impersonal.

Durkheim also argued that, as work becomes more complex in the course of the transition from mechanical to organic societies, it is possible to distinguish between abnormal and normal forms of labour. For most people work will be experienced as normal, but there is the possibility that in 'exceptional' circumstances work will take on abnormal forms. As Rojek (2000) points out, Durkheim identified three forms of abnormal work. First, he felt that sudden societal change could give rise to what he called the *anomic division of labour*. Anomie refers to a breakdown of social norms and it is a condition where norms no longer control the activities of members in society. With the *anomic division of labour* also comes the *uncoordinated division of labour* whereby individuals are affected by social and economic upheaval to the extent that they cannot find their place in work because there are not yet any clear rules to help guide them. Third, when individuals are assigned to jobs not fitting to their skills and interests through the *forced division of labour* this is also likely to bring about greater anomie. In a nutshell, Durkheim was suggesting that changing conditions of work can lead to both dissatisfaction and conflict. In terms of its specific significance for the study of 'deviance' this concern with 'anomie' was developed in relation to a study of the ultimate 'deviant' act, *Suicide: A Study in Sociology* (1952 [1897]). In this work Durkheim argued that suicide was inversely related to the degree of integration in society.

From this position Durkheim's key concern was to analyse the prospects of securing social cohesion in the face of rapid social and economic change. In resolving this problem, he conceived of the social world through the metaphor of a biological organism and the use of similar terms to those employed by scientific investigations of the natural world. Notions of 'normalcy' and 'pathology' were offered as substitutes for 'health' and 'disease' such that Durkheim proffered that 'crime is normal . . . It is a factor in public health, an integral part of all healthy societies' (1964 [1895]: 67).

Crucially then, functionalists' positivistic concern with *science* and the broad formal workings of society left them without a theory of 'deviance' as such, since 'deviance' was only deemed worthy of consideration because of its role in maintaining the wider social system and 'its ability to illustrate the latent functions of what seemed incapable of having any such function' (p. 95). Functionalists conceive of 'normal' or 'functional' levels of crime whilst viewing an absence or excess of crime as pathological, resulting in turn in social stagnation or breakdown. It is through the awareness of the threat that crime poses that societal norms and values are reinforced. For Mead this re-establishment of social order is enacted in dramatic form through the subjection of criminals to a form of punitive justice (1918).

Whilst functionalism has faced heavy criticism for its apparent failure to account for change and avoidance of any conceptualisation of structural conflict, a key contribution which emerges from this perspective is an awareness of societal complexity and the extent to which 'deviant' behaviour can overlap with the conventional and 'normal' even when inspired by similar moralities and motivations. Its unpopularity is however bound up in a wider failure to grapple with the complexities in social life that it reveals in terms of everyday lived experience, since issues are only evaluated in their own context. As Mary Douglas argues, functionalism:

> depends on a form of sociological determinism that credits individuals with neither initiative nor sense. It was partly for this failing that sociological

functionalism has been in low repute for the last thirty years. It had no place for the subjective experience of individuals willing and choosing. To suppose that individuals are caught in the toils of a complex machinery that they do not help to make is to suppose them to be passive objects, like sheep or robots.

(1986: 32)

Nevertheless, as a constitutive element of the tendency towards dichotomisation within sociological thinking its presence has remained within many associated debates, both contemporary and historical, which 'returns us to the most ancient antinomy of all: that good can be known only in relation to evil, its mirror image' (Downes and Rock, 1998: 103). As such, from this perspective, 'deviance is not just what is left over from conformity: it is inextricably bound up with the preconditions for conformity to exist' (ibid.: 106).

Like sociology, the realm of sport might similarly be considered as a legislative project (Bauman, 1987) which has sought to establish societal norms and reveal the 'deviance' of the minority whilst setting itself the task of facilitating conformity to shared values and rules. Despite being increasingly contested (Kenyon, 1986), it is for this reason that it is widely held that the sociology of sport as a sub-discipline has been heavily influenced by and has clung on to a series of structural–functionalist assumptions, long since marginalised from the sociological mainstream (Barnes, 1995) and wider critical discourse. This is most clearly evidenced in the collection of essays in Lushchen and Sage's *Handbook of Social Science of Sport* (1981).

The most pertinent strands of functionalist thinking for the sociology of sport appear to have been Talcott Parsons' functional imperatives model (1966) and Robert Merton's (1938) reworking of Durkheim's theory of anomie which have been applied to sport in relation to its role within the 'socialisation process' and the production of 'deviant behaviour' (see Loy and Booth 2000 for an extended discussion). In part this is related to Spencer's (1861) original endorsement of the Victorian concept of 'muscular Christianity' (see Money, 1997) which advocated approval for the moral value of sports and games and set the tone for the missionary zeal with which 'modern' sports were developed over the course of the following century; a perspective which is elegantly articulated in the quotation from *Cassell's Book of Sports and Pastimes* with which we began this chapter.

In keeping with this position a number of North American studies have provided some empirical support for the notion that participation in sport serves as a deterrence to delinquency and 'deviance' (Schafer, 1969; Buhrmann, 1977; Hastad et al., 1984). As such, whilst there remains little definitive evidence of a direct causal relationship between involvement in sports, moral outlook and criminal or 'deviant' behaviour (Long and Sanderson, 2001; Collins et al., 1999; Snydor, 1994; Robins, 1990; Coalter, 1989), this perspective retains its rhetorical authority on many social policy agendas. Agendas which are at least implicitly related to functionalist perspectives which see sports, in Parsonian terms, as social systems with important socialising influences (Stephenson, 1975; Heinila 1969; Luschen, 1969) or, in Merton's terms, as offering alternative sources of reward which mitigate against the strain towards anomie and 'deviant' behaviour caused by structural imbalances in society (Luschen, 1976; Loy, 1969).

Robert Merton's work originally refined Durkheim's notion of anomie as a state of 'normlessness' brought about through dramatic social change in the face of the apparent failure to realise the American dream of self-determination and popular affluence during the economic depression of the 1930s. Acknowledging growing aspirations prompted by the emergence of mass production and advertising, in contrast to Durkheim's focus on social change, Merton argued that anomie was created by a social structure that holds out the same goals to all its members without giving them equal means to achieve them. The result being a 'strain to anomie' as distinct from conformity. This was illustrated through four types of deviance distinguished through a matrix of acceptance/rejection of societal goals such as 'money success' and socially accepted means of realising those goals such as hard work or education (Merton, 1938).

Under this model, which retains clear parallels with Durkheim's study of suicide, the first strain was named *innovation* which involves the use of illegitimate means to attain culturally accepted goals, or in sporting terms 'cheating'. The second strain, *ritualism*, is characterised by the opposite formulation whereby an attachment is made to the institutional means at the expense of achieving cultural goals, when considered in sporting terms, fruitlessly 'playing by the rules' or advocating that it is the taking part and not the winning that counts. *Retreatism* involves the rejection of both goals and means, as characterised by 'dropping out' or non-participation. Finally, *rebellion* is seen as involving a similar rejection of goals and means but also the attempt to replace them with alternatives. Within the realm of sport individualised 'extreme' sports or the Gay Games which emerged in opposition to the perceived heterosexism of mainstream sport provide good examples.

Merton's key empirical observation was that given the greater disparity between cultural goals and the means to achieve them at the lower end of the social hierarchy, deviance is inversely related to social status. This conclusion has produced a compelling criticism such that in Box's view Merton reduces anomie theory to one of 'relative deprivation' (1971: 105–6). Furthermore, such a positivist, over-arching theory offers an over-essentialised account of cultural goals and means of attainment whilst failing to account for the complexities involved in understanding the origins, forms and consequences of 'deviant' behaviour. Crucially for labelling theorists, whilst the theory may account for the *forms* of 'deviance' it does not account for why certain *persons* or *populations* are termed 'deviant'. Most pertinently for us though this approach fails to account for the individualism, diversity, contingency, uncertainty, immediacy and ambivalence that characterises contemporary social formations. In such conditions it is hard to conceive of collectively understood cultural goals in anything other than the most general sense. Indeed in the sporting sphere, where aspirations and the means to achieve them are increasingly wrapped up in mediated representations of celebrity and superstardom, the overnight achievement of untold wealth and fame might generate strain just as readily as deprivation.

'Mean' meanings: interpretive sociology, figurationalism and the legacy of functionalism in discussions of sport

In contrast to the scientific positivism of functionalism, interpretive sociology derives from hermeneutics, or the philosophy of interpretation of meaning, although it is most commonly associated with the work of Max Weber, who along with Durkheim and Marx is widely considered to be one of the founders of modern sociology. Weber was concerned with achieving an interpretive understanding of human action which recognised it as 'social insofar as by virtue of the subjective meaning attached to it by the acting individual or individuals, it takes account of the behaviour of others and is thereby oriented in its course' (1947: 88). Yet whilst this position has proven to be extraordinarily influential within the development of sociology as a discipline it is the sociologies of 'everyday life' and more particularly symbolic interactionism that have proven most pertinent to the study of 'deviance' and the sociology of sport. Indeed, symbolic interactionism was the dominant perspective within the sociology of deviance during the 1960s and early 1970s until it was superseded by the more critical accounts that we will consider later.

Symbolic interactionists, following the path of their antecedents within the early-twentieth century Chicago school (Park and Burgess, 1925), have been concerned with the descriptions of the full range of social worlds, or subcultures, occupied by street corner gangs to beach-bums and football hooligans. Crucially, they are concerned with the interactions that go on within those social worlds and a search for the meanings that those involved give to their actions as revealed by anthropological participant observation, or 'ethnography'. Within this scheme there is an understanding that meanings are established subject to constraints, principal amongst which are the names and symbols upon which definitions are built. As Howard Becker articulated in his classic study, *Outsiders: Studies in the Sociology of Deviance*:

> Social groups create deviance by making the rules whose infraction constitutes deviance, and by applying those rules to particular people and labelling them as outsiders. From this point of view, deviance is not a quality of the act the person commits, but rather a consequence of the application by others of rules and sanctions to an 'offender'. The deviant is one to whom that label has successfully been applied; deviant behaviour is behaviour that people so label.
> (Becker, 1963: 9)

As we will see later this position had a profound influence on the early radical criminology of the Birmingham Centre for Contemporary Cultural Studies (BCCCS) and the work of Cohen (1971, 1972) and Young (1971) in particular, but interactionists should not be confused with radical criminologists. For whilst radical criminologists' conception of social structure demands political action and transformation, interactionists do not recognise the existence of a self-evident superstructure. Instead they are motivated by a desire to observe people doing things in the quotidian and providing detailed revelations of the complex processes through which 'deviant' practices emerge outside of fixed structures.

As such, emerging from the work of Greg Stone (1955, 1957) and colleagues at the University of Massachusetts during the 1970s, early interpretive studies of sport subcultures tended to emphasise the significance of 'agency' and the concept of 'career' over 'structure' (Ball and Loy, 1975). Hermeneutic approaches have been employed in a number of studies considering media coverage of high-profile 'deviant' sporting incidents (see Donnelly, 2002) but most interpretive studies, influenced by Clifford Geertz's concept of 'thick description' (1973), have tended to focus on the apparent contradictions of participants' actual behaviours which are seen to both challenge and reproduce dominant ideologies. For example, Beal's analysis of skateboarding subcultures (1995) reveals how the practices of these groups challenge mainstream values such as competition, at the same time as reproducing sexist male cultural forms. For Peter Donnelly, arguably the leading exponent of subcultural analyses of sport in North America (1985, 1993), the relationship between dominant cultures and the resistance embodied in subcultures is fluid. Oppositional characteristics change over time depending on the dominant cultures' willingness to incorporate subcultures.

Along with Peter Donnelly (2000), Jay Coakley similarly claims to adopt a largely 'interactionist' perspective in focusing on sport and the concept of social-isation, emphasising a two-way process through which people make decisions that shape their own lives. In this sense, in the midst of the wider paradigmatic conflicts within the sociology of sport, Coakley has emerged as the leading exponent of attempts to synthesise approaches, particularly in relation to the study of 'deviance'. Ultimately, Coakley rejects the universalism of functionalism and what he refers to as 'conflict' perspectives by revealing a more complex interactive process in which sports are seen 'as sites for socialisation experiences, not causes of social-isation outcomes . . . [or] changes in the character traits of athletes or spectators' (1998: 102). Nevertheless, a critical appraisal of this work reveals the traces of functionalist perspectives or the emergence of a 'neo-functionalist' position articulated through notions of 'positive' and 'negative' character traits (1998: 113) and a rather limited reappraisal of positivist notions of 'deviance' in sport, generally, which do not disrupt the search for effective 'control'.

Coakley's approach makes some grand claims on the basis of an appreciation of the difficulties of interpreting 'deviance' in sport but ultimately delivers little in the way of theoretical insight. He suggests that there are two main ways in which 'deviance' in sport has been theorised: the absolutist – 'its either right or wrong' – and the relativist – 'it all depends on who makes the rules' – approaches (1998: 148–9). The absolutist approach is represented as structure functionalist, laying emphasis on the identification of 'deviance' as a deviation of behaviour from a predetermined social norm. By contrast the relativist position is represented in an over-simplified and theoretically naïve fashion as emanating from conflict theorists who present 'deviance' as a 'label' relating to certain behaviours or people which are identified as 'bad' or undesirable on the basis of rules made by people in positions of 'power'.

For Coakley, who in this instance appears to consider 'sport' independently of its wider social context, the main problems with these conceptualisations is that they ignore 'deviance' which involves an overcomformity to rules and norms, or 'positive deviance' (Hughes and Coakley, 1991), and do not account for the ways athletes use these norms to evaluate themselves and others. As such, Coakley offers an alternative schema which draws on what he calls a 'critical normal distribution approach' to distinguish between 'positive deviance' involving overconformity or unquestioned acceptance of norms, and 'negative deviance' involving under-conformity or a rejection of norms.

Ultimately though, this position echoes with Durkheim's assertion that when 'the crime rate drops noticeably below the average level' the forces of social control have become too strong whilst criminal 'excess is undoubtedly morbid in nature' (1964: 66–72). Coakley's position similarly produces two ends of a continuum which in their extreme manifestations are seen to lead to fascism (or excess control) and anarchy (excess deviance) on either side of the 'normal' accepted range of behaviour (1998: 151). This position might also be related to Merton's strain theory, with 'positive deviance' identified as a form of *innovation* and 'negative deviance' an example of *retreatism*. This criticism is anticipated by Coakley (Hughes and Coakley, 1991), who suggests that rather than rejection of accepted means, 'positive deviance' involves an 'overdetermined' commitment to both goals *and* means. If this is the case it is hard to see how any boundary between 'norms' and 'positive deviance' can be established at all, since no transgression is implied. From our perspective it would seem that for anyone fitting the dubious category of the 'positive deviant' the 'normal' means to achieve goals are insufficient and in need of augmentation or *innovation*. Otherwise the category is surely left redundant.

Whilst undoubtedly showing a more sophisticated appreciation of the varieties of 'deviance' in sport than many other studies, Coakley's approach is ultimately too abstract, offering an objectivist, top-down analysis which (despite his interactionist credentials) essentialises certain types of 'deviant' behaviour and their sources. Through reliance on the available literature there is an uncritical identification of certain forms of 'off the field' behaviour including the rather vaguely defined concepts of delinquency, academic cheating, alcohol use and sexual assault as examples of 'negative deviance'. Similarly, drawing on the work of Ewald and Jiobu (1985) relating to the addiction-like overconformity to norms in sport, self-injurious overtraining (Nash, 1987), unhealthy eating strategies (Franseen and McCann, 1996) and a willingness to play sports regardless of pain and injury (Nixon, 1993, 1996; Young and White, 1995) are identified as examples of 'positive deviance' when performed in pursuit of competitive sporting 'success'.

In this sense there is an assumption of the pre-eminence of the 'sport ethic' which underpins the analysis. The belief systems which are seen to constitute this sports ethic (Coakley, 1998: 152–3), which it is suggested has become part of the mindset and culture of athletes, states that competitors:

- make sacrifices for the game
- strive for distinction
- accept risks and play through pain
- accept no limits in the pursuit of possibilities

but ignores the point that most people in sport are not involved at an élite or even seriously competitive level and that even those who are will not necessarily blindly follow the logic of the 'sport ethic'. Indeed, it is clear that contemporary social theorists from the sociological mainstream, including Bauman (2001), Giddens (1991) and Beck *et al.* (1994), argue that people are guided by a discourse of individualism and that they are reflexive individuals who are guided by their own will rather than meta-discourses such as the sports ethic. The point that we want to develop is that whether or not behaviour is considered 'deviant' – 'positive' or 'negative' – will always be contingent on the context in which the 'act' takes place and the interpretations of it which follow.

In this light Snyder's study of 'deviance' among college athletes, while drawing on aspects of Coakley's framework and Durkheimian notions of group solidarity, is more firmly grounded within the Weberian interpretive tradition (Snyder, 1994). In an interpretive consideration of the causes of burglary among a group of college athletes Snyder rejects the functionalist 'sport builds character' dictum in drawing on McCall and Becker (1990) to reveal the contingent, fluid nature of interaction between the actors in particular social situations. Crucially, invoking Lyng's (1990) notion of 'edgework' and Csikszentmihalyi's (1975) concept of 'flow' which we discuss further in the next chapter, he alludes to the 'motivation to commit some crimes for the thrill of it' (1994: 243). Asserting that 'behaviour that appears to others as irrational is subjectively defined as fun, play, thrilling and exciting. In some respects this is consistent with Geertz's classic interpretation of the Balinese cockfight in which he argues that:

> it is in large part because the marginal disutility of loss is so great at the higher levels of betting that to engage in such betting is to lay one's public self, allusively and metaphorically, through the medium of one's cock, on the line. And though to a Benthamite this might seem merely to increase the irrationality of the enterprise that much further, to the Balinese what it mainly increases is the meaningfulness of it all.
>
> (Geertz, 1973)

This notion of the 'quest for excitement' (Elias and Dunning, 1986) has also been a cornerstone of figurational sociology which has attempted to offer a sustained theorisation of one aspect of 'deviance' in sport, namely violence. Figurational sociology stems from the work of the German sociologist Norbert Elias and was built up around a group of researchers at the University of Leicester in the UK. It is not a 'new' school of thought, but a meta-theoretical synthesis of elements of Comte, Durkheim, Marx, Simmel, Weber and Freud. It places an emphasis on how the present has emerged out of the past whilst the concept of figuration itself refers to the webs of interdependence which link and both constrain and enable the actions of individuals. From this perspective the long-term structure and dynamics of figurations cannot be explained solely in terms of the properties of individuals or 'classes'. Rather, power relations are seen as a structural feature of all human interdependencies with networks marked by a series of power balances that contain elements of co-operation and conflict.

It is these interdependent polarities or 'tension-balances' which are regarded as helping not only to explain the dynamics of sport but also its appeal to human beings and their 'quest for excitement'. This ties in with Elias' concept of the civilising process (1994) which, at least in the UK, emerged as a paradigmatic, if increasingly challenged, concept during the 1980s and early 1990s, in relation to sociological discussions of violence in sport (see Dunning and Rojek, 1992). Elias was concerned to trace the development of both the personality structure of individuals and the social standards that have been formed in European societies since the Middle Ages. He suggested that changes in manners and etiquette revealed a trend towards greater control over expressiveness and emotion including a progressive refinement of outward manners, a strengthening of the thresholds of shame, embarrassment and repugnance and a gradual internalisation of self-restraint and feelings of guilt and remorse. In a similar vein to Lyng's 'edgework' (1990) and Rojek's 'wild leisure' (2000) this was also seen to involve a transfer of emotions from direct participation in acts of aggression and violence to 'mimetic' activities, the mimicry of 'danger' and the increasing preference for the visual pleasure of witnessing more controlled acts in the sports arena (Smith, 1983).

Through a focus on the exemplar of the English football hooligan those who continue to indulge in public violence and displays of the body were then seen as the antithesis of the 'respectable' or 'civilised'. In contrast to the work of Peter Marsh whose social psychological ethogenic approach concluded that much of what is referred to as violent disorder is, in fact, highly ritualised orderly behaviour constrained by tacit social rules (Marsh *et al.*, 1978), the 'Leicester school' identified the rise of 'football hooliganism' as being predominantly related to 'uncivilised' behaviour within the 'rough' working class (Dunning *et al.*, 1988). It is suggested that this grouping has been less influenced by the civilising process and been the victims of a 'decivilising spurt' that produced wider social inequalities in the period since the 1960s.

Employing Suttles' notion of ordered segmentation as originally applied to Chicago street gangs (1968), in the *Roots of Football Hooliganism* Dunning *et al.* stress the need to focus on the social relationships typically generated by the life experiences of people from 'lower working class communities' which are regarded as being characterised by relatively high levels of open violence (1988). Rather patronisingly, they argue that members of the 'rougher' working class traditionally place strong emphasis on ties based on kinship and locality, display hostility towards outsiders, and find it normal for boys to form street corner gangs that fight with others, since for them fighting is one of the few available sources of excitement, meaning and status. According to Armstrong and Harris then 'the basis of the argument . . . is that *the* significant factor in hooligan behaviour is the generation of violence in a particular sub-cultural environment' (1991: 431).

However, whilst Elias's underlying metaphysics implies that football hooligans will be drawn from specific elements of the social hierarchy, Armstrong's (1998) research with *Blades* 'hooligans' in Sheffield suggests that such violence is very much contingent upon time and context, rather than being a universal attribute of particular sections of working-class men. As a vociferous critic of the 'Leicester school' researchers, Armstrong's work suggests that despite their efforts to overcome the duality of structure and agency, the figurationalists' synthesis emphasises similarity rather than difference, fixity rather than contingency; an incongruity that undermines and disrupts the coherent order of the concept of the civilising process.

As Blackshaw (2002) has argued elsewhere, for Armstrong, without stating it as such, figurationism seems to be all too typical of the arrogance that pervades modern, legislative reason. He seems to be arguing that the figurationalists have corrupted intellectual work on football hooliganism in order to make it fit their rationalistic, linear form of reasoning. He implies that Dunning *et al.'s* arguments are weak because they subscribe to universal truth claims (figurationalism) and are logocentric (the theory of the civilising processes).

For us, and for different reasons, neither figurationalism nor Armstrong's interpretive position provides an appropriate model of intellectual enquiry for the sociology of sport to pursue as they each reflect the two extremes of the continuum across the intellectual activity of the field of study. With regard to the former, this is quite simply because the metaphysical structure that figurational sociology has inherited from Norbert Elias demands that interpretation be made secondary and subservient to its theory. Only once the break with the 'master' trend of the theory of the civilising processes is recognised can both continuity and change be seen to operate through a plurality of socially, culturally, politically and economically determined logics, which may be 'progressive' or not.

At the same time, what Blackshaw (2002) describes as Armstrong's apocalyptic anthropology can be criticised as a programme of interpretation which offers only limited new theoretical developments. Nevertheless Armstrong's approach works better for us than the figurationalist's because its mode of enquiry is thoroughly self-absorbed and the autobiography of Armstrong, the interpreter who is local to Sheffield, intrudes throughout, offering an intimate 'seeing' of a 'local' variety. By contrast, in Dunning and his colleagues' work little effort is made to connect the civilising process with examples of 'real' social interaction. As Giulianotti elucidates:

> [O]ne might say that the figurationalist's use of Elias is rather weak ethnographically. They make no meaningful attempt to employ Elias's figurational approach at the everyday level. The Leicester researchers fail completely to examine the complexity of figurational dynamics within a football hooligan group, such as the interdependency of individual hooligans or the fluidity of power relations within the group generally.
>
> (1999: 47)

Aside from its 'latent evolutionism' (Horne and Jary, 1987: 101) and despite its protestations towards synthesis, for us, the Eliasian approach can be justifiably further critiqued on account of the dubiousness of its break with the more positivist strands of sociology and the latent functionalism that this implies. As Layder argues, figurational sociology sees itself as 'inherently superior to other forms of sociology because it "resolves" the numerous false problems and false dichotomies that plague conventional approaches' (1986: 386). However, as he goes on to point out:

> Instead of transcending epistemological disputes Elias merely refuses to recognise them, and thus unknowingly becomes impaled on the horns of the dichotomies he wishes to go beyond . . . By its inability to transcend the empiricist versus rationalist, inductivist versus deductivist philosophical debates Elias's figurational sociology, and the theory of knowledge which underlies it, suffers from the very same limitations which he claims to have 'gone beyond'. The main effect of this is to undercut the explanatory power of the concept of figuration itself, an explanatory power which is possessed by those objectivist conceptions of structure which the concept of figuration is designed to replace'.
>
> (ibid.: 381–4)

'Whose side are you on?' Marxist, radical and subcultural theories

Partly as a reaction to the perception of orthodox functionalism's continuing authority, despite its seemingly uncritical, ahistorical, non-comparative and conservative stance (Jarvie and Maguire, 1994), functionalist accounts increasingly came under attack during the 1960s and 1970s in the face of marxist, neo-marxist and feminist critiques.

Whilst it was Edwin Sutherland who made the first concerted criticism of the extent to which functionalist analysis had neglected the diverse social distribution of crime and deviance in his article 'White Collar Criminality' (1940: 10) it was Steven Box's marxist-inspired critique which revealed how policing focuses much more on public 'working class' than private 'middle class' criminality (1971, 1986). He pointed out that the identification, or revealing, of criminal actions is often related to the victim's awareness of their 'victim status'. Most 'ordinary' crimes, such as burglary, robbery and assault involve a victim who will fairly rapidly recognise their status as such. By contrast, 'for the most part, corporation crimes remain hidden, the victims, being an abstraction, unaware that they have been victimised' (Box, 1971: 63). He also points out that even in those circumstances where 'ordinary' crimes involving 'ordinary' victims (such as the exchange of a forged match ticket) have been committed they are not always reported or revealed to the authorities. Victims may feel the authorities will not be sufficiently interested; that the incident was a private matter between themselves and the offender; that the crime cannot be proved, or even embarrassed or unwilling to expose a private matter to public gaze.

Just as 'ordinary' crimes such as robbery, assault and theft are reported more readily than 'respectable' crimes such as embezzlement, fraud, forgery and tax evasion because of their very visibility, so we might see that in the sports world the 'deviance' of athletes and spectators, who are widely subjected to an official and televisual gaze, is more readily reported and policed than corporate crime. In Box's terms it is the crimes of the powerful that remain less visible, less open to public interpretation, moral prescription and punishment when compared with the practice of 'on the field deviance'.

From this perspective the identification and definition of 'deviant' and criminal behaviour is, at least partially, related to the degree of power that the offender possesses, both to maintain the invisibility of their own 'deviance' and to label and judge others' behaviour as 'deviant'. This power, it is suggested in marxian terms, is located much more strongly among those individuals who occupy 'white collar', middle-class management positions, or in terms of sport, those who own and run sport as opposed to those who play and watch.

This position has been criticised by Hazel Croall (1992), who argues that rather than 'white-collar' or 'respectable' undetected crime being the product of the power of capitalist property relations, it is more related to opportunism, people finding themselves in exploitable positions and cultural definitions of acceptability. If we consider the scandal surrounding 'bungs' in English professional football (cash payments made to intermediaries and managers in order to 'ease' the passage of player transfers) from this perspective, it is the everyday nature of the practice and managerial codes rather than marxist power relations which long maintained its unremarkability and consequent public 'invisibility' (Bower, 2003).

Nevertheless, perhaps given that the wealthy have a surfeit of criminal opportunities as well as legitimate ones (Ruggiero, 1996), we can identify a series of examples of institutional corruption and 'deviance', corporate crime and 'closure' within the world of sport where the interests of those with access to institutional forms of power are privileged over the sports performer and spectator. The issues of racial inequality, racist practice and sexual abuse within the institutions of sport are characterised by processes of denial and silencing which can leave the sporting 'hardman' (Back et al., 2001) or victim of abuse (Brackenridge, 2001) isolated and vulnerable. The whole question of collective negotiation or 'the cartel' operated by sports competitions such as the NHL, NFL, NBA and FA Premier League has remained largely unquestioned (Hamil et al., 2000). The abuse of 'monopoly' power by sports teams which have a unique psychological hold over their fans or 'customers' and which has enabled spectacular increases in sports event ticket pricing over the last decade, remains unchecked (Greenfield and Osborne, 2001). The organisation of ticket distribution systems which enable touts, scalpers and 'corporate hospitality' agents to prosper at the expense of 'fans', and the organisation of policing regimes which impose restrictions and discomfort on travelling spectators have become routine (Brown, 1993; Stott et al., 2001). The corruption and 'politics' surrounding decisions on where to locate international sporting events such as the Olympics and the men's football World Cup remains largely outside public view (Jennings, 1996; Sugden and Tomlinson, 2003). The whole question of corporate responsibility in cases such as the Hillsborough stadium disaster continues to be neglected (Williams and Smith, 1999). The manipulation of athletes, the media and public to serve corporate ends in the promotion of boxing and other sports events is largely accepted as part of the sport (McRay, 1988).

A kind of corporate-acceptable versus non-corporate-unacceptable dichotomy is implied by these interpretations of white-collar crime. The very definition of sporting 'deviance' might be characterised by the following juxtapositions whereby athlete or spectator 'deviance' is visible, individual, sensational, related to the spectacle and demonstrating a clear violation of rules/ethics while corporate 'deviance' is non-visible, institutional, unremarkable, peripheral to the spectacle and having an ambiguous relationship to rules and law.

It was, however, the growing interest in and visibility of what were termed the 'crimes of the powerful' (Pearce, 1976) that enhanced the appeal of radical approaches within criminology more generally and which, through a grand critique of existing approaches and the recovery of a fully marxist model of 'deviance' and control, came to be defined under the banner of radical or 'new' criminology (Taylor *et al.*, 1973). For its adherents this new approach ultimately advocated the need for a society embodying the principles of socialist diversity as the only means of eliminating crime which was seen to be intimately tied up with capitalist property relations. Similarly, within the sociology of sport 'rather than seeing themselves as technocratic servants of sport-forms which they uncritically accepted as "good", many began to see themselves as critics whose principal goal was to use research and action to "purify" the "pathological sport-forms produced under capitalism"' (Coakley and Dunning, 2002: xxix).

Nevertheless, the early neo-marxist interpretations of sport, which drew upon the critical theory associated with key Frankfurt school theorists such as Horkheimer, Adorno, Marcuse, Benjamin and Habermas, still retained elements of structure functionalist thought even if they were considered more critically. For Rigauer (1969), in industrial capitalist societies, sport was seen to reproduce social behaviour which is functionally and normatively consistent with the needs of capitalism whilst maintaining the illusion of sport as an autonomous liberatory domain. Similarly, both Vinnai (1970) and Prokop (1971), in different sporting contexts, saw sport as taking over socialisation functions within an authoritarian framework which ultimately undermines social autonomy through the production of technical and disciplined behaviour which leads to individual alienation. Perhaps most significant though is Jean-Marie Brohm's book, *Sport: A Prison of Measured Time* (1978), in adopting the terminology of 'deviance' and its control, which offers the most straightforwardly structural marxist account, seeing sport in Althusser's terms (1971) as part of the ideological state apparatus.

Brohm argues that sport participation in capitalist societies ultimately leads athletes to become alienated from their own bodies. In line with the medicalisation thesis developed in John Hoberman's *Mortal Engines* (1992), the body is seen to be experienced by the athlete as an object and an instrument, a technical means to an end, and a machine with the task of producing the maximum work and energy. The result of this is that the body ceases to be a source of pleasure and fulfilment in itself. Instead, pleasure and fulfilment depend on what is accomplished with the body – satisfaction comes in terms of competitive outcomes rather than the physical experience of involvement.

This perspective echoes the concepts developed in the more generalised critical theory offered by Morgan (1994) in his *Leftist Theories of Sport*, which has argued that the institutionalisation of sport has corrupted the 'practice' of sport. From a romanticised historical perspective Morgan identifies market norms, or the competitive pursuit of financial reward, as undermining the intrinsic value and glory of sports participation. From this perspective athletes can be expected to cheat and break rules since it is the commercial goal not the sporting principle which is all important.

Whilst retaining a critical stance and neo-marxist orientation, others have criticised the extent to which these accounts over-simplify the interface between structure and agency and their overreliance on economic considerations of social class in the establishment of sport's meanings and functions. In his work Gruneau (1983) prefers to see sport and leisure forms as sites of conflict, struggle and a means of self-representation. Clarke and Critcher (1985), in their seminal critique of the sociology of leisure, *The Devil Makes Work*, recognise the widespread interpretation of sport's role in challenging 'deviant' behaviour among unoccupied working-class young men. They suggest that state-sponsored sports interventions are organised around the perceived need to deal with the 'problem of working class youth' by keeping them 'off the street', 'under supervision' and with 'something constructive to do' (1985: 135). However, they also recognise leisure as an arena for cultural contestation between dominant and subordinate groups (ibid.: 227).

Drawing on the historical accounts of E. P. Thompson (1963) and the theoretical frameworks offered by Gramsci's hegemony thesis (1971), British sociologists such as Critcher (1971, 1979), Clarke (1978), Hargreaves (1986) and others based at the BCCCS developed a cultural studies position which was concerned with 'speaking up' for the marginalised and which placed an emphasis on subcultural counter hegemonic practice.

Whilst subcultural studies had originally emerged out of the Chicago School's interest in youth gangs and the fostering of 'deviant careers' (Cohen, 1955) which provided a basis for Luschen's functionalist analysis of sporting delinquency (1971), cheating (1976) and doping (1984) and the interpretive approaches considered earlier, the new focus shifted the interest in subcultural studies in a more critical direction. Relating to the changes in youth culture in post-war Britain, the Birmingham researchers began to focus on 'style'-based youth cultures, such as Teddy boys, mods and skinheads through the adoption of a subcultural model. For them the deviant behaviour of such groups had to be related to the collective reaction of working-class youth themselves to structural changes in British society (Hall and Jefferson, 1976).

Cultural studies at this time were greatly concerned with the processes by which dominant ideologies are created, accepted and challenged and how they affect the structure of people's everyday lives. Subculture within this perspective is an area in which groups of people challenge dominant meanings assigned to cultural products. The style and images used by groups of working class youth promote an opposing definition of reality, one which challenges the assumed naturalness and, therefore, the legitimacy of the dominant groups' definition of acceptable behaviour.

(Crosset and Beal, 1997: 76)

According to Phil Cohen's *Subcultural Conflict and Working Class Community* 'the latent function of subculture is this – to express and resolve, albeit "magically", the contradictions which remain hidden and unresolved in the parent culture [by attempting] to retrieve some of the socially cohesive elements destroyed in [the] parent culture' (1972: 23). John Clarke's study of skinhead culture echoes this view by arguing that this style represents 'an attempt to re-create through the "mob" the traditional working-class community as a substitution for the real decline of the latter' (Clarke, 1976: 99). Elements of this perspective were integrated into one of the first academic interventions to consider the issue of 'football hooliganism' which was related to the commercialisation of the game and, more particularly, changes which were occurring in the relationship between working-class supporters and their home team (Taylor, 1971). This early treatise on spectator violence defined the 'football hooligan' in romanticised terms as a working-class resistance fighter opposing the commercialisation and embourgoisement of the game.

Beyond methodological concerns, the key criticism of subcultural theories then is a contested perception of their continuing historic reliance on narrow notions of class-based resistance to dominant ideologies. There is also a sense that the theories tend to focus almost exclusively on male cultural forms and exclude any discussion of the shifting behaviour patterns of members of 'subcultural' groups as they move between subcultural setting and family home. In turn these omissions help to reinforce the somewhat dubious representation of subcultures as tight, coherent groups (see Gelder and Thornton, 1997; Hargreaves, 1994; Rojek, 1992; Hargreaves and Tomlinson, 1992; Horne and Jary, 1987 for a full consideration of the debate). For Redhead there is a political determinism in the perspective which leads him to conclude that '"authentic" subcultures were produced by subcultural theorists, not the other way around' (1990: 25). In essence, he suggests that the 'idea' of the subculture served a particular political and academic purpose which did not necessarily have much to do with an accurate understanding or representation of the subject. As such the theory has lost much of its explanatory value since the cultural studies approach still ultimately rests on the relationship between the pursuit of hegemonic power and the resistance to it. The use of the terminology of subcultures within this framework then may well overstate the oppositional qualities or transformative potential of sport (Crosset and Beal, 1997: 78–80).

In this light the work of Pierre Bourdieu has become increasingly influential within cultural studies and among the former advocates of subcultural theory. Bourdieu (1984) developed a unified sociological theory which is supported by historical research and classical empirical sociology. His work focused in particular on the analysis of culture and, unlike many other contemporary social theorists, has given consideration to sport as a cultural form which has prompted a growth of interest in his work within the sociology of sport itself (Clément, 1995). While no orthodox marxist, fundamentally Bourdieu was interested in the ways in which sport reproduces dominant social and cultural relations and analyses this process through the notion of habitus.

For Bourdieu 'the notion of habitus expresses first and foremost the rejection of a whole series of alternatives into which social science has locked itself, that of consciousness and of the unconscious, that of Finalism and of Mechanicalism etc.' (Bourdieu and Wacquant, 1992: 12–13). Bourdieu used the concept to account for the ways in which all social structures are generated in practice by participating social agents and argued that all humans 'inherit' dispositions to act in certain ways. In this sense they possess a concept of society which they then modify, generating a new concept which is attuned to their own local conditions and experiences. Garry Robson's work is significant here in its application of Bourdieu to the thoroughly demonised habitus of supporters of Millwall football club. In this work Robson (2000: xi) demonstrates how the:

> Millwall myth . . . chimes closely with the broader mythology and sense of dramatized and notorious social identity long familiar to working class men in south east London. The development and negotiation of the Millwall myth, from within the fan-community, should therefore be understood as a particularly intense, rather than novel, experience of dialectically inflected and experienced social identity.

For Bourdieu the adaptations that this implies were physical as well as attitudinal, denying any notion of body/mind separation since physical behaviour and deportment were seen to express the systematic functioning of the socialised body. As Wacquant describes in relation to the increasingly 'deviant' sport of boxing through his observation of life in a Chicago ghetto gym whilst seeking to disrupt perspectives that reduce boxing to a brutal and uncivilised practice involving inherently violent individuals:

> Boxing is an individual sport, perhaps the prototype of the individual sport insofar as it puts into play – and in danger – the sole body of the fighter, whose proper learning is nevertheless quintessentially collective, in particular because it presupposes a belief in the game which . . . is born and lasts only in and through the group that it defines through a circular process . . . to become a boxer is to appropriate through progressive impregnation a set of bodily and mental dispositions that are so intimately interwoven that they erase the distinction between the physical and the spiritual.
>
> (Wacquant, 1992: 224)

In some respects these approaches allow us to 'see' social practices from the subject positions of those engaged in them rather than through the discursive formations which might categorise them as 'deviant' elsewhere, such that even Jay Coakley, who states his opposition to professional boxing 'for health reasons', recognises that the stories that emerged from Wacquant's work 'tended to challenge popular beliefs' (1998: 186).

In *Policing the Crisis* (Hall *et al.*, 1978) BCCCS researchers turned their attention back to the role of authority figures and institutional arrangements in the assignment of 'deviant' categories through an extension of their critique of the reproduction of order in capitalist Britain through a focus on societal reaction to youthful 'deviance' in the specific form of 'mugging'. This was achieved through an adaptation of the concept of the 'moral panic' (Cohen, 1972; Thompson, 1998), itself developed from Becker's symbolic interactionist 'labelling theory' of 'deviance' (1963) discussed previously. This work argued that the media does not simply report events which are 'naturally' newsworthy, rather there is a systematic sorting and selecting of events and topics according to a socially constructed set of categories and routine structures of news production that tend to reproduce the definitions of the powerful. In a similar vein Stuart Hall was also concerned with how the prominence of categories such as the 'football hooligan' were related to the organisation of sport in the media. Representations of sport are in some senses located within a world of their own on the back pages, at the end of the news and on the sports channels. Accordingly, it has been suggested that when a sport story like 'hooliganism' breaks out of these boundaries to appear as 'news' it only serves to emphasise its apparent importance (see Hall, 1978).

'Hooligan' stories have performed this role in England for 30 years to the degree that the very term now evokes a set of accompanying characteristics. Indeed, the four main themes located in the descriptive language used in relation to 'hooligans' by Whannel (1979: 331–2) 25 years ago – that they are mindless/senseless; maniacs/ lunatics; foul/subhuman; minority/so-called supporters – seem equally prominent today. Whannel argued that these viewpoints are 'mediated' through the process of news production and the codes of selection and presentation associated with it and that this process has helped to establish the vocabulary of football hooliganism since it is 'once primary definitions are in play [that] the media can transform these by translating them into their own public language' (Hall and Jefferson, 1976: 75). It is in this context that the 'football hooligan' was seen to emerge as a new 'folk devil' leading to the development of a 'moral panic' and future incidents appearing within this framework as evidence of a trend which is increasingly newsworthy in its own right:

> The space opens for papers to launch a campaign, to call upon the authorities to act, to demand stricter policing and tougher punishment. The football hooligan story becomes a law and order crusade. Any subsequent governmental response can be taken up by the press as a token of both the importance of, and the success of, its campaign. Stricter policing will tend to lead to greater arrest figures, providing a statistic that the press can appropriate as 'evidence' of an escalating problem (adding further legitimacy to the campaign).
>
> (Whannel, 1979: 333)

Whilst such perspectives have increasingly been subjected to criticism in the face of the ubiquitous stage-managed moral panic (McRobbie, 1994) and recognition of the media role in the constitution of sporting realities (Crabbe, 2003), Whannel went on to argue that the existence of an established frame of reference does tend to privilege facts and explanations which support and reinforce it. Alternative explanations and stories may appear but they do not affect the structure of the dominant form of explanation.

Left realism, feminism and the dangerisation thesis

Radical criminology itself underwent something of a reappraisal during the 1980s through the emergence of a more pragmatic outlook that showed a greater sensitivity to the practical consequences of crime, which Jock Young has termed 'left realism'. Downes and Rock suggest that the dominant model within this perspective 'bears an imprint of the earlier "fully social theory" of the new criminology, a parallelogram composed of the State, society and the offender, but which is fuller still because it now makes provision for the victim' (1998: 300). A principal influence on this reassessment was the contribution of feminist criminologists who, through their assessments of crime from the standpoint of female victims rather than male offenders, forced criminologists of the left to take the effects of crime seriously rather than merely seeing them as a consequence of wider capitalist property relations.

Downes and Rock (1998) argue that the emergence of feminist criminology is generally assigned to the publication of Carol Smart's (1977) *Women, Crime and Criminology* which critiqued the neglect of female criminality and the positivist biological determinism which underpinned what analysis there was. Ten years on, in the face of a growing body of literature, Gelsthorpe and Morris argued against the notion of a single feminist criminology and espoused the need 'to talk of feminist criminologies, or, better still, feminist perspectives within criminology' (1988: 225). However, the fundamental point that 'theories of crime should be able to take account of both men's and women's behaviour and to highlight those factors which operate differently on men and women' (ibid.: 231) remained central.

Reflecting wider trends within sociology, ultimately feminist studies of crime evolved in two directions along the axis of the empirical and the theoretical. The left realists took their cue from the former branch which concerned itself with the history and sociology of women's experiences of, and involvement in crime, and more recently, a wider conceptualisation of gender and the crimes and controls of men and how they are nested within social constructions of masculinity. It was in recognition of this work that Jock Young claimed that feminism was 'the major contributor to the contemporary radical practice of exposing the invisible victim' (1988: 171) where previously there had been a tendency 'to idealise oppressed groups and an inability to see antisocial behaviour and divisions within them' (ibid.: 174).

In a sporting context this shift was illustrated by Ian Taylor, who in his early work on football hooliganism had defined participants in romanticised terms as defenders of football's traditional working-class communitarianism against a growing embourgoisement of the game. This position was then reassessed, with support from Robins (1984), after considering the emergence of the skinheads (see Clarke, 1973) and other 'fighting gangs' associated with 'racist-populist politics'. Taylor argued that 'the repertoire of some of these [hooligan] groups now extended far beyond the "taking of ends" and the property vandalism of the 1960s to involvement in National Front-inspired attacks on blacks' (1982: 158) and other violent activities. The 'hooligan' was now depicted as a member of a lumpen 'underclass', ripe for manipulation by fascist elements. In classic 'left realist' fashion, whilst the marxist-influenced analysis remained sympathetic to members of this class, whose lived experience is described as one of 'material and psychic frustration', the 'hooligan' was no longer held up in the same romanticised 'class fighter' terms. Rather, the popular fear of 'hooligans' was now seen as a rational response to their actual behaviour.

The 'left realist' project was a largely empirical one which, adopting a consensual notion of criminality, sought to reveal the 'true' nature of crime, deviance, victimisation and social control by paying closer attention to the experiences of women and minority ethnic groups whilst providing more radical 'solutions'. Despite the inspiration from feminist empirical studies and the advocacy for 'victims' that this approach implies it has nevertheless itself been the subject of a concerted feminist critique (Schwartz and DeKeseredy, 1991; Walklate, 1992).

This critique has emerged out of the alternative branch of feminist grand theory which would claim that preoccupation with empirical detail essentialises criminal women as a category, missing the point that it is women's relationships to patriarchal society that should form the cornerstone of academic enquiry. From this perspective criminology is itself reduced to a 'masculinist master discourse' (Young, 1991). As Ngaire Naffine points out, citing the work of Young and Rush (1994):

> left realists invoke the concept of the universal victim to establish a common concern about crime . . . but in the process the features of the victim blur and she loses her specificity, even though one of the major stated concerns of the realists is with the criminal victimisation of women.
>
> (1997: 65)

Within the realm of sport, feminists have offered a broader conceptualisation of 'deviancy' and notions of difference than that demonstrated within criminology and penology generally, through a focus on gendered and racialised issues of power, domination and resistance (Scraton, 1995; Messner and Sabo, 1990; Messner, 1992). However, feminist cultural studies of sport have themselves been blighted by a rather narrow theoretical focus through their documentation of resistance to the dominant heterosexual masculine hegemony which they conceptualised within sports practices (Birrell and Richter, 1987; Hargreaves, 1994).

Whilst this has produced some productive descriptions of 'deviant' behaviour among women in sport, through an interest in gay and lesbian studies (Kaskisaari, 1994; Griffin, 1998; Lenskyj, 1986), considerations of female subcultures

(McRobbie, 1991), and the subversion and occupation of 'men's' rugby songs (Wheatley, 1994) and body-building spaces (Mansfield and McGinn, 1993; Bolin, 1992), we would suggest that these studies continue to be hampered by a preoccupation with binary understandings of gender difference. The point is well illustrated in Celia Brackenridge's pioneering explorations of sexual exploitation in sport (2001). In some respects, through its engagement with actions which excite the greatest moral repugnance and unreflexive condemnation, it is unsurprising that 'rationalist' notions of 'deviance' are woven into a text which starts 'where sport is'.

In attempting to establish a 'realistic' policy agenda Brackenridge acknowledges the dilemmas presented by contemporary theoretical deconstructions of gender (Butler, 1990) for institutions that have been built on sex segregation. However, it is significant that discussions of 'how the dominant ideologies of "heterosexual masculinity" and "family" combine inside sporting subworlds to preserve male power and to stifle female autonomy' (p. 99) provide the *starting point* for the consideration of theory. Ultimately, whilst a contingency model of sexual exploitation is offered it is centred on the (positivist) assertion that 'sexual contact with an athlete is always wrong and always the responsibility of the coach or authority figure' (p. 240) whose judgements are a factor of the 'gender order of sport' (p. 238).

In many respects this can be related to wider populist concerns with rising levels of 'crime' and its material consequences which has evolved into what Downes and Rock refer to as a 'practical administrative criminology of the left' (1998: 301). A criminology which has now moved beyond its marxist roots and, in the face of the increasing 'normality' of crime, has abandoned the search for 'causes' preferring to fall back upon the functionalist pursuit of social cohesion. For Young:

> the new administrative criminology openly criticises 'dispositional' theories; instead it explains crime as the inevitable result of a situation where the universal state of human imperfection is presented with an opportunity for misbehaviour. The task is to create barriers to restrict such opportunities and to construct a crime prevention policy which minimises risks and limits the damage. An actuarial approach is adopted which is concerned with the calculation of risk rather than either individual guilt or motivation . . . It is not an inclusionist philosophy which embraces those found guilty of an offence and attempts to reintegrate them into society. Rather it is an exclusionist discourse which seeks to anticipate trouble whether in the [sports ground] or in the prison and to exclude and isolate the deviant . . . Such an administrative criminology is concerned with managing rather than reforming, its 'realism' is that it does not pretend to eliminate crime but to minimise risk.
>
> (1999: 45–6)

Echoing Foucault's (1988) exploration of the implications for judging 'dangerous individuals' through expert knowledge, other recent analyses (Lianos, 2000; Lianos and Douglas, 2000) have been equally concerned with the ways in which public perceptions have become more sensitised to danger and how the right to censure as a result of dangerisation has come to feature more extensively in relation to crime control. Lianos and Douglas (2000: 103) suggest that this 'new attitude to deviance is a side effect of new forms of social regulation' based on dangerisation, which has seen society develop 'the tendency to perceive and analyse the world through categories of menace' (p. 110) and invokes the tacit assumption that the world 'out there' is unsafe and that as a consequence it becomes essential 'to continuously scan and assess public and private spaces in terms of potential threats by other people' (p. 111).

Indeed, what the anxious majority cannot abide above anything else 'is difficult people and dangerous classes which it seeks to build in the most elaborate defences against, not just in terms of insiders and outsiders, but throughout the population' (Young, 1999: 390). For Young, with the development of a risk society, what we see is the dwindling tolerance for difficulty and difficult people. Basically, calculations of risk (Beck, 1992) take-over issues of responsibility for social inequality, and at the same time, difficult 'problem' populations replace the 'deserving' and 'undeserving' poor as targets of dangerisation.

As a result of these factors threats of danger are exaggerated – as are the identities of individuals perceived as threatening – to the extent that the probability of becoming a victim of a dangerous crime seems to be omnipresent. Nowhere is the ubiquitous probability of victimisation felt more than in relation to the threat of sexual abuse by 'paedophiles' in sport. According to Celia Brackenridge sport faces two particular problems in relation to this threat. First, committed paedophiles use it as a way to get access to young people, and second, a culture has developed in sporting circles under which sexual liaison and banter is widely and sometimes inappropriately tolerated. For Brackenridge, sport must be much more efficient in its management of this problem of risk:

> There should be a move towards the situation in medicine or therapy where there is a professional distance between client and practitioner . . . the problem has been that, particularly in Britain, sport has traditionally been seen as something of a moral oasis, with a pure, Chariots of Fire values system.
>
> (Brackenridge quoted on the BBC Online Network, 9 August 1999)

As much as is possible, Brackenridge's technico-administrative approach to abuse in sport aims to eliminate the subjective and value judgements associated with paedophilia in order to concentrate on the known 'facts' about the problem in sport. This approach typically involves studying the probability of risk through the statistical distribution of abuse in sport, or comparing a group of known abusers with a group of non-abusers in order to identify and isolate the factors that make it more likely that some coaches will abuse young people under their care. It is in all probability impossible to provide firm figures on sexual abuse in sport, but Brackenridge defies this 'reality' to demonstrate that research in Canada has shown over 20 per cent of young athletes have been sexually abused. She thinks the UK could mirror this experience. In a recent publication, she cited the case of one coach who regularly abused more than 30 boys at a community club and she says that swimming authorities are currently investigating at least 40 alleged abuse cases (Brackenridge, 1999).

However, the key problem with this techno-administrative approach is that it evidences an *essentialist* and *absolutist* view of sexual 'deviance'; that is, it assumes that sexual 'deviance', including sexual abuse, is behaviour that violates accepted values and public morality and there is absolutely no room for debate. The problem of paedophilia is thus seen to be shaped by intrinsic, instinctual and overpowering forces in the individual that not only shape the personal but the social as well. From this perspective, then, it is biological and instinctual forces – which are basically male – that form the perversion for paedophilia. Consequently, the question of whether sexual abuse is really an autonomous realm or 'natural' force which the 'social' controls is never really considered.

This approach to managing the risk of paedophilia in sport reflects what Feeley and Simon (1992: 188) have described as the new penology, which is basically concerned with the efficient administration of danger in contemporary societies. The problem is that this approach not only increases public perceptions about the probability of paedophiles operating in sport, but it also provides the general public with tangible targets of dangerousness that 'can be handled, tied down, locked up, neutered, even destroyed – unlike most threats, which tend to be disconcertingly diffuse, oozy, evasive, spilt all over the place, unpinpointable' (Bauman, 1999: 10). Ultimately this technico-administrative approach ends up paying exclusive attention to coaches and 'abused' sportsmen and sportswomen at the expense of including the study of the 'experts' and others who are charged with the identification and protection of young people at 'risk' of 'danger' in sports.

Conclusions

In this chapter we have been concerned to demonstrate that in striving to find the 'truth' about 'deviance' in sport through explicitly and implicitly positivist theoretical frameworks, writers have been stuck in a realist paradigm which has underplayed the complexity and relativities associated with the construction of sports-related 'deviance'. We are also conscious that this has led to an undue focus on the essentialised 'deviant' practices of 'men' involved in one way or another in élite competitive sports.

In the following chapter we intend to consider the emergence of some more insightful frameworks associated with the work of Michel Foucault and other post-structuralist writers which have become increasingly evident within the sociology of sport (Rail and Harvey, 1995). We also seek to reveal the significance for studies of sport and 'deviance' of more conventionally 'sociological' theoretical developments within the field of leisure studies which appear less restrained by the conceptual straitjackets which have tended to contain the sociological imagination within our area of enquiry. Disappointingly for us, however, we remain attentive to the realisation that these developments tend in the main to be limited by a continuing, albeit alternative, focus on the social uses and disciplining/schooling of the body offered in the initial functionalist accounts considered above.

3 Beyond grand narratives

Poststructuralism, new directions and functionalist legacies

Watching the game: Foucault, poststructuralism and the normalising gaze

Foucault, archaeology and the panopticon

Given that David Downes and Paul Rock's (1998) *Understanding Deviance* claims to provide the reader with an 'extensive coverage' of 'the principal theories of crime and social deviance', it is somewhat perplexing to us that there is not even a relatively brief survey, never mind an extensive discussion of the significance of the work of Michel Foucault for the sociology of 'deviance'. This is not to dispute the quality of the scholarship – which incidentally is good – but is more than a little surprising to us because Foucault's *œuvre* is replete with insights, both ordinary and extraordinary, for understanding 'deviance'.

Indeed, it is difficult for us, in such a short space, to do justice to the work of Foucault. His erudition is not only wide-ranging; it is also at times bewildering, contradictory, and antithetical. In many ways his writings are also dystopic or nightmarish. He was also obviously in love with the idea of exploring heterotopias, particularly in his own personal life (Miller, 1993) and in this regard he was fascinated with sex, but in this respect he was also always the theorist of the underdog, such as the mad, the bad, the perverse and the sexually 'deviant'. Certainly, Foucault visits some insistent themes within all his published works, which in our view more often than not have pertinence for the sociology of deviance. And it is to these that we now turn.

Foucault's early 'archaeological' writings, *Madness and Civilisation* (1967) and the *Birth of the Clinic* (1975), arguably provided the platform for his most compelling contribution to the sociology of deviance, *Discipline and Punish: The Birth of the Prison* (1977). The earlier works which laid the foundations for his theory of surveillance, developed in *Discipline and Punish*, sought to question the discursive origins of the 'truth' about, on the one hand, 'madness' and, on the other, the power associated with the emergence of the bio-medical 'gaze' (*le regard*) in modern society. In *Madness and Civilisation* Foucault explored how madness came to be constructed through a modernist discourse in which religion, but also now 'science', in the form of medicine, became dominant. Correspondingly, in the *Birth of the*

Clinic, he began to uncover the myth of the clinical 'gaze', which emerged with the 'opening up of a few corpses', when it materialised that the medical physician could now see into the very 'heart' of the problem of the human subject in order to diagnose it, treat it and monitor it.

As has been well-documented, the theme of the 'gaze' and its role in controlling and maintaining 'docile' minds and bodies in the modern 'disciplinary society' is developed more extensively in *Discipline and Punish*. It is in this book that Foucault (1977) suggests that in modern societies there has been a historical movement from brutal, overt repression and social control to rational, scientific and bureaucratic control of 'deviant' populations through surveillance. In this most illuminating work Foucault evokes the image of Jeremy Bentham's panopticon in order to argue that the all-seeing 'gaze' comes to serve as a metaphor for the power/knowledge and surveillance connected with governmentality in the modern state.

Foucault suggested that in the modern state, surveillance replaces the medieval 'spectacle' of public law enforcement and the goal of this new form of social control is to administrate and make good the problem of social 'deviance'. Echoing his marxist forebears, for Foucault, the ultimate goal of surveillance was to pacify and secure a stable and predictable work-force for the nascent modern capitalist industry. Weber's concern with the growing bureaucracy of modern *Iron Cage* rationality can also be detected here as Foucault suggests that modern capitalism no longer required as many workers, so there was a greater need to regulate the population even more efficiently. From Foucault's perspective, then, there has been a significant shift in the ways in which populations in modern capitalist societies are controlled socially, which was conjured up in pernicious fashion in George Orwell's seminal novel, *Nineteen Eighty-Four*:

> The telescreen received and transmitted simultaneously. Any sound that Winston made, above the level of a very low whisper, would be picked up by it; moreover so long as he remained within the field of vision which the metal plaque commanded, he could be seen as well as heard. There was of course no way of knowing whether you were being watched at any given moment.
>
> (Orwell, 1979: 6)

A significant feature of panopticonism is that like Orwell's 'Big Brother' surveillance, it is indiscernible: those under surveillance are always unsure whether or not they are being watched. This model of surveillance keeps those being watched subordinate by means of uncertainty, and as a consequence the 'watched' simply act in accordance with the panopticon, because they never know 'when' or 'who' might be watching. Flynn outlines the implications of the panopticon for the all-pervasive nature of modern social control, which, for Foucault, comes to establish itself at the heart of the social fabric of modern societies:

> Foucault's famous description of Jeremy Bentham's Panopticon relates power and knowledge, norm and surveillance, in an interplay of architecture and

social science to reveal the self-custodial nature of modern society, where 'prisons resemble factories, schools, hospitals, which all resemble prisons'.

(Flynn, 1994: 41)

Foucault himself never mentions the role of sport in this process, but as Jean-Marie Brohm, writing from a marxian perspective was to argue, sport is perhaps the social practice which best of all exemplifies the all-pervasive nature of surveillance in the modern 'disciplinary society' (Andrews, 2000). Indeed, had he cared to discuss it, Foucault would without doubt have recognised the disciplinary techniques of the emerging institutional regime of sport as a crucial part of the 'carceral archipelago' described by Flynn.

Perhaps missing the point of his understanding of discursive power, a number of critics have questioned the historical accuracy of Foucault's (1977) theory of surveillance and social control. Nevertheless, his less than convincing investment in historical accuracy has not prevented a significant number of interpreters from applying the panopticon model. In sport, one of the earliest applications emerged alongside the British cultural studies tradition with John Hargreaves' consideration of the British physical education system as a disciplinary regime which acts as a means of social control through the schooling of bodies to reproduce specific class, gender and ethnic divisions (1986). Similarly, Brian Pronger draws on Foucault's work to illustrate how scientific–medical knowledge has contributed to the transformation of the human body into a machine in the service of contemporary consumer capitalism (1995, 2002), while Rinehart identified the swimming pool as a mechanism of surveillance which when 'divided into areas for lessons (or lanes for the swim practice), became the symbolic of "hundreds of tiny theatres of punishment"' (1998b: 42).

Bale's pioneering work in the field of sports geography has also been important in revealing how 'the sports place . . . has changed from being one of open, public space to one of segmented and panopticised confinement' (1994: 84). This point has been developed in Giulianotti's considerations of social control at football grounds (1999: 80) and Armstrong's (1998) work which focuses on the development and extension of social control among English football supporters through the use of technologically advanced rational systems of surveillance and control. As he argues, in a quite literal reading of Bauman's classic text, *Legislators and Interpreters* (1987), recent tactical and technological changes in the policing of football hooligans amount to a transformation from legislative law enforcement policies to interpretive surveillance strategies. Armstrong argues that, 'the police are no longer using legislation to neutralise phenomena but are now interpreters, and use the most recent technology and surveillance techniques to watch hooligans' (p. 313).

Feminist critics have been quick to point out the neglect of women in Foucault's work (see for example, Hartsock, 1993 and Sawacki, 1994) but as Andrews' (2000) discussion of poststructuralism's influence on the sociology of sport shows, it is feminist-inspired analyses of sport, surveillance and 'deviance' that have emerged most powerfully in the writings of scholars of sport rather than work concerned with 'the relationship between sport and the male/masculine form' (p. 125). (An extended discussion of these Foucauldian-inspired feminist studies is beyond the scope of this book. For a more thorough discussion see Andrews (2000).) Generally speaking, however, these feminist analyses have been organised around two central themes: the bio-technicopower associated with the discursive constitution of women's bodies (e.g. Markula, 1995; Cole and Denny, 1994) and the ways in which the patriarchal media spectacle is implicated in the power/knowledge regimes of truth underpinning the omnipresent male 'gaze' (e.g. MacNeill, 1998). As Andrews argues then, 'sport is thus implicated as an optic of modern disciplinary power: a mechanism of surveillance which renders visible and intelligible the normal body and the abnormal body against which the norm is constituted' (2000: 124).

It is important to note here though, that in revealing how modernist conceptual-isations placed their faith in the 'pedagogical and spiritual transformation of individuals brought about by continuous exercise' (Foucault, 1977), in common with many of the perspectives we reviewed in the last chapter, these aspects of Foucault's work have more than a fleeting coincidence with functionalism. As Garland (1990) suggests, his understanding of 'deviance' is unable to identify with the irrational and counter-productive features which tend to accompany actual processes of social control. Further, in taking the unintended consequences of penology as its *raison d'être*, Foucault, like the figurationalists, can be criticised for offering a 'configuration' of social control that is not only latently functionalist but built on retrospective wisdom and an unsubstantiated form of reasoning. Finally, his conclusion that surveillance is directed not at punishing 'deviants' as such but socially controlling the working classes by creating 'deviants' through the discursive category of the criminal, merely offers a more sophisticated functionalist conception of modern surveillance.

What is distinct and what points us forward though is the quintessential point of Foucault's work that there are myriad ways in which people think about and know their own sense of reality and that how the world is experienced is a matter for someone at some time and in some place. While many sporting discourses continue to emphasise sport's 'functional' role as an agent of 'normalisation', a force for 'good', Foucault's work alerts us to the fragility and contingency of such conceptualisations, an attentiveness which was applied particularly well in his later work focusing on the power of discourse, technologies of the self and the 'confessional'.

Foucault, genealogy and the confessional

While a detailed discussion of the evolution of Foucault's project would be too great a task to take on here, it might be useful at this stage to discuss very briefly the theoretical orientation of his later publications. Foucault himself always attempted to deny for his work any form of categorisation. But this has not stopped him being described in the main as either a 'poststructuralist' or a 'postmodernist'; this despite the paradox that, as we have suggested, much of his early work was structuralist in its orientation. It would be wrong of us then to give the reader the impression that Foucault's work is synonymous with poststructuralism and post-modernism. However, it cannot be denied that there is a great affinity between the two sensibilities and that Foucault's work resonates with each of them. Trying to distinguish between these different positions is, however, a futile business and should not be allowed to detract our attention from the general theoretical assumptions that all poststructuralists and poststructuralisms share.

Crucially, Foucault's approach to social enquiry inverts the conventional wisdom of systematic rational accounts to give priority to 'society' over the individual and culture over nature (Harland, 1987). Ritzer (1997: 39) emphasises most clearly what this means in relation to 'doing' Foucauldian social enquiry:

> Foucault takes as his goal the creation of 'a method of analysis purged of all anthropologism'; his work is anti-humanistic . . . In fact, even in terms of his own work, Foucault seeks to avoid the sense of a human subject or author . . . instead of focusing on people and what they say, Foucault (1983) focuses on discourse as *practice*. . . . he is looking for the unities of discourse in the population of discursive events, *not* in people and what they say. In other words, he has disengaged discursive events (as objects) from people (subjects) who might engage in them.

Contrary to his critics and what Hammersley and Atkinson (1995: 14) would argue then, Foucault's shift towards a genealogical view of social enquiry is not 'anti-realist'. Just the reverse is in fact the case. This is *why* Foucault focuses on discourse as practice, instead of on what people say, because for him what people say cannot be relied upon since *everyone* is discursively positioned. For Foucault, to suggest that things are not as they appear serves only to fix their meaning in a positivist sense when what is at stake is the *effects* of their surface appearance in specific contexts. Harland elucidates in a further sense what this transformation in Foucault's project of social enquiry involves: 'The most obvious aspect of the difference between "archaeology" and "genealogy" is that the latter puts the emphasis upon power rather than upon knowledge, upon practices rather than upon language' (1987: 155). In this sense, Foucault (1981, 1986, 1987) is not denying self-reflexivity; on the contrary, his later work was concerned specifically with the existential nature of individual, self-to-the-self relationships and self-relationships to others, as 'arts of living'. But what Foucault is emphatic about is that individual selfhood and self-reflexivity is in all instances shaped through discourse, in the context of people's relations to others. The individual is always situated discursively in the sense that 'certain bodies, certain gestures, certain discourses, certain desires, come to be identified and constituted as individuals' (Foucault, 1973: 18). These incarnations of self and identity emerge from configurations of power, within which some forms of discourse become normalised, while others are silenced and marginalised (Foucault, 1977).

In the *History of Sexuality* Foucault (1981) develops this idea of discursive normalisation in relation to sexuality. In this book, once again paying homage to Max Weber, Foucault suggests that the history of sex in modern western civilisation is one associated with subjugation whereby sex comes to be repressed because it is incompatible with the work ethic. At the same time though, there is a 'discursive explosion' in society's need to talk about sex and consequently what we see emerging in the eighteenth and nineteenth centuries is 'a steady proliferation of discourses concerned with sex' (Foucault, 1981: 18), which in the main took the form of institutional discourses on 'deviant' and marginalised sexual differences (McNay, 1994).

The unities of discourse implied by 'sexual acts' themselves and the very intensity of the 'pleasures' and 'desires' involved in sex provided the basis for the problematic of 'sexuality', and the outcome was that sex came to be 'placed by power in a binary system: licit and illicit, permitted and forbidden' (Foucault, 1981: 83). Juxtaposition was pivotal to Foucault's critical writings and as Dreyfus and Rabinow (1982: 141) suggest, the binary system underpinning this process of disciplinary power was to become a necessary and important 'tactic' of bio-power. By which Foucault meant the power that is able to dictate its own seemingly 'natural' law in the policing of sex, which he called the 'sexual' confession.

As the experiences of Justin Fashanu, a black English professional football player, show, the 'sexual' confessional involves those under the 'normalising gaze' in a process of self-deconstruction in response to its 'disciplinary technologies'. And this self-deconstruction is not merely about disclosing once and for all one's sexual 'deviance', it involves the 'deviant' individual standing in the spotlight and confessing their vulnerability in the face of their failure to conform to the contingent power/knowledge of the 'normalising gaze'. Justin Fashanu describes, in his own perceptive account, the way in which he was not only required to confess to the powerful world of the football tabloid press his 'queerness', but also the wretchedness associated with this 'dirty little secret':

> . . . my world is based around *Sun* and *Daily Star* readers . . . I genuinely thought that if I came out in the worst newspapers and remained strong and positive about being gay, there would be nothing more they could say. Of course, I was wrong and lost three years of my career.
>
> (quoted in Garfield, 2003)

What is significant about Fashanu's 'queerness' is less the actual repression of his sexuality – because in a western democratic society he is as 'free' as he likes to be 'queer' – but more the contingency of the myth of repression associated with football in the tabloid press. Seen in this way Fashanu's 'sexual deviance' was not just regarded as something to be judged, but something that required regulation and administration. This myth and its corresponding ritual of confession, implicitly operated to calculate Fashanu's sexual experiences within a discourse which brought to bear to those more powerful than himself the 'truth' about his 'shame' in order to somehow set him 'free'. According to Foucault this type of disciplinary power is exerted implicitly in all such discourses, and the penalties for 'coming out' in professional football are absurdly plain to see. Indeed, Justin Fashanu remains the only professional football player in England to openly 'come out' about his 'queer' sexuality since, as Brian Pronger has argued, the open expression of sexual identity by gay men is rare in traditionally heterosexist male sport (1990). In this context, after a highly promising career was cut short through the normalising power of football's dominant discourse, Fashanu ultimately committed suicide in 1998.

With the 'sexual' confession the 'deviant' is always subject to systematic enquiry, through the disciplining, marginalising and subordinating effects of social control. Nevertheless, as a pioneer of 'queer' theory, in her deconstruction of the hetero-sexual matrix of sex, gender and sexuality, Judith Butler (1990) draws explicitly on Foucault and linguistic theorists to consider the production of selves as effects, specifically identifying gender and sexuality not as an expression of what one *is* but something that one *does* 'performatively'. As such 'hegemonic heterosexuality is itself a constant and repeated effort to imitate its own idealisations' (Butler, 1993: 125), whilst the act of 'dragging up' has a transgressive political potential such that as Gail Hawkes observes:

> If 'drag' is the verbal shorthand for the performative use of gendered dress codes to subvert the hegemonic twinning of gender and sexuality, then we can speak, in this sense, of dress as performance, of women 'dragging up as women' . . . Dressing-up as performance allows rereading of all dressing up as playful . . . [where] the readings of the male/masculine/heteroxesual, female/ butch/lesbian, male/camp/homosexual, are not reversed but deliberately scrambled.
>
> (1995: 269 cited in Lloyd, 1999: 198)

In this respect within the realm of sports studies the emergence of the gym, body-building culture, and more specifically, women's body-building has provided a productive site of investigation which focuses more readily on the transformative, transgressive potential of sport in the age of performativity and consumption. In her review of the literature Cole (2000) reveals how Bolin (1992) and Mansfield and McGinn (1993) focus on the ways in which women's body-building is made 'safe' through the maintenance of a stylised masquerade of 'femininity' designed to satisfy the normalising gaze of male judges. Whilst Patton points to the limited authority of such a disciplinary regime in the face of the irony of dressing up muscled women body-builders in order to erotise them to the point that 'one wonders how heterosexuality can survive its own gender construction' (2000: 12). More radically, for Haber (1996) the 'shock' produced through the display of women bodybuilders ultimately has the potential to make spectators aware of the artificiality of sexuality, sex and gender; whilst analysis of the *Pumping Iron* films reveals the desire to visualise sexual difference and reconsider what it is to be a 'woman' (Robson and Zalcock, 1995).

Building on Sedgwick's work on the 'exercise addict' (1992), Cole has gone on to integrate Derridean deconstruction techniques into such analyses which further reveal the shortcomings of the more positivist interpretations of 'deviance' offered by Coakley (1998) and others. In this work, which compliments Franklin's exposure of the contradictory logic of appeals to the 'natural' in sport (1996), Cole points to the impossibility of the 'exercise addict' being an essential entity by demonstrating how both sides of the healthy/unhealthy, pure/corrupt, natural/unnatural binary oppositions which constitute sport inhabit the subject position of the 'exercise addict' through the fluctuations of sporting discourse (1998).

Cole has also challenged the pervasiveness of conventional neo-functionalist understandings of modern sport as a means for 'channelling otherwise instinctual, aggressive, unproductive and criminal drives and desires' (1998: 445) through the concept of the sport/gang dyad, which she identifies as a central dynamic governing the national imagination in 1980s' America (1996). Similarly, Sloop sought to identify the discursive constraints through which Mike Tyson was popularly read in relation to the pejorative categories 'boxer' and 'African American' (1997) during his trial for the rape of Desiree Washington, such that his guilt was viewed as 'highly feasible indeed probable' by the majority of the trial's audience. This point seems to echo with Butler's concern with the performative politics of visuality in the technological age which she has discussed in relation to the video recording of police officers beating Rodney King in Los Angeles:

> I do think that there is a performativity to the gaze that is not simply the transposition of a textual model onto a visual one . . . It seems to me that this is a modality of performativity, that it is racialisation, that the kind of visual reading practice that goes into the viewing of the video is part of what I would mean by racialisation, and part of what I would understand as the performativity of what it is 'to race something' or to be 'raced' by it.
>
> (quoted in Bell, 1999: 6)

But there is a further twist in these rituals, which relates to the 'hidden' excitement and fascination about what makes sexual 'deviancy' and violence what it is, which is suggestive of all of our fetishisms and desires to consume a bit of the 'deviant' other. For the purposes of our own analysis, Bauman's (1992a) work emerges as important here in drawing on Foucault's theory of surveillance to suggest that, in our contemporary world, it is consumption that has emerged as the new 'inclusionary reality'. We will consider this work in greater depth in the following chapter but before doing so we wish to turn our attention to alternative theories from within the sociological tradition which deal with this 'desire for deviance' through 'abnormal leisure'.

On the edge or in the flow: leisure studies, abnormal leisure and the legacy of functionalism

In their acknowledgement of these new perspectives and the collapse of the dualisms which have pervaded social scientific thinking, leisure theorists and some social psychologists have recently provided a number of useful concepts in relation to efforts to move beyond the dichotomies of work and leisure which had previously stifled the discipline. Interestingly, and perhaps somewhat perversely, whilst

showing a greater imagination and degree of sophistication, these new developments are also far more firmly rooted within the regimes of conventional sociology
than those ideas associated with the 'poststructuralisms' and 'postmodernisms'. In
some respects what we have witnessed is a move backwards, which may also provide
greater possibilities for moving forwards. In contrast to the previous fetish for
'endings', of which Sumner's (1994) work is an exemplar, we are now witnessing
a fascination with retrieval which presents both shortcomings and opportunities.
In the following sections we aim to review some of these developments before
assessing their usefulness for our own project.

Stebbins and serious leisure

Attempting to get to grips with a fast-changing world in which work appears to be
becoming less meaningful for a significant number of people, Stebbins (1992, 1997
and 1999) distinguishes between, on the one hand, 'serious leisure' and, on the other
hand, 'casual leisure'. For Stebbins (1997) casual leisure is in the main consumptive
and involves largely non-productive leisure activities, such as 'hanging around',
drinking and smoking. Serious leisure, as the term suggests, is essentially a form
of leisure participation which is productive and allows the individual to develop a
sense of career from their free time activities. Stebbins (1999) discusses three types
of serious leisure: amateurism, hobbyist pursuits and volunteerism.

Each of these types of serious leisure has a special capacity to support enduring
careers of leisure which are marked by historical turning points and stages of
achievement. Serious leisure also tends to be built on the kind of perseverance,
which although at times experienced as particularly challenging for those involved,
enables its participants to build special skills and knowledge and this in turn tends
to engender self-confidence through achievement where they are successful. There
are also other long-lasting benefits to be had through engaging with serious leisure,
which go beyond individual personal self-enhancement, such as material products
and long-lasting personal relationships. As Rojek observes, serious leisure is built
on a strong sense of moral foundations of social behaviour and tends to give primacy
to integrative dimensions of companionship and community. Consequently, for
Stebbins, it is plain to see that serious leisure plays a largely integrative function,
and as such it should be understood as 'a vehicle for the cultural and moral
reaffirmation of communities as places in which the individual recognises relations
of belonging' (Rojek, 2000: 18).

Stebbins takes the debate about leisure in a new direction from other more
conventional approaches, which largely tend to focus their critical gaze on the
dichotomy between work and leisure. However, there are some problems with his
analysis. As Rojek (2000: 19) points out, Stebbins's predilection for serious leisure
tends to 'emphasize the integrative effect of leisure in reinforcing the social order',
at the expense of recognising the efficacy of casual leisure for individuals and social
groups. As Rojek concludes, he ends up reducing serious leisure to being merely
a 'rational-purposive activity'. Consequently his use of the concept, has a conservative bias and, as such, it is underpinned by an ideology of functionalism: that is

the assumption that its contribution to the larger whole of social life makes serious leisure a 'good' thing.

While this may be so in terms of the way Stebbins has used the concept it is worth recognising that both Rojek and Stebbins himself may have underplayed the usefulness of the idea. For our purposes the notion of serious leisure might well be more widely applied than Stebbins anticipated, and might indeed be applied to forms of leisure and styles of engagement that have otherwise been seen as 'unproductive' or 'deviant'. The 'work-like' characteristics of this classification lend themselves to comparison with social psychological categories of obsessive behaviour and notions of 'positive deviance' whilst the integrative elements might be associated with the commitment found within any number of 'deviant sub-cultures' which extend beyond the morally laden categories originally defined.

Indeed, the notion of serious leisure might be regarded as a theory of the quintessential 1990s' 'deviant' leisure category of the 'anorak' or 'trainspotter'. The irony of which is revealed by the insightful title to Irving Welsh's (1993) classic novel *Trainspotting*, which deals with an underworld friendship network in Edinburgh characterised by heroin users, petty criminals and conmen, and offers a dark and ironic take on young junkies enjoying the highs and suffering the lows of heroin addiction which subverts the judgemental gaze of the usual documentary approach to such issues by presenting the everyday lived experience of the principal characters. The film presents drug-taking within a 'serious' live for today leisure culture which reveals the commitment, initiative and communal practices required to persevere within this life world whilst rejecting the middle-class values which permeate and discipline modern work–leisure formations. In this fashion we are offered an insight into the complexities which surround contemporary leisure spaces and the agents who operate within them.

Liminality, edgework and the carnivalesque

Despite his critique of the functionalist assumptions in Stebbins' work, Rojek (2000) himself develops an approach which conceptualises a notion of 'abnormal' rather than 'deviant' leisure which takes Durkheim's (1938 [1893]) classic distinction between 'abnormal' and 'normal' forms as its intellectual reference point. Rojek does still take Durkheim to task regarding the empirical reliability of his thesis although this critique is in the main not relevant to our discussion, except for the rather futile point that Durkheim's model is problematic for scholars of leisure because he 'failed to anticipate the challenge that leisure would mount to work as the central life interest' (2000: 144).

Building on Durkheim's theme of the society in transition Rojek draws on the work of Bryan Turner (1984) and Foucault to demonstrate the argument that with the Enlightenment what was deemed 'abnormal' behaviour now tended to be explained in terms of medical science rather than myth. Rojek stresses that with this change the medical profession takes over issues of 'abnormal' behaviour, presenting non-religious solutions – in the form of both informal and legal discourses – for all manner of 'deviant' behaviours and 'illnesses', from drug abuse to alcoholism, masturbation to prostitution and so on. However, the key point Rojek makes here is that one consequence of this shift towards the establishment and re-enforcement of medico-legal 'truths' about 'deviance' has been that leisure studies have in the main come to accept that 'the subject of abnormal leisure is the responsibility of criminologists and medical practitioners [and that this has in turn] contributed to the legalization and medicalization of abnormal leisure' (2000: 146). For Rojek, abnormal or 'deviant' leisure is the example *par excellence* of the unresolved, disturbing forms of our desires and our fantasies. 'Deviant' leisure may belong to the forbidden and the deadly, but it should not escape the notice of scholars of leisure that it *is* leisure all the same.

Now drawing on the alternative terminology of 'deviance', Rojek (ibid.: 147) goes on to challenge this culpability to demonstrate the propinquities and continuities between 'deviant leisure practice and ordinary, "normal" leisure practice'. However, before he takes this argument a step further in discussing what he identifies as the three major forms of abnormal leisure – the invasive, the mephitic and the wild – he seeks to contextualise his core argument around the concepts of liminality, edgework and surplus energy.

As Rojek suggests, for Victor Turner, the concept of liminality literally means a 'threshold', a place 'in an out of time', which provides the individual with a:

> spatial separation from the familiar and habitual, constitutes a cultural domain that is extremely rich in cosmological meaning, conveyed largely by nonverbal signals. Liminality represents a negation of many of the features of preliminal social structures, and an affirmation of another order of things, stressing generic rather than particularistic relationships.
>
> (Turner, 1973: 213–14)

All liminal leisure experiences include both personal and transpersonal elements. Yet the liminoid, while reaching beyond the experience of the individual, depends on a unique existential (and by implication individual) encounter. Indeed, Fulgham (1995) argues that the most powerful dimension of liminality is its solitariness; the way it emphasises the individual's separateness from others. As Hill suggests, evoking Durkheim's original notion of anomie, 'liminality is thus dislocation, and can therefore be a period of risk when the individual might reject social behaviour and lose bearings, suffering a state of "normlessness" when the customary codes of conduct are dispensed with' (2002: 115). Rojek goes on to argue that Turner's work is important too 'because it shows that "deviant", abnormal leisure values and practices are expressed habitually as part of the ordinary relations of everyday life' (Rojek, 2000: 149).

Like Foucault's (1998) heterotopia, Turner's liminal stage of margin is at the same time both 'mythical' and 'real' and it operates at the 'edge' of everyday life as a temporal discontinuity. It is a borderline 'integratory and interstitial space' where identities are performed and contested. As a 'borderline work of culture' it 'renews the past, refiguring it as a contingent "in-between" space, that innovates and interrupts the performance of the present' (Bhabha, 1994: 7). In the context of sport, liminal spaces have been interpreted as putting

> civility and culture . . . up for grabs. In . . . the sometimes violent crowd behaviour after a big game win, rioters in the streets insert themselves into history performatively, with their bodies, in the way that they can make, as Paul Connerton says, 'society remember' (1989). Rioters are in a liminal space, a seductive swirl of celebrity, of sport.
>
> (Sydnor, 2000: 236)

In this sense, liminal leisure is not dissimilar to the festival world of the carnivalesque.

The carnivalesque is a blanket term that refers to those traditional, historical and enduring forms of social ritual, such as festivals, fairs and feasts, that provide sites of 'ordered disorder' (Bakhtin, 1984; Stallybrass and White, 1986), where social rules are broken and subverted; and where one can explore one's 'otherness', secret desires and most intimate pleasures. Drawing on Barthes' (1957) work, Fiske offers wrestling as an example of the carnivalesque, suggesting that 'wrestling is a parody of sport: it exaggerates certain elements of sport so that it can question both them and the values that they normally bear' (1990: 86). Within the sociology of sport Giulianotti has employed the concept of the carnivalesque in his considerations of the transformative potential of the performative styles of Scottish football fans (1991, 1995). By contrast Crabbe and Wagg (2000) have considered the commercial use, distortion and vacuousness of the term in relation to the staging of the 1999 ICC Cricket World Cup. In similar vein, Presdee (2000) suggests that in the contemporary period the carnivalesque has been fragmented and in the detritus, people's pleasures and desires for disorder are now found in acts of 'deviance' and 'crime', where they can transgress the quotidian through 'edgework'.

The concept of edgework, whilst introduced by the journalist Hunter S. Thompson in his dealings with the negotiation of boundaries between life and death, consciousness and unconsciousness, and sanity and insanity (1971, 1979), first entered sociological debate through the work of Stephen Lyng on voluntary risk-taking (1990). He was concerned with the contradiction in western societies between the public agenda to reduce the risk of injury and death, and private efforts to increase such risks, and the failure of psychological models to account for how 'some people place a higher value on the experience of risk taking than they do on achieving the final ends of the risky undertaking' (p. 852).

From their ethnographic study of skydivers Lyng and Snow (1986) identify three categories associated with edgework: activities, skills and sensations. Lyng suggests that as an activity edgework requires a threat to physical or mental well-being as illustrated by dangerous sports such as sky-diving or motorbike/car racing (see Sato, 1991) but also dangerous occupations such as test piloting and stunt work. In the context of these activities Lyng stresses the importance that 'edgeworkers' assign to the development and use of skills and an élitist orientation, which maintains that such skills are possessed by only a select few who identify with one another on the basis of their perceived status. Finally, the experience of edgework is said to produce a sense of 'self-realisation', 'self-actualisation' or 'self-determination', which in its pure form leads 'individuals [to] experience themselves as instinctively acting entities, which leaves them with a purified and magnified sense of self' (Lyng, 1990: 860) as a kind of 'hyperreality', more real than the mundanity and senselessness of everyday life.

For whilst the spectre of risk increasingly hangs over us (Beck, 1992) it is the secure, monotonous, repetitive character that more often characterises our contemporary condition and it is this mundane orderliness that enables individuals to experience what Baudrillard calls 'ecstatic experience' (1993) through an engagement with risk and the public display of 'risky behaviour'. With this vision in mind a variety of extreme or 'whiz' sports have been represented as a conscious assertion of the continuing vitality of the self which stands against the perceived risk aversiveness, monotony and emptiness of our times (Midol and Broyer, 1995).

Lyng himself draws parallels between edgework and alternative considerations of risky behaviour such as Goffman's conceptualisation of risk-taking as 'action' (1961) whilst drawing the distinction that ultimately edgework is about achieving control rather than abandoning it. More sympathetically, he also acknowledges the connections with Csikszentmihalyi's concept of 'flow' (1975), which has focused on activities such as rock-climbing and refers to an experience of total involvement in one's activities, unselfconscious movement, distorted sense of time, feeling of personal transcendence and uncertainty of outcome allowing for creativity. Indeed, in the principle application of the concept to sport it is suggested that:

> Athletes who are good at finding new opportunities for action in whatever they do, and who are prepared to put themselves on the line, are more able to set the stage for flow to occur than athletes who simply follow routines and play it 'safe'. Taking risks puts you *on the edge* of the challenge-skills balance equation, extending challenges (and thus skills) beyond comfort zones.
> (Jackson and Csikszentmihalyi, 1999: 38, emphasis in the original)

Pilz (1996) has also used the term to make sense of German football hooligans' articulation of their achievement of a sense of unselfconscious adventure and excitement which transcends the banality of contemporary social relations. Yet for Lyng, whilst edgework involves experience of elements of the flow phenomenon, ultimately it stimulates a sense of self-actualisation as revealed through moments of uninhibited behaviour and spontaneous expression rather than a loss of self-consciousness.

Similar to the 'borderline work' associated with the notion of liminality however, edgework is placed firmly within the sociological mainstream through its concern with 'the boundary between order and disorder, form and formlessness' (Lyng, 1990: 858). Invoking a social psychological synthesis of the work of Marx and Mead, Lyng centres his analysis on an exploration of the spontaneity/constraint dialectic such that 'on one level, [edgeworkers] seek a highly structured experience in which hazards can be anticipated and controlled, while on another level they attempt to place themselves in a highly unstructured situation that cannot be planned for' (ibid.: 875). Crucially, edgework is seen to call 'out an anarchic self in which ego is manifest but the personal, institutional self is completely suppressed . . . Thus edgeworkers experience this action as belonging to a residual, spontaneous self – the "true self"' (ibid.: 878–89).

In contrasting ways this approach alerts us to two of the key concepts, namely individualism and consumerism, which we consider in more detail in the following chapter. Whilst offering in Mead's terms an over-essentialised conceptualisation of the self, Lyng's analysis does acknowledge the primacy of notions of individualism within contemporary social formations in recognising the absence of the social 'me' in the face of the elevation of the more narcissistic 'I', even if it is only a perceived 'I'. However, Lyng perhaps misses the point that in a consumer society even 'risky' 'leisure' experiences are increasingly characterised by a quick fix 'I want it all now' quest for immediacy and instant gratification, which points to the contingency of surface experiences rather than 'authentic' career-based attainment of skill levels.

Presdee's work within the emerging field of cultural criminology (Ferrell, 1995) is in this respect rather more insightful by drawing out the connections between 'crime', carnival and consumer culture and highlighting that 'what is important, as in all consumption, is the immediacy of the experience' (Presdee, 2000: 60). Referring to practices as seemingly diverse as sadomasochism, rave culture and the 'sport' of joy-riding, Presdee is able to demonstrate how in 'the ever-expanding realm of commodification and consumption, acts of hurt and humiliation, death and destruction, all become inextricably woven into processes of pleasure, fun and performance' (ibid.: 65).

In less ubiquitous terms Rojek draws the reader's attention to the idea of 'limit-experience'. Basically, limit-experience involves the pursuit of a series of 'limits' or 'higher' pleasures which by necessity involves the individual foregoing restraints in order to reach that 'limit' at the expense of their own self-destruction or the destruction of others. Rojek discusses the private life of Michel Foucault in the context of explaining this idea and uses Miller's (1993) argument that Foucault may have been prepared to risk the lives of others in the pursuit of his own sexual gratification despite the knowledge that he was at the time HIV positive. Rojek concludes his discussion by suggesting that if liminal and edgework leisure experiences are about testing limits in order to experience intense moments of pleasure and excitement, they are also about expending surplus energies and they are always likely to be so in societies which set moral limits on what is and is not acceptable 'normal' behaviour.

Abnormal leisure and the polysemic self

In the light of his discussion of liminality, edgework and surplus energy Rojek goes on to formulate his own understanding of abnormal leisure. He suggests that abnormal leisure involves 'pushing the limit experience so that it threatens the self and others' and it arises when the 'individual refuses to bestow respect or trust on the other' (2000: 176). And individuals who engage in abnormal leisure as a response to the other tend to deal with that other in an oppositional way. This takes two forms. Either the other is experienced as threatening so it must be expunged or the individual experiences a desire to devour the other as a form of personal pleasure. This aspect of Rojek's analysis brings to mind Bauman's application of Lévi-Strauss' strategies of *anthropophagia* and *anthropoemia*.

Bauman (1995: 179) argues that at every level of society, social groups employ, conjointly, *anthropophagic* and *anthropoemic* strategies of oppression towards the other: the two strategies are only effective precisely because they are used in conjunction. Those employing *anthropophagic* strategies, gobble up, devour, and assimilate outsiders who they perceive to carry 'powerful, mysterious forces'. In marked contrast, those employing *anthropoemic* strategies (from Greek: to vomit) towards others, metaphorically throw them up, casting them into exile, 'away from where the orderly life is conducted . . . either in exile or in guarded enclaves where they can be safely incarcerated without hope of escaping' (ibid.: 180). The two strategies work as one:

> The phagic strategy is *inclusivist*, the emic strategy is *exclusivist*. The first 'assimilates' the strangers to the neighbours, the second merges them with the aliens. Together, they polarize the strangers and attempt to clear up the most vexing and disturbing middle-ground between the poles of neighbourhood and alienness – between 'home' and 'abroad', 'us' and 'them'. To the strangers whose life conditions and choices they define, they posit a genuine 'either-or': conform or be damned, be like us or do not overstay your visit, play the game by our rules or be prepared to be kicked out from the game altogether. Only as such an 'either-or' the two strategies offer a serious chance of controlling the social space. Both are therefore included in the tool-bag of every social domination.
>
> (ibid.: 180)

Rojek's analysis goes on to problematise the idea of the contradictions implied in the management of self and identity in relation to our leisure choices and in so doing brings to our attention the series of selves we are in our lives and the consequences of this for interpreting abnormal leisure. Indeed, Rojek recognises that after postmodernism the Cartesian duality of mind and body is replaced by a more complex understanding of the polysemic sense of self and identity. For Rojek these aspects manifest themselves as abnormal leisure as a reflection of the self as personal failure and are applied to aspects of the self that the individual perceives as worthless. For example, self-body loathing evidences that the body is loathsome, a living symbol of disgust, and a typical response to such self-loathing is drug and alcohol abuse.

Rojek then explores what he describes as the three key types of abnormal leisure forms: invasive, mephitic and wild leisure. Rojek's discussion of *invasive leisure* basically extends the reader's understanding of abnormal behaviour associated with self-loathing and self-pity and the ways in which disaffected selves tend to experience anomie and personal alienation from the rest of society. Rojek then catalogues the extent to which some individuals are prepared to attempt to step beyond the limits of this sorry existence in their leisure lives by 'punishing this invalid element of the personality' through drink, drug or solvent abuse in order that they can 'turn their back on reality'.

Mephitic leisure encompasses a wide range of pursuits and activities from mundane encounters with prostitutes to the buzz of murdering through serial killing, but mephitic experiences involve the individual's self-absorbed desire for gratification at the expense of others. Why Rojek calls these leisure activities and pursuits mephitic is that they are generally understood to be 'noxious', 'nasty', 'foul' and 'morally abhorrent' by most 'normal' people, to the extent that they cause major offence to the moral order of things.

Rojek's third category of abnormal leisure is *wild leisure* which involves limit-experiences through edgework and as such tends to be opportunistic in character. However, very much like mephitic leisure it involves the individual's self-absorbed desire for instant gratification. The experience of 'limit' is the name of the game with wild leisure and a good example of this is extreme sports, particularly when they are still interpreted by the moral majority as acts of 'deviance' rather than sport. Rojek spends the greater part of his discussion of wild leisure focusing on crowd behaviour such as rioting, looting and violence, particularly at sports events. However, in the latter part of the discussion he suggests that new technology has presented people with even more opportunities for wild leisure in the form of pictures and video clips of anything from sexually depraved acts to genocide, which present individuals with the vicarious 'delight of being deviant' (Katz, 1988). As Rojek puts it: 'The expansion of network society lays the foundation for the enlargement of wild leisure patterns. For, it renders rational-legal limits permeable and simultaneously neutralizes the identity of the viewer. The opportunities for voyeuristic and vicarious experience are significantly enlarged' (2000: 191).

Indeed, within sport, extremes and risk are not monopolised by individualist subcultural formations; in other contexts it is their private consumption rather than their public production which has attracted most interest from those concerned with extreme phenomena. Numerous studies of media coverage of North American sport have shown how electronic and print media technologies have exploited aspects of sports' crowd and player violence (see Young, 2000) whilst Baudrillard (1993: 75) has argued that:

> the most striking thing about events such as those that took place at the Heysel Stadium, Brussels, in 1985, is not their violence per se but the way in which this violence was given worldwide currency by television and in the process turned into a travesty of itself . . . Today's violence, the violence produced by our hypermodernity, is terror. A simulacrum of violence, emerging less from passion than from the screen: a violence in the nature of the image.

The demand for such spectacles, is not new since as Baudrillard (ibid.: 77) goes on to point out:

the Romans were straightforward enough to mount spectacles of this kind, complete with wild beasts and gladiators, in the full light of day. We can put on such shows only in the wings, as it were – accidentally, or illegally, all the while denouncing them on moral grounds. (Not that this prevents us from disseminating them worldwide as fodder for TV audiences: the few minutes of film from the Heysel Stadium were the most often broadcast images of the year).

Perhaps now, driven by media expansionism and the breakdown of collective consumption patterns, TV is becoming less candid in its pursuit of such extreme phenomena within the world of sport. The increasingly bizarre and 'really' violent displays associated with contemporary wrestling and 'Jack Ass' TV, along with the hyperbole and media fascination with the behaviour of Mike Tyson and other celebrity sporting 'deviants', offer up our very own contemporary 'extreme' gladiatorial spectacles which appear unfathomable to the legislative meta-theories reviewed in the previous chapter. Indeed, Tomlinson's critical engagement with Guy Debord's situationist polemic on consumerism, *The Society of the Spectacle*, manifestly illustrates the ordinariness, 'normality' and popular embracement of sporting 'spectacle' (2002). Similarly, as we suggested earlier, perspectives within the emergent field of cultural criminology have highlighted the commodification and eager consumption of broader conceptualisations of 'deviance' in ways which conflate the easy dichotomies between cultural and criminal practice (Ferrell, 1995).

Rojek concludes his own analysis by raising some important metaphysical issues surrounding what actually constitutes 'normal' life, 'normal' leisure and 'normal' people. He makes the point that not everybody is in the game of rationing everyday life to comply to the ordinariness of the dominant moral order and 'from the standpoint of someone caught up in invasive, mephitic or wild patterns of leisure, the behaviour of ordinary people seems transparently inauthentic and life-destroying' (2000: 192). As he suggests, it is those who voluntarily submit to the 9–5 routine who are in all probability the 'abnormal' ones.

As a recent article in *Leisure Studies* shows (Bramham, 2002), the work of Rojek deserves special attention, not least because his impact within this field of study has been enormous. His *Capitalism and Leisure Theory* (1985) brought together a full range of theoretical insights and in doing so helped to establish leisure studies as a serious area of academic study. Such is Rojek's strength as a theoretician, his *Decentring Leisure* (1995) was the seminal publication in relation to introducing postmodernism and poststructuralism to leisure studies. As we have shown in the foregoing discussion we have found Rojek's work refreshing in the way he has been brave enough to deal with difficult questions, such as the controversies surrounding violence and abuse as realms of leisure activity, which feature prominently in *Leisure and Culture* (2000).

The problem with Rojek, however, as Bramham's discussion shows, is that his palimpsestuous love of tangents – for example, postmodernism in *Decentring Leisure* and classical Durkheimian sociology in his more recent works – constantly threatens to destabilise his arguments as they are developed in each of his new publications, to the extent that there is no coherent 'sociology of Rojek'. Perhaps Rojek himself would respond that he is not claiming coherence, and that he believes that sociology should be allowed to remain a little puzzling. All the same this incoherence is not without a cost and as we show is inimical to the efficacy of the arguments he makes about 'deviance' and leisure.

In a nutshell the major problem with Rojek's analysis of abnormal leisure is his overreliance on Durkheim's functionalism – a problem, it is worth pointing out, we have encountered in the sociology of sport time and again throughout this first section of the book. First of all, Durkheim's emphasis on the structure-functionalist nature of social life is never acknowledged by Rojek and as a consequence he never offers a corrective to Durkheim's position. This problem is exacerbated by Rojek's own tendency to focus too heavily on the individualist and by definition largely existential nature of abnormal leisure experiences and as a consequence he reduces his analysis in the main to a discussion of the practices of single historical actors.

The second issue regarding functionalism, is that Rojek's analysis of leisure, as for Durkheim's analysis of work, comes divided into two forms. Indeed, Rojek makes the dichotomy between 'abnormal' leisure and 'normal' leisure central to his sociology, at the expense of recognising the undecidability of meaning implied in many contemporary leisure practices. In our view the following quotation from Bauman offers a curative interpretation, which while retaining the concept of the 'abnormal', offers more clarity to the meaning of the undecidability surrounding the use of the concept by taking into account the contingency and ambivalence associated with contemporary social life. As Bauman puts it:

> 'Abnormal' stands for any departure from the favoured pattern; it turns into 'deviation', which is an extreme case of abnormality, a conduct calling for therapeutic or penal intervention – if the conduct in question does not differ somewhat from the preferred pattern, but transcends the boundary of tolerable choices. The distinction between mere 'abnormality', a matter of attention, treatment and cure, and the much more sinister 'deviation', is never clearly drawn and when drawn tends to be hotly contested . . .
>
> (2000: 24)

The above criticisms notwithstanding, we have shown that Rojek's analysis has a good deal to offer, its strength is not merely located in his discussion of invasive, mephitic and wild leisure, but also in the importance he puts on the *responsibility* of sociology to continue to research and theorise 'deviance' in relation to leisure and sport. His critique in regard of the latter point is constructed as a response to those in leisure studies who are not prepared to engage with the more pernicious forms of 'abnormal' leisure. In this respect Rojek's analysis bears out our own view that sociology does not operate in a vacuum, and he supports our recognition that if we do not research and theorise 'deviance' in sport and leisure, others outside the sociology of sport are still going to do so. If this was allowed to be the case what we would have is not only 'half a story' about leisure, as Rojek himself suggests, but also a rather distorted and for the most part badly theorised understanding of 'deviance' to boot.

Conclusions

It is in response to this concern and our wider disappointment that even the more insightful accounts within the literature on 'deviance' have largely failed to provide any bold new terms of reference, focusing on notions of individualism, performativity, consumerism and transgression, that we have written this book.

In a context where socio-cultural diversity has all but replaced conformity or 'normalcy' and its binary opposite 'deviance', rather than explaining 'deviance', the determination of 'normalcy' or providing solutions to the 'problem' of 'deviant' behaviour in sport, we wish to offer a form of critical sociological analysis that allows us to get beyond the protocols that have tended to divide the 'isms' in the sociology of sport. We wish to question the focus on conventional notions of sporting 'functions' and explore the complex and multi-levelled ways in which particular behaviours are normalised in certain settings and demonised in others, and how both hidden and overt forms of regulation operate to sustain those understandings.

Our interpretative framework aims to build on the disciplinary notion of the 'normalising gaze' in a more imaginative fashion by considering how sport disciplines athletes and spectators through an omnipresent but decentred gaze: a gaze which has a multiplicity of popular and individual forms, which is both feared and desired, evaded and sought out and which increasingly polices inclusion and exclusion within specific sporting cultures and contexts.

Part II
Re-imagining theory and 'method'

4 Understanding sport and 'deviance' in liquid modernity
A conceptual 'toolkit'

Introduction

While understanding 'deviance' in the sociology of sport remains largely focused within the confines of the social theories that once served as watchwords for a whole generation of criminologists and sociologists (and which we discussed in Chapters 2 and 3), the sociology of deviance itself has in the main moved its focus away from ideology, theory and abstract thought. Indeed, despite arguments emerging in the field that have been contrary to Sumner's (1994) eschatological position, there has emerged in the main a reticence to theorise 'deviance' anew (Downes and Rock, 1998). Those who have continued to try to theorise 'deviance' in more imaginative ways in an effort to take into account recent societal changes have suffered from a neglect of the epistemological, ontological and methodological problems posed by Sumner's critique (see, for example, Ferrell, 1995).

If there is a 'big' idea underpinning contemporary understandings of 'deviance' since Sumner's attempt to put the concept to bed once and for all it is the idea of what has variously been called late modernity (Garland and Sparks, 2000; Garland, 2000), reflexive modernity (Beck *et al.*, 1994), postmodernity (Bauman, 1992a) or liquid modernity (Bauman, 2000). We want to suggest in this chapter that this over-arching focus on late modernity has emerged because, not only have many of those in the fields of criminology and the sociology of deviance lost their faith in the efficacy of extant social theories and their attendant methodological approaches, but they have also been, to say the least, guarded against developing 'new' ways for theorising 'deviance'. Indeed, the majority of commentaries have tended to interpret the field of study on the basis of administrative agendas, preferring empirical or 'common sense' judgements. Most of the key protagonists in the field have shifted their focus to the idea of 'late modernity' as a 'new' kind of socio-cultural force to be reckoned with in relation to these administrative agendas. This kind of approach is evidenced in the first chapter of a recent, edited book on *Criminology and Social Theory* by David Garland and Richard Sparks (2000). Indeed, rather than theorising contemporary criminology as such, Garland and Sparks identify the idea of late modernity as a social and cultural transformation of such significant proportions that it must 'necessitate some intellectual response on the part of criminologists' (2000: 14). Accordingly, they set themselves the task of outlining the ways in which 'late modern' conditions underpin what they describe as the contemporary 'crime complex'.

We want to argue that the idea of late modernity is a beginning worth exploring in relation to theorising 'deviance' anew, but our reading of Garland and Sparks' article leads us to suggest that because these authors merely use the idea of late modernity as a starting point they have little to offer other than some ready-made guidelines – not a set of theories as such – for understanding the quotidian of 'crime' and 'deviance' in our contemporary world. It is our contention that what we already know about the idea of late modernity has to be translated into social theorising about 'deviance', and specifically for our purposes, into social theorising about 'deviance' in sport.

The second major problem with Garland and Sparks' approach is that, although they identify two of the most important factors related to the emergence of late modernity – the interlacing nature of social, cultural, economic and political change and the fragmentation of social class – they never consider in any particular depth the significance of the rise and establishment of consumer culture for understanding 'deviance'. Indeed, much in common with other criminologists and deviancy theorists, their work has a narrow 'law and order' agenda which is pursued at the expense of exploring crime and 'deviance' in more imaginative ways than have hitherto been developed.

It is our contention that in a sociality where few things are considered to be 'deviant' anymore, it has become even more desirable to get involved in 'dangerous' and 'illicit' activities and it feels so mouth-wateringly, lip-smackingly naughty to do so – a trend that advanced consumer capitalism has been quick to recognise: hence its fascination with inventing risks (Baudrillard, 2001) and fashioning ever new opportunities for 'deviance'. It is our view too that what constitutes 'deviance' is complicated all the more once we begin to recognise that in many ways what we perceive to be 'deviant' is often nothing more than a sophisticated commodity form. It is generally accepted in the sociology of sport that the 'deviance' of and within sport has always provided both its participants and consumers with a passport to relatively safely transgress the boundaries of the permissible, allowing unmitigated access to what 'outside' sport is conventionally repressed or forbidden: the speeding Formula 1 racing car providing its driver with the ultimate adrenalin rush whilst the voyeuristic gaze of millions of TV viewers anticipates a potentially lethal 'smash' as readily as a slick pitstop; the desire to witness the destructive power of the media's monstrous pet figure 'Iron' Mike Tyson . . . the list is endless.

However, it is inconceivable that 'deviance' in sport could have found such an excess of commercial favour in the past as it has today. Particularly in the last 10 or 15 years or so the demarcation between 'real' 'deviance' and that for consumption has blurred the line between 'fact' and 'fiction', as 'deviance' has increasingly been turned into yet another marketable commodity. Indeed we want to argue in this chapter that much so-called criminal activity and 'deviant' behaviour in sport is just that: all surface, flow and attention-seeking without the exit wounds whose consumption in Presdee's terms 'becomes a blissful state of "non-responsibility", a sort of never-ending "moral holiday", where we can enjoy, in private, immoral acts and emotions' (2000: 64). We also want to argue that another striking difference between what has conventionally been understood as 'deviance' in sport in the past and today is not just the way 'deviance' is staged for consumption and the sense of the spectacular that is often involved, but also the mass and the calibre of the audience for it.

It is with the task of exploring and putting some flesh on the complexity of understanding 'deviance' in sport – and by this we mean sport in its widest possible sense – against the backdrop of mass consumer culture that the final part of this book is primarily concerned. We approach it with the knowledge that if we cannot hope to offer a wholly convincing theorisation of 'deviance' in the legislating manner (Bauman, 1987) of extant social theories of deviance, at least we can offer the next best thing: a sense of what 'deviance' in sport means today and the ways it is understood and acted out within contemporary social formations. To begin with, though, we must set out the central tenets of a 'new' sociological theory made to the measure of understanding 'deviance' against the backdrop of the conceptualisation of a 'late' modern era subsumed by consumer culture. It is with this topic that the current chapter is concerned.

In the first instance, we will make our task easier by saying that, 'late' modernity, 'post'modernity, 'reflexive' modernity, 'liquid' modernity – however it is understood – as an economic, political, social and cultural configuration, is properly viewed as a specific historical event which is in the process of superseding 'early' or 'solid' modernity. Moreover, for the sake of consistency and without wishing to essentialise or lineate this process we will from this point adopt the terms 'liquid' modernity and 'solid' modernity (Bauman, 2000) as opposed to 'late' modernity and 'early' modernity or 'postmodernity' and modernity. For Bauman (1991: 272), liquid modernity proceeds from the point solid modernity begins to contemplate itself: liquid modernity is solid modernity 'coming to terms with its own impossibility; a self-monitoring modernity, one that consciously discards what it was once unconsciously doing'.

Following in the footsteps of Weber's (1930) classic analysis of the emergence of industrial capitalism from traditional society, we also presume that liquid modernity and solid modernity form an interlacing contrast, and that neither can be discussed in isolation. This is more so given that for us the illustrative force of these concepts is far from complete, for who are we to talk of the certainty and relative stability of times in which we did not live? Certainly we must recognise not only contrasts but also a degree of overlap, a seeping of one into the other. Equally though we are sure of a shift in the balance of authority or dominance of one set of formations, sentiments and aesthetics over another and, for us, this is best exemplified through the concepts of, at least relative, solidity and liquidity. As Bauman would say, we do not live in either solid modernity or liquid modernity. Both of these 'worlds' are:

> but abstract idealizations of mutually incoherent aspects of the single life-process which we all try our best to make as coherent as we can manage.

Idealizations are no more (but no less either) than sediments, and also indispensable tools, of those efforts.

(Bauman, 1992b: 11)

As is well known, in *The Protestant Ethic and the Spirit of Capitalism* Weber suggested that the 'Puritan ethic' played a key role in bringing about the monumental historical transition of traditional society to industrial capitalism, and by definition, solid modernity. Paradoxically, however, according to Weber, this religious moral code was soon to be extinguished by the very ethic it had produced: 'Puritanism' was no longer necessary to industrial capitalism after it had become established. Weber not only spells out this distinctive turn, but expresses his uneasiness with the subordination of the masses in industrial capitalism and reveals his concomitant disenchantment with the new modernity. Weber's is both a sombre and powerful narrative, and as his analysis showed, the solid modern bureaucratic state redefined problems requiring public attention as technical and administrative ones, which now required bureaucratic solutions.

Very much like Weber's nascent solid modernity, liquid modernity is still guided by the omnipresence of rationality, but as the work of sociologists from Giddens (1991, 1992) to Bauman (2001) to Lash (2002) to Beck (1992, 2002) shows, the liquid modern *puissance* (Maffesoli, 1996) is one that has become increasingly *individualised* through a discourse which stresses the narrative of reflexive selfhood (Giddens, 1991). In liquid modernity, reflexivity takes on a specific discursive form, 'a radical individualism . . . not a utilitarian but aesthetic individualism: not an individualism of a controlling ego but the individualism of a heterogeneous, contingent desire' (Lash, 1994: 144). Liquid modern individuals become 'hedonistic sensation seekers' who are governed by the 'will to happiness' (Bauman, 1997) rather than the coercive impact of the past (Bauman, 1992a).

As we have previously suggested, Max Weber's sociology is important to our analysis because it provides us with a specific exemplar for our own task. Using Weber's two-pronged approach as a springboard – he traces institutional processes and uses the idea of a 'religious complex', whereas we turn our thoughts to institutional processes and use the ideas of individualism and reflexivity – in the following sections we outline the central institutional features of liquid modernity as they relate to 'deviance' in sport. Corresponding to Weber's account, this analysis will be crucial to what follows in the rest of the book, for it will provide the groundwork for the arguments made with regard not only to the commodification of 'deviance' in sport, but also to the new forms of social control emerging with liquid modernity.

Liquid individualism and 'deviance'

The 'events' which mark the transition from solid modernity to liquid modernity are, for Garland and Sparks (2000: 14), no less monumental than Weber's account of the transition from traditional society to modernity. As they suggest: 'the world we inhabit today is no longer quite the same as the world out of which modern criminology emerged, nor even the world that the sociology of modernity was developed to explain'. As Garland and Sparks (ibid.: 16) go on to argue, liquid modernity is the product of an amalgam of post-Second World War social, political and economic changes that has been accompanied by a cultural transformation, which has brought with it 'new freedoms, new levels of consumption and new possibilities for individual choice'. In the process the 'solid' taken-for-granted social class systems of yesteryear with their centralised, hierarchical authority have gradually been deconstructed and superseded by a mediatised and technology-driven society of horizontal social networks (Castells, 1996). Presenting the *illusio* (Bourdieu, 2000) that anybody and everybody – if they 'choose' to draw on their own individual 'talents' – can be anything they want to be; and that it is simply down to 'bad luck' that the majority will never be rich or famous or powerful, however hard they try. Indeed, as Bauman's project shows, liquid modernity is above all else the *individualisation* of social inequality underpinned by a snatching individualist pursuit of wealth, power and status. In the event, liquid moderns are condemned to live this individualised existence *de jure* (Bauman, 2000) – judged responsible for their own individual choices and charged with the responsibility of the consequences of those choices. In this sense, liquid modernity makes all being contingent and accordingly an individualised predicament, which not only heightens individuals' awareness of who they are, but reconstitutes identity as an object of individual self-reflexive activity (Bauman, 1992a).

If in solid modernity people's perception of their place in the world was not ascribed, they at least generally knew where they stood. The respective directors' and players' entrances, directors' boxes and terraced kops at football stadiums denoting a hierarchy based on patronage and 'status'. In liquid modernity these symbolisations become blurred and uncertain. Instead of simply inheriting their place in the world, people are now compelled to find one for themselves.

For Giddens (1991: 32), what further differentiates the liquid modern condition from traditional society (and solid modernity), is that reflexivity extends itself into our conception of who we are, and 'the self becomes a reflexive project'. Giddens argues that, in post-traditional society, the self is essentially disembedded from the local community. With liquid modernity, a postulated unity of interests gives way to more specialised *habitats* and associated life styles and individuality. From this viewpoint, people can be seen to have been 'liberated', in the sense that modern, cosmopolitan urban areas with their highly developed communication and transport networks facilitate multiple interest-based social groupings. The rationale underpinning this argument suggests that 'people are not so much antisocial or gregarious beings as they are *operators* who are willing to forego a secure source of fruit for a chance to connect more of the world' (Wellman *et al.*, 1988: 134).

These operators exist only in their assertion of themselves as individuals. Liquid men and women realise too that they are no different from anybody else and that to perform their individuality is the only game in town. Consequently they are destined to live a life as a 'casino culture' (Bauman, 2000) or a 'dice-life' (Baudrillard, 2001): athletes procrastinating over whether to take cold remedies that may contain banned substances, shop window football players forgoing the security of a new contract or an education in the hope of securing better terms with a new club. As Baudrillard pithily suggests, just as programming the deregulation of the *dice-life* is impossible so is the possibility of predicting what the *dice-life* holds in store: the illusory nature of the *dice-life* is its only possibility: 'the dice-life and its willed *dé-viance* . . . is superfluous. In this sense, constructing an artificial destiny with dice operates almost to protect you against the unpredictable fatefulness of the world as it is' (Baudrillard, 2001: 62).

In Bauman's (1997: 25) terms, Baudrillard's 'dice-life' demands above all else a *palimpsest* identity, 'the kind of identity which fits a world in which the art of forgetting is an asset'. Perdurability is not the name of the game in liquid modernity and selves become more than the sum of their parts: the individuals you see do not really determine who we are and what we do together. In this regard, post-structuralists, such as Jacques Derrida, emphasise the contingency rather than the fixity of the self. For Foucault, as for Derrida (1973), the liquid modern, self-reflexive individual cannot be understood as solid, because a self that can think in terms of *différance* cannot be unitary. Both Foucault and Derrida then, with Deleuze and Guattari (1983), remain committed to a decentred self, which is both poly-semic and schizophrenic.

These poststructuralists can undoubtedly be criticised for reaching a level of abstraction which is unsurpassed in the literature. Yet the themes and issues which we are concerned with here suggest possibilities for engaging poststructuralism on a less abstract level, bringing it down to a more concrete level to engage with issues regarding the apparent fixity of selfhood. Yes, we are sportsmen and -women, but we are also sons, daughters, fathers, mothers, lovers, people with sexual fetishes, with our own ready-made perversions and so on. Indeed, the relationship between the different aspects of an individual's life in liquid modernity is complex, borne out of the ability to make individual choices *de jure* (Bauman, 2000), but also made manifest by a 'generalized and structurally induced *destabilization* of identity' (Dunn, 2000, quoted in Bauman, 2002b). This results in a liquid version of the ritual performance of our rebirth. Quick-fix transformation, the sort that results from a new job, a different lover, meeting up with the 'girls', a night out with the 'lads' or playing your favourite sport is ubiquitous in liquid modernity. Selfhood today is by default contingent and temporary.

Consequently, as Smith (1999: 154) notes, Bauman argues that living in liquid modernity is permeated with 'the contingency of events and the insecurity of being'. As Rojek (1995) has argued, the fact that liquid modern individuals are reflexively aware of the utter meaningless of their own sense of place in the world means that all too often self-dissatisfaction and ennui become overwhelming features of their existence – life seems much more interesting where other people are at. The grass always seems greener on the 'other' side.

'Deviance', too, emerges as an evanescence of the complexity of self and identity rather than being understood as what orthodox sociological approaches see as merely a manifestation of power/knowledge (Foucault), labelling (symbolic inter-actionism) or social control between social groups (Durkheim, Weber and Marx). In what Dean McCannell (1992) describes as our contemporary era of senile capitalism the complexity of self and identity emerges as a battleground for reality plays which evince 'deviance' and 'deviants'. Orthodox sociologising about 'deviance' never really contemplated the complexity of the self. However, if we explore interpretations from Freud to the poststructuralists to Bauman and Beck, we begin to understand that what we once simply understood as the self had to be rethought out. Indeed, since the work of Freud it has been recognised that we are often divided against ourselves. As Phillips (2003: 7) suggests:

> If what we once wanted was to live a good life, or to be redeemed by God's grace, what we now want, in Freud's view, is an object that is by definition forbidden. And this is going to make our so-called selves at best ironic and at worst horrified.

Freud was stressing not only the importance of the forbidden for our sense of self but the significance of the ways that we interpret and present our selves in multiple ways, which are often in conflict – all of which is too complex for most orthodox sociological interpretations of the self to cope with.

The sociology of deviance has been slow, too, to acknowledge the series of selves we are in our lives and the consequences of this for interpreting 'deviance' more directly. However, as we saw in Chapter 1, queer theory has been much more successful in highlighting the complexity of the self in these processes. With the emergence of poststructuralism, postmodernism and queer theory the Cartesian duality of mind and body is replaced by a more complex polysemic sense of self and identity. We also witness the redefinition of identity and the self as a commodity, which reaches its ultimate expression in the commodification of the body. This latter issue is given particular attention in this chapter, but before we turn to the aspects concerned with consumer culture we must discuss the consequences for sport of the individualisation of identity.

The individualisation of identity, the individualisation of sport

As Baudrillard (2001) suggests, in liquid modernity individual identity-seeking is a form of dream-making that is pathetically absurd. Yet the idea of individuality, like authenticity, emerges at its most potent when it transpires that there is no such thing: existentially individuals may be unique, but uniqueness or 'being' the 'real thing', is fated to be no more than fleetingly significant in the marketised consumer culture that is liquid modernity. In the event, individuals set themselves a circle that they can never hope to square: the ambivalence of being authentic in a consumer culture where authenticity is just another life style choice. Yet this does not, nor could it prevent individuals seeking out the significance of their own personal individuality through the task of performativity, which is brought on by the damning fear of invisibility.

Baudrillard (1989) describes those who participate in individualised sports and leisure pursuits, such as the skate-boarder, the jogger and the body-builder as those who regard the body with the same kind of blank solitude, the same narcissistic obstinacy. For Baudrillard, the cult of the body is extraordinary. It is the only object on which everyone seems to be able to concentrate, not as a source of pleasure, but as an object of frantic concern, in the obsessive fear of failure.

> The body is cherished in the perversed certainty of its uselessness. Pleasure is an effect of the resurrection of the body, by which it exceeds that hormonal, vascular and dietetic equilibrium in which we seek to imprison it, that exorcism by fitness and hygiene.
>
> (Baudrillard, 1989: 34)

Consequently, the body has to be made to 'forget pleasure as present grace, to forget its possible metamorphosis into other forms of appearance and become dedicated to the utopia of preservation of a youth that is already lost' (ibid.: 35). Baudrillard suggests that the way that we are phobically concerned with the body prefigures the way in which it will be made up in the funeral parlour on our death: 'where it will be given a smile that is really "into" death'.

'Into' death, 'into' the body, 'into' sport

Baudrillard argues that being 'into' sport, the body, or whatever, is key to all of this. The point is not to be, nor even to have, a fit body, but to be 'into' your own body, 'into' your sexuality, 'into' your desire. The hedonism of the 'into': the body is a scenario and the curious hygienist threnody (lamentation for the dead) devoted to it runs through the innumerable fitness centres and gyms, bearing witness to a mass individualist asexual obsession. As he suggests:

> This is how it is with body-building: you get into your body as you would into a suit of nerve and muscle. The body is not muscular, but muscled. It is the same with the brain and with social relations of exchanges: body building, brainstorming, word-processing.
>
> (Baudrillard, 1996, quoted in Horrocks, 1999: 54)

According to Baudrillard (1989: 37–8):

> you can stop a horse that is bolting. You do not stop a jogger who is jogging. Foaming at the mouth, his mind riveted on the inner count down to the moment when he will achieve a higher plain of consciousness, he is not to be stopped.

He continues to run straight ahead, or even on the spot when forced to stop moving by the presence of road traffic, because he has lost the formula for stopping.

> If you stopped him to ask the time, he would bite your head off. He does not have a bit between his teeth, though he may be carrying dumbbells or even weights in his belt . . . What others in the past saw in self-privation, and

proud stillness, he is seeking through the muscular exertion of the body. Jogging is a form of self-torture . . . Like dieting, bodybuilding and so many other sports, jogging is a new form of voluntary servitude (it is also a new form of adultery).

Consequently, our expenditure of energy is no longer related to sex or work but to leisure, to gym-time, where the virtually disabled . . . can work off 'stress' in body-building, step-classes or other novel exercise regimes. In the gym, as we work-out, the video screens dominate, and everyone is aware of this. According to Baudrillard, no performance can be without its control screen and what he describes as the New International Hygienic Order wants to be seen and is:

everywhere jogging or walking, phobically concerned with bodies, self-maximisation and self-inflicted servitude . . . Glory, destiny and conquest, and all the risks nature would have supplied us in this scenario, have become the challenge of the body against itself in ever finer grades of performativity and experimentation. This is why disabled Olympic athletes mutilate themselves (DRUGS) to improve their chances . . . The millennial neo-individual *invents* risks rather than faces them in destiny. The fight for survival disappears as he artificially recreates the conditions of survival. There are no more heights – just dangerous sports.

(Horrocks, 1999: 55–6)

Baudrillard is concerned here with a contemporary obsession with risk which is symptomatic of liquid modernity in two important senses (Beck, 1992, 1994; Giddens, 1991). First, material risk is individualised as the responsibility of the nation state to its populace diminishes while at the same time the global network of capital and commodities continues to grow independently of international borders. Second, 'new' risks abound in liquid modernity. Liquid modernity is the age of global warming, terrorism, AIDS, CJD, BSE, SARS, to name but a few 'new' risks. These risks take on an added dimension when we take into account the central importance of *body-cultivation*, which means that we now not only pay more attention to the body, but also to anything that it is consumed by, or that comes into contact, with it: what Bauman (1994: 154) calls the liquid modern 'horror of disease and toxic substances that [may vandalise the individual] by entering the body or touching the skin'.

Baudrillard (2001) takes Bauman's observation one step further by suggesting that predestined to exact both physical and symbolic violence on the self, the individual invents extreme risks rather than face their destiny and in the process fritters away in an 'exhaustion of possibilities'. As the following quote shows, 'deviance' through sport has a key role in this process:

This is how it is with all those who deliberately submit themselves to extreme conditions: solitary climbers or sailors, cavers and those who play jungle wargames. All risk-situations, which were once man's natural lot, are today re-created artificially in a form of nostalgia for extremes, survival or death. A technical simulation of pain and sacrifice – and this includes the humanitarian compulsion to take others' suffering on oneself in order to find it in a substitute destiny. Everywhere we find the same symbolic mortification . . . Right down to 'boosting', that very specific method employed by the disabled athletes in the Atlanta Olympics who deliberately inflicted injury on themselves to improve their results. Not to mention drugs and other forms of mind-bending – anything goes in the attempt to achieve this violent deconstruction of the body and thought . . . And the price to be paid is a mortification of the gaze, the body, the real world.

(Baudrillard, 2001: 49–50)

Consumer culture and 'deviance'

As the work of existentialists from Kierkegaard to Jaspers to Sartre has argued, the individual liberated through reflexivity is burdened with choice, and is at every turn faced with the need to make decisions: it is up to the individual to choose the life they think is best. And in their droves, liquid modern individuals, according to Bauman and Baudrillard, now free to choose, choose to consume. As Baudrillard puts it: 'you want us to consume – O.K., let's consume always more, and anything whatsoever; for any useless and absurd purpose' (Baudrillard, 1983: 46).

If the major accomplishment of the centred 'roots of order' underpinning solid modernity was to turn life into a regimentality in which the work of *homo faber* and the leisure of *homo ludens* was divided (Rojek, 1995), the major accomplishment of the decentred disorder sustaining liquid modernity has been its ability to turn the attention of *homo faber* and *homo ludens* to the life of *homo consumens* (Bauman, 2003). Indeed, as Bauman argues, it is the instantaneity of consumer culture and its ability to 'take the waiting out of wanting' in delivering *homo consumens'* hopes and dreams that is today what is imagined as the measure of the success of a life worth living.

For Bauman liquid modernity is constructed through consumption, and as such, we are all consumers today, and it takes a 'heroic constitution' (Bauman, 1994) to concede that one is not part of the consumer game. As we have said already, the upshot of this is that liquid modern inequalities are best seen as consumer inequalities: in a society of consumption you are what you can afford. Consumers appear to be free to choose any life style they wish, because the market flaunts consumer choice so lavishly. However, the purported equality perpetuated by the free market forcefully dupes the masses by hiding the accomplished inequalities of consumers, even though these inequalities are materially visible to even the untrained eye.

Bauman (1992a: 225) goes on to suggest that consumer capitalism gives an undertaking to deliver what it cannot – equality. Differently from its predecessor, production-orientated industrial capitalism, consumer capitalism is bereft of any openness and honesty – at least with industrial capitalism you pretty much knew where you stood. Bauman accords consumer capitalism a second two-facedness. It reduces the notion of freedom to consumerism; it leads people into thinking that they can liberate themselves by simply 'buying' a new identity.

A long time before Bauman and Baudrillard were charting contemporary consumer culture, Adorno and Horkheimer (1979), two of the most perceptive philosophers of modern times, were suggesting that it is not possible to separate human consciousness from the material existence of people's lived condition. They offered their own theory of the modern world, which suggested that everything we see is mediated through the filter of the 'culture industry'. As is well known, Adorno and Horkheimer asserted that we may think that we are free, but we are only free 'to choose an ideology – since ideology always reflects economic coercion – everywhere proves to be freedom to choose what is always the same'. But if, for Adorno and Horkheimer, it was 'monopoly' and 'sameness' that were the two important defining features of the 'culture industry' which related to individuals in their role as consumers, in liquid modernity it is 'polysemy' and 'difference'. More than even those early critics of consumer culture could ever imagine, the denizens of liquid modernity stagger under the weight of an accumulation of consumer culture which is thoroughly 'individualised' in order to cater for differentiation.

Contra both crude marxian interpretations and even the more sophisticated version put forward by Adorno and Horkheimer, the thing is that liquid moderns today *know* that they are living in a virtual consumer reality 'fabricated', not by some invisible committee in a darkened room, but by the decentred and disproportionately distributed effects of global capitalism. Indeed, as Bauman asserts, liquid modern contingency-consciousness *is emancipation from false consciousness* (Bauman, cited in Rojek, 1995: 157). Adorno and Horkheimer were right, however, when they suggested that we live in an infantilised world for much of the time – cushioned by prosperity, only occasionally awakened into difficult ethical choices of maturity – which is not to say that there is never time for direct political drama. In a consumer world, liquid moderns live perpetually on the edge of violent change and there is always demand for drama. Even here, though, direct action is usually no more than play acting, however well intentioned. Voices are insistent on being heard, but as Bauman (1999, 2002a) observes, these belong to the television, not the political platform or the polis.

As Connor (2003) suggests, the liquid modern consumer world is one that is best described as an age of *extimacy*: 'a fizzing mist of complex and changeable identifications and interactions'. A hybrid world that is at once abstract and intimate, 'out there' but instantly always looming 'close-up'. And with this consumer reality is a quite specific 'style' of being in the world, a stage-managed style of fractured, erratic, fluid and above all else palimpsest dispositions towards a world wary of anything which attempts to exist beyond its 'sell by date'.

Bauman's sociology suggests that the rise of this consumer sociality has been underpinned by the emergence of a majority who are cash-rich or credit worthy and time-poor and who are under ever increasing pressure to reconcile being both 'good' workers and 'good' consumers. The trick is in consumer capitalism's ability constantly to keep moving the goalposts and the upshot is that this liquid version of consumerism 'creates' individuals who appear to be not so much intrinsically greedy as intermittently greedy. Just when they think they have arrived 'where it is at', they find that 'it' has shifted, moved somewhere else; and so their search must begin once again. This is because the obsolescence built into consumer goods means that they date hopelessly, and are guaranteed to do so.

What is more, as Natoli (1997: 179–80) argues, there is (no)thing that is uncommodifiable in liquid modernity and even that:

> popular culture [including sport] self-commodifies. It doesn't resist the power of the market. It can't. Popular culture doesn't pretend to be outside the culture; it's already inscribed in the flux of culture, including, of course, the market metanarrative. Unfortunately for that metanarrative, however, is the fact that popular culture, with a passport to go anywhere it can to make a profit, often finds itself reflecting unsettled, problematic values and meanings. Nothing is meant to counter market values but the possibility yet remains that countering values can be made conceivable.

People's emotional engagement with consumer culture is all-pervasive in liquid modernity. As a consequence, 'liquid moderns' are destined to live their lives on the surface. They have to, since there is nothing much below it. They have no credible history they are aware of – only the nostalgia for a marketwise DIY ready-made historicity – and no culture other than a consumer culture that is their own. The major accomplishment of this culture is that when they enter this marketwise dream world of consumption they can be anything they want to be – just like the footballers who adorn the back pages of the tabloid press: 'good' or 'bad', 'normal' or 'deviant', all they need is the transformative touch of a 'Changing Rooms' style bought makeover.

Wrapped up with consumption is the subversion of linear narratives, such as age and time, so that we can be 40, a teenager, parent, grandparent all at once. Indeed, as we have already suggested, the liquid modern aphorism of the self is equally not what it used to be and becomes instead a series of episodes rather than a self-constancy. Moreover, when the self is palimpsest and polysemic it means that there is no necessary conflict between the most dirty and scopifilic desires of our 'deviant' self and other aspects of the self, such as our personal relationships and professional personas.

Liquid modernity suggests a consumer world that allows people to become self-indulgent, so rich and so powerful as to submerge, dissolve and liquefy – for the moment at any rate – all linear narratives. The almost pathological enthusiasm to consume is chiefly the work of living out fantasy; a fantasy involving a desire turned into a wish (Bauman, 2003). Indeed, in a consumer sociality the 'will to desire' (the desiring gaze) and the 'will to be desired' (through the gaze of others) struggle unabashed to hold our attention. This is because of the intense, intricate and incomparable feelings of being desired and of desiring that come with the synopticon 'gaze' which we consider in more detail below. And in a consumer society the narcissistic mirrored walls of gyms and 'fitness' centres staffed by personal trainers espousing positive affirmations of self ensure that the power of the 'gaze' does not go unreciprocated. For the horror of the synopticon is not the fear of being watched but the fear of not being watched and not being desired, which manifests itself in self-loathing and the perversion of introversion.

Consumer culture, celebrity culture and 'deviance'

If this consumer world is in many ways defined by individual narcissism, it is also defined by individuals' neurotic obsession with authenticity, the blind worship of celebrity, the frantic urge to consume. We want to argue that implicit to the idea of consumer culture is celebrity culture and the relationship between the two suggests that they have to be understood in the same manner that Foucault understood power and knowledge: they are two sides of the same coin.

If consumers of sport love celebrities, they love their very own, home-bred celebrities even more. As Conrad (2003) shows, the most loved sporting celebrity of them all, David Beckham, is a free-floating signifier who is an expert in self-reincarnation:

> he is a pair of trainers, you wear him till you wear him out, then you throw him away . . . If he is a meatball, you gobble him up, absorb his goodness, and then excrete what's left . . . Consumerism is greedy and fickle, and Beckham . . . is fast food.

But the key to Beckham's success as a celebrity is that he is able to continually reinvent himself and his existence is *several* – not *one* – and is pronounced by a series of transubstantiations. Should they fall from the public's 'gaze' liquid modern celebrities, like David Beckham, have no qualms about reinventing themselves, including inviting persecution out of the fear of invisibility.

Celebrity individuals in a consumer age are tele-visual people and they perceive that the body is a surface that can display itself in different ways at different times, the self becoming a renewable resource in a world where radical discontinuity has become the lived reality. In the cut-throat world of liquid modernity, competing is really the only way to get noticed, to gain a profile: to be someone in liquid modernity is to be a celebrity. What is more, to be hated makes celebrities feel more 'real', authentic; that they have made their presence felt. In liquid modernity, to be 'deviant' is to be unforgettable. This is why sport is key for ordinary 'celebrity' individuals, who in their own sporting activities hope to become in one inglorious inversion their very own everyday DIY versions of the celebrity 'deviants'.

This is a tangible remedy to the frenzied task of living the dice-life in which the security of a fixed identity is exchanged for the palimpsest life-strategy of what Baudrillard (2001) has dubbed the 'double life'. For each and every one of these 'celebrities' – 'authentic' or 'pretending' – knows that the only 'truths' that really matter in liquid modernity are the exaggerations made possible by the 'double life' – hyper-celebrity, hyper-deviancy, hyper-bole, hyper-masculinity, hyper-trophy, hyper-sexuality, hyper-anything as exemplified by the exaggeration and extremity which underpins the competitive 'sports' format of TV shows such as *Gladiators, Pop Idol, Big Brother* and *I'm a Celebrity Get Me Out of Here*. Since, as Baudrillard suggests, the liquid consumer world in which we reside is itself a hyper-real world.

Consumptive 'deviance' and sport

Consumptive 'deviance' is hyper-real. It is any form of 'deviance' that has featured in the mass media, on television. It is the 'deviance' that the celebrity seeks to endorse. It is 'deviance' that buyers decide to buy. It is 'deviance' denounced by establishment forces – sporting bodies, the FA, the BBC. Consumptive 'deviance' reflects Baudrillard's (1989) culture of the 'into' – 'into' sport, 'into' sex, 'into' death as well as Presdee's 'carnival of crime' (2000). It authenticates a style, a fashion, a thrill; it provokes media attention. Consumptive 'deviance' is not a disease of the mind, of some disturbed inner state, but a kind of performance. It may have all the hallmarks of deviance, including its violence, its unpredictability and dangerousness, but it is scripted, a stage-managed DIY or ready-made version of 'deviance', to be consumed and to be consumed by.

With consumptive 'deviance' individuals can leave the drama of the really dangerous world for the world of consumer culture. The hallowed world of 'real deviance' is invaded by consumer culture, for example, the 'new' virtual football hooligans who on their computers can now choose to do the 'business' at a cool distance. No place is left now for the 'deviant' imagination as orthodox sociology knew it. No insane suggestions. No dreams of possibility embodied in the collective euphoria of the drama – only staged, marketised intimations of a 'deviant' identity.

Consumptive 'deviance' begins where authenticity, perversity, filth and sickness leave off, end, cease to exist. It inhabits a different territory, a marketised cultural desert, and we for the most part live in that desert. The wonderful thing about consumptive 'deviance' is just that: it is consumptive, nothing more than an excruciatingly staged-performance act. It is for the moment. And you can do anything with it – if you can afford the 'costs'. Consumptive 'deviance' is compelling in a profound way, because it is imagined to be all the things that 'real' deviance is. It allows those who 'buy' into it to witness or feel subversive, dirty, sexy and desired. It can momentarily promote hurt, fear, pain and entertainment without the exit wounds. Consumptive 'deviance' entertains at the same time as making itself feel like the 'real thing'. It works ingeniously through strategies of entertainment, with comprehensive engagement not required. It celebrates the unextraordinary moment, that familiar quality of consumption, which is the defining existential feature of liquid modernity. In the end, consumptive 'deviance' works because it cuts to the quick at warped speed; and it is able to provide intimations of the ecstasy of the dirty, the foul, the perverted, the sublime – the 'feeling' of 'deviance'.

In this context, sport, whilst a janus-faced pursuit, an expedient of both freedom *and* an instrument of repression, has always offered spaces for the pursuit of the different and the 'deviant', from the ritualised and largely socially acceptable rule-breaking activities, such as foul play, to the more abhorrent forms of crime against the vulnerable, such as sexual abuse. And in its commodified and mediatised contemporary form it offers consumers of it even more choices. Indeed, it is through images and representations that the market economy offers for our consumption sport as 'deviance' and it is through sport that our desires for the 'deviant' other tend more and more to be fulfilled. In a culture in which consumption is paramount consumptive 'deviance' in sport becomes yet another life style choice. Just as the market is able to freeze-frame and capture for every new generation the most important sporting moments – Bobby Moore lifting the World Cup, Mohamed Ali and George Foreman's 'Rumble in the Jungle', Shergar crossing the line at Epsom – it is also equally effective in the ways in which it is able to absorb and regurgitate 'deviance' – the feel, the smell and the taste of it – for their consumption.

Yet the consumption of 'deviance' always has meaning for those implicated. And this involves the perceived sense of something being done which is morally wrong and the ubiquitous aesthetic thrill that comes at the moment of revelation. This consumption of 'deviance' seeks to capture a sense of the phantasmagoric nature of existence which eludes people in the mundane quotidian of their everyday lives. In a nutshell, this consumption of 'deviance' offers its performers and consumers alike the 'perfect' simulacrum of the very disorder they are in the process of celebrating.

This consumption of 'deviance' also involves its protagonists in a process of self-identification with the 'real' perpetrators, calling to mind gratuitous pleasures as they watch them. The authors of these imaginings revere the link with the 'dirtiness', the 'perverse' and the 'filth' associated with these 'deviant' acts – the 'juicy' tackles, the 'big' hits, the 'dirty' tactics and so on. This search for 'dirtiness' and 'filth' is then a search for escape from the 'cleanliness' and 'morality' associated with the mundane quotidian in sport for a world in which the 'ugliness' of 'deviance' is both championed and celebrated whilst being simultaneously and hypocritically condemned.

This sort of 'deviance' acquires a consumer form which allows its perpetrators, like dying old men, to see the fragments of other lives imagined in subliminal rushes. Except of course these rushes do not, like the dying old men's, call to mind what went before, but take the form of invented or carefully stage-managed risks. For those living in liquid modernity it would seem are often too juvenilely unable to live with their everyday 'normality' to escape the need to invent their own 'deviance'. As Baudrillard suggests the neo-individual 'invents' risks rather than facing his or her destiny head-on. DIY 'deviance' kits, then, are utilised not only to inflate images and reputations, but also to compensate for all that is otherwise not happening, as if to distract individuals from an underlying ennui that pervades their everyday lives when they are not consuming. It is as if for Baudrillard it is through the 'performativity' of consumptive 'deviance' that liquid moderns can usurp that which was once assumed to be the 'real' itself. And in order to better understand the implications of this critical perspective for theorising 'deviance' in sport it is to the major theories of 'performativity' that we must now turn.

The performativity of 'deviance'

Presentation of the self in everyday life: Goffman and the ethnomethodologists

Erving Goffman (1959, 1961) was one of the first major theorists to explore the idea of performativity in some critical depth. Goffman's sociology is located in the symbolic interactionist tradition, which seeks to explain social action by understanding the 'interaction order' of particular 'life-worlds' relating to individual actors themselves. As Ritzer (2003) points out, Goffman focused on the dramaturgical nature of social life, which led him to explore symbolic interaction as an endless sequence of dramatic performances similar to those performed on stage. Drawing on a number of theatre analogies, Goffman set out a categorisation of dramaturgical contingencies through which he identified the key 'stage props' or strategies individual actors might draw on in order to negotiate their way through everyday life.

At the same time that Goffman was developing these ideas about performativity, studies in ethnomethodology (Cicourel, 1964; Garfinkel, 1967), which set out to uncover the 'methods' by which actors construct their everyday lives, were being developed. These sought to show that, during performances, individuals are not only able to convince others about their social identities – through the structures of everyday activities which they ordinarily and routinely produce and maintain – but can also disrupt tacitly agreed and taken-for-granted assumptions about everyday life through 'breaching experiments' (see Garfinkel, 1967).

Like the ethnomethodologists Goffman centred his own analysis on individual actors and the ways they present themselves in everyday life, but differently to them what he was also offering was a sociology which took more account of the institutional and structural aspects of the interaction order. In this respect Goffman was alert to the point that although individual actors can draw on a range of techniques in order to maintain the presentation of the self, performativity comprises, not merely singular acts in order to perform a 'personal front', but also established or institutionalised roles. For Goffman, then, dramaturgical performances tend to be embedded in an already existing reality and are selected rather than individually created (Ritzer, 2003).

These latter points notwithstanding, the social construction of the self remained at the very heart of Goffman's analysis, and from Butler's (1990, 1993) perspective this reflects the major weakness of his sociology. Even though Goffman takes into account both institutional and structural aspects of the interaction order, he understands the individual presentation of the self as a performance rather than the 'front end' of performativity. Goffman's solidly modernist understanding of the self is 'fixed' and 'deep' rather than 'liquid' and 'aesthetic'; he constructs an understanding of the self at the 'centre' of things and this understanding is underpinned by a foundationalism which, in Butler's terminology, 'presumes, fixes and constrains' the individual subject.

What Butler is suggesting is that conventional wisdom in sociology tends not only to be preoccupied with the 'individual' or 'individual experience' but also understands the human *habitus* as something that lies deep in the human condition; like some sort of trace which is deep rooted and a seemingly 'natural' basis for people's interaction with the world. Yet, what her critique of Goffman's interpretation of the self is suggesting, is that there is actually nothing below the surface and the individual does not exist outside discourse – what you see is what you get – and what the self performs is merely performativity, which contrary to conventional wisdom actually turns assumptions about the 'natural' back on themselves. As Butler (1990: 186) argues, 'just as bodily surfaces are enacted as natural, so these surfaces can become a site of dissonant and denaturalized performance that reveal the performative status of the natural itself'. Contrary to Goffman, from Butler's perspective it is a waste of time attempting to find or uncover the 'true' or 'real' self; the self is always defined in the performativity of the business of everyday life and this performativity is always a transaction with others. This is the central difference between Goffman and the poststructuralist interpretations of individual subjectivity and performativity which we will discuss in more detail below. However, it is to Lyotard's post-modernist inspired understanding of performativity that we must turn first of all.

Lyotard and the performativity of truth

According to the postmodern theorist Lyotard (1984), the idea of performativity is coterminous with the new 'generalised spirit' of knowledge underpinning the social, cultural, political and economic shift to a 'postmodern' society. Lyotard stresses that, in keeping with these 'postmodern' changes, performativity marks a conspicuous shift in the way in which knowledge claims come to be legitimated. In a nutshell, modern knowledge – as opposed to postmodern knowledge – established its monopoly of *truth* through the use of grand narratives or big stories, which were able to legitimate themselves in such compelling ways that they were hardly questioned. In modern society, science was the chief criterion by which the most convincing of these knowledge claims were made.

However, for Lyotard as for Baudrillard, with the advent of 'postmodern' society, capitalism becomes so pervasive that there is nothing left that is not commodifiable. Inevitability science becomes merely another commodity and in turn 'truth' is now determined, not by its ability to tell the 'truth', but by its exchange value. Basically, if modern society stood for the language game of denotation (the difference between true or false), postmodern society stands for an alternative, 'technical' game of efficiency versus inefficiency. As a result performativity becomes the new criterion of the legitimacy of knowledge claims. In postmodern society everybody seems to have a view about what constitutes the 'truth' and as a result various 'language games' or knowledge claims are made, and these are played out through the 'techniques and technologies' of performativity. For Lyotard, this plurality of competing voices is made possible by the 'performativity criterion' which invokes an 'incredulity to metanarratives' – in short, scepticism towards any idea or theory which posits universal truth claims.

To sum up, for Lyotard, in 'postmodern' society the status of knowledge is altered and performativity comes to represent a kind of neo-capitalist efficiency which is able to bring the 'pragmatic functions of knowledge clearly to light and elevate all language games to self-knowledge' (Lyotard, 1984: 114). In Austin's (1975) terminology, truth is now performative rather than constative and the most convincing truth claims are those which the market will determine are the most performatively efficient. Yet despite his deep scepticism about the further consolidation of capitalist values in 'postmodern' society, Lyotard remains ambivalent about performativity. This is because performativity is more acceptable than the legislating kind of 'truth' which was the hallmark of solid modern society. Consequently, for Lyotard, performativity is sublime precisely because it acknowledges its own limits; that is, it is inspired by that which is not presentable and takes its pleasure in the existential awareness of recognising the impossibility of its own totality.

Judith Butler and the performativity of drag

Butler also develops the linguistic notion of performativity found in the edited collection of the philosophy of J. L. Austin's (1975) *How to Do Things with Words*. Following Austin (and Foucault), Butler (1990) argues that performativity must be understood as a discursive mode by which subjectivity is effected. Butler uses drag as an example of performativity and in so doing suggests that it is a serious business, even when it is ostensibly comedic. Butler does not think that if we 'dragged out' more, 'gender life would become more expansive and less restrictive'. On the contrary, she argues that there are limits to the subversive efficacy of drag. For Butler, drag, like many other aspects of social life has its own morose side. Some people have mistakenly understood that Butler identifies drag to be a paradigm for performativity, and she finds this interpretation of performativity interesting as it evinces an apparent public desire or fantasy with the 'theatrical remakings of the body' associated with drag (Butler, 1994) .

Butler (1994) argues that it is important to distinguish 'performance' from 'performativity'. As we have stressed already, this is because the notion of performance presumes a solid subject, i.e. it is me – a solid self – who puts on a performance. Evans (2003: 17) misses the point of this argument when she suggests that, Butler merely focuses her attention 'on the performance by men and women of differentiated gender identities' rather than also exploring social class and ethnicity, which are equally important. Presdee (2000) too focuses on the expressive nature of the performance of the 'carnival of crime' rather than exploring its performativity as such. As we have already seen, for Butler, the concept of performativity decentres or 'contests the very notion of the subject' *behind* the performance. As she argues, 'just as bodily surfaces are enacted as the natural, so these surfaces can become the site of dissonant and denaturalized performance that reveals the performative status of the natural itself' (Butler, 1990: 146). For Butler the commonsensical understanding of the solid world of gender relations (and for that matter social class and ethnicity) turns out to be not so solid after all. Butler is making the point that discourses are not without foundation; that is they might not have any privileged or clear direction, but they at all times emerge at some time from somewhere.

Butler also argues that performativity is always nuanced with otherness; that is, it must be understood as a kind of 'deviance' from the other. She also suggests that it is the act of performativity that makes the world of gender relations 'apparently' solid. For Butler, this is the point when discourses become productive in specific ways. Performativity is 'that aspect of discourse that has the capacity to produce what it names'. Subsequently, and borrowing from Derrida, she suggests that this production always happens through a certain kind of repetition, recital or story. In this sense, performativity is a form of theatre through which ontological *effects* are established. In a nutshell, 'identity is performatively constituted by the very "expressions" that are said to be its results' (Butler, 1990: 23). Yet Butler also wants us to understand that the 'norms' through whose recurrence performativity works must always have a history and be recognisable. Finally, Butler brings our attention to the ambivalence that makes performativity always mutable, always needing to repeat through reiteration the *effects* of its own performativity – of what it is and what it is not – in order to reinforce its own aesthetics of existence. As she puts it: 'The reconceptualisation of identity as an effect, that is, produced or generated, opens up the possibilities of "agency" that are insidiously foreclosed by positions that take identity categories as foundational or fixed' (Butler,1990: 147).

Diamond (1997: 47) challenges Butler's propensity to over-simplify the 'complexity of practices that constitute cultural and social existence' by reducing our understanding of performativity and its 'iterative sites' to theory and the theorist's critical gaze at the expense of exploring in more imaginative ways the wider performance within which performativity is constituted. As Diamond's critique implies, the idea of performance need not mean foundationalism – performance matters because it 'is the site in which performativity materializes in concentrated form, where the "concealed or dissimulated conventions" of which acts are mere repetitions might be investigated and reimagined'.

We revisit the ideas of 'performance' and 'performativity' in Chapter 7, to critically explore the consumptive 'deviance' associated with the 'sport' of cruising. However, before we move on to the final section of the book it is imperative to discuss the 'new' forms of surveillance, power and social control that emerge with liquid modernity. The purpose of this discussion is not only to provide the final part of the jigsaw which constitutes our own reinvigorated discourse for the sociology of 'deviance', but it is also achieved in order to provide a critical starting point for our analysis of 'liquid' social control through community sport, which is the major focus of Chapter 8.

The 'new' liquidity of 'deviance', power and social control

Repression and seduction: from the panopticon to the synopticon

As the reader will recall, in Chapter 3 we suggested that, for Foucault, in modern societies there is no single power source and society operates as a giant panoptic mechanism which achieves social control through the disciplining, marginalising and subordinating effects of the normalising gaze. In line with our own analysis,

Bauman (1992a) has drawn on this aspect of Foucault's theory of surveillance to suggest that, in our contemporary world, consumption has emerged, for the masses, as the new 'inclusionary reality' or normalising constraint.

Bauman argues that, contrary to the postulations of the critical theory of Habermas (1976), in the postmodern sociality, the 'weapon of legitimation' – the hegemony by which the state acquires its *raison d'être* – has been supplanted 'with two mutually complementary weapons: this of *seduction* and that of *repression*' (Bauman, 1992a: 97–8). Bauman adds, *vis-à-vis* Giddens (1991), that experts and expert systems play a crucial role in the liquid modern sociality, but not in Habermas's sense. They are no longer needed to serve the needs of capitalism to 'legitimate' the dominant hegemony, rather, in Bauman's critical theory, experts and expert systems become crucial to the enforcement and preservation of the weapons of *seduction* and *repression*. In a consumer culture, the market accomplishes its ideal the minute it 'succeeds in making consumers dependent on itself' (Bauman, 1992a: 98).

Bauman suggests that today if we are all consumers, it is only the minority, the 'flawed consumers' (Bauman, 1995), whose subordinate position prevents them from participating freely in what has become for the masses a dream world of consumption. Consequently, today it is only the poor who experience the hard edge of exclusionary and repressive surveillance. As Bauman (1992a: 98) points out, '*repression* stands for "Panoptical" power, as described by Foucault. It employs surveillance . . . and is indispensable to reach the areas *seduction* cannot, and is not meant to, reach'. A crucial role that repression carries out in this respect is to elucidate the unappealing traits of non-participation in the realm of the free market, by reforging 'the unattractiveness of non-consumer existence into the unattractiveness of alternatives to market dependency'.

Ultimately, it is the prevailing presence of repression that manifests itself in the form of the welfare services – the reforms that once aimed to destroy the 'five giants' of want, disease, squalor, ignorance and idleness – which makes seduction the secure vanquisher in this game of domination. Rather than being emancipatory the welfare services today constitute a second-rate and repressive regime, which have recourse to the expert and governmentalised 'gaze' of those employed by the state: the DSS officer, the community sports development worker, the GP, the social worker, the probation officer, and so forth that collectively 'police' the 'flawed consumers'. In Feeley and Simon's terms this approach is 'concerned with techniques to identify, classify, and manage groupings sorted by dangerousness. The task is managerial not transformative' (1992: 452).

As Foucault (1977) points out, this modern form of repressive social control which always operates at a distance has been made possible through the construction of what Anthony Giddens (1991) has identified as 'experts' and 'expert systems' which claim the necessary authority to command the power/knowledge of governmentality. For Bauman (1995: 100), 'distance' is of the utmost importance here since it is not merely used to differentiate 'us' from 'them', it also allows 'us' to construct 'them' as 'the objective of aesthetic, not moral evaluation; as a matter of taste, not responsibility'. This process is what Bauman describes as idiaphorisation, which essentially marks the comfortable but anxious majority's disengagement with a commitment and responsibility for the poor. As he puts it, the principle of this type of social distancing is 'making certain actions, or certain objects of action, morally neutral or irrelevant – exempt from the category of moral evaluation' (1995: 149).

A point no better exemplified than through Presdee's consideration of the joyriders on the Blackbird Leys estate in Oxford, an otherwise invisible underclass whose illegal car chases he argues might have 'occurred because for those on the estate, there is no other site of carnival' (2000: 51), no access to the legitimised transgressive potential of the market-place. In this sense, following Rose, the repressive regime might be:

> better understood as operating through conditional access to circuits of consumption and civility . . . [which] may succeed in producing enclaves of contentment and encouraging the pursuit of pleasure, [but are] grounded in an exclusionary logic: those who are excluded – the new 'dangerous classes' – are forced to consume elsewhere.
>
> (Presdee, 2000: 190–5)

This new centrality of consumerism and the performative 'deviance' which it has spawned also points us to Bauman's (1998a) later work on the theme of seduction and repression, which draws on a paper by Thomas Mathiesen (1997), to argue that the logic of the repressive apparatus of the panopticon has largely been supplemented by the seductive allure of synopticon watching. For in our present-day society it is by and large not the few *who watch the many* (panopticon), but rather *the many who watch the few* (synopticon). For Bauman, as for Mathiesen, the power mechanism of the synopticon, facilitated as it is by new technologies, allows the many to watch the few, and the few who are most keenly watched are the celebrities, including those from the world of sport:

> They may come from the world of politics, of sport, of science or show business, or just be celebrated information specialists. Wherever they come from, though, all displayed celebrities put on display the world of celebrities – a world whose main distinctive feature is precisely the quality of being watched – by many, and in all corners of the globe: of being global in their capacity of being watched.
>
> (Bauman, 1998b: 53)

What is also significant about the synopticon, however, from the point of view of our own analysis, is that unlike the repressive apparatus of the panopticon it 'needs no coercion'. But at the same time the penetrating and scopophilic eye of the synopticon is also malicious, disrespectful: it specialises in spying on what ought not to be seen and what those under its 'gaze' feel they must reveal or confess themselves. It is also through the wider public's desires for 'a bit' of the deviant other that the synopticon seduces the many into watching the few. And with this synopticonal 'gaze' come 'new' and 'cool' ways of imagining 'sport', 'deviance', 'sex', 'gender', 'violence', 'fitness', 'the self', 'bodies' and the like, which follow on from and join the extant discourses of power/knowledge, such as 'the work ethic', 'scientific truth', 'sexual emancipation' and 'health control', which undergirded the panopticon 'gaze' as Foucault imagined it.

When two became one: the 'reality principle' and the 'pleasure principle' strike a deal

For Bauman (2002a) the major achievement of the modern world underpinned by the panopticon 'gaze' was its ability to suppress the 'pleasure principle' associated with people's desire for 'deviance'. For Freud (1920), the 'pleasure principle' is a tendency inherent in the unconscious of all individuals, and involves their 'wishes' to seek their own satisfactions regardless of all other considerations. In what Bauman has described as solid modernity the suppression of these 'wishes' operated through what Freud called the 'reality principle'. However, the price of the triumph of the 'reality principle' was the temporary suspension of the 'pleasure principle', which had to be put off *ad infinitum*. In the event, solid modernity achieved its status quo by 'allowing' its incumbents to achieve the utmost possible expression of their desires with 'normalising' conditions. Basically shame was what maintained the 'reality principle': the shame of being found with one's pants down in a compromising situation unworthy of somebody 'normal'. That is individuals had to be sure they knew the differences between 'fantasy' and 'reality' in accord with the demands of the 'reality principle'. People were of course wont to take some risks but this did not ultimately ever lead to the complete undermining of the moral order, because with the 'reality principle' intact:

> rather than complete suspension of morality one finds the lifting of the curtain of morals followed by embarrassed or guilty returns to moral codes (Shields, 1992: 8). And so the attempt to escape perishes because it depends upon the very conventions that make everyday life possible. By searching for the total sexual encounter, the orgy of freedom and self-expression, the unbridled carnivalesque and the other 'real' experiences which lie beyond civil society, we collide with the antinomies of our desire.
>
> (Rojek, 1995: 88)

As such the guiding feature of the 'reality principle' was procrastination. Phillips (2003: 9) suggests that desire is the watchword for a society dominated by the 'reality principle', because it is another word for a risk not taken: 'the unlived life that seems the only life worth living'.

The guiding feature of the 'pleasure principle' on the other hand is instant gratification. As Bauman suggests, liquid modernity is a world where the overriding view is that people must have what they desire as a 'wish' and have it now, this very minute. As he adds, the stock in trade aesthetic of consumption is its ability to abolish delay by taking 'the waiting out of wanting' (Bauman, 2000: 159). If, for Freud, the central goal of life was death, for Bauman, as for Baudrillard, the central goal of life today is to consume. Therefore it was inevitable that in a society where the individual is first and foremost *homo consumens* – rather than *homo faber* or *homo ludens* – that the 'pleasure principle' would come to the fore. Indeed, when the central goal in life is the pleasure of self-indulgence through instant gratification, putting off until later what is presently being denied through the 'reality principle', if not becoming an altogether redundant life-strategy has increasingly been cast in the shadow of the 'pleasure principle'. And when the 'normal' lost its authority, shame, if not disappearing, took on a different but equally meaningful role in people's lives.

Liquid modernity is a world committed, passionate one might say, on people revealing themselves; it is the world of *Big Brother*. With liquid modernity came the individuals' need to shed the burden of their shame, in order to ease the pain: the need to share the anxiety of their distress, to have someone else to carry the burden, not *for* them – in a society of individuals that is too much to ask of anybody – but *with* them. This type of confessional takes two forms because in what is an increasingly visual culture we are all of us under an obligation to show, not just tell, our stories. Here, it is the celebrity, the ubiquitous tele-visual figure, who performs the central role; delivered directly from the clutches of *Alcoholics Anonymous* and 12-step celebrity rehabilitation programmes such as the former England football team captain Tony Adam's *Sporting Chance* charity to confess their alcoholism, drug addiction and depravity before millions of viewers eager to see how low our idols and super-heroes can go. In the fashion of our times the celebrity pays for treatment before putting the results of their treatment, their shame, up for sale in commodity form before the evaluative gaze of an audience obsessed with celebrity and its 'deviance'.

With liquid modernity, 'normalisation' is thus replaced by 'precarisation' as the 'reality principle' and the 'pleasure principle' strike a deal. As Bauman (2000) puts it, with liquid modernity it was as if the 'reality principle' and the 'pleasure principle' were destined to make each other's acquaintance, basically because consumer capitalism in its quest to maintain its prosperity now found a market for 'deviance' and it 'needed' its incumbents to live out their impulses, irrationalities and perversions ('sport' inevitably has come to play a key role in this process). In so doing he marked out that ambivalent territory at the beginning and the end of procrastination. He elucidates:

> The two kinds of space . . . are strikingly different, yet interrelated: they do not converse with each other, yet are in constant communication: they have little in common, yet stimulate similarity. The two spaces are ruled by sharply dissimilar logics, mould different life experiences, gestate diverging life itineraries and narratives which use distinct, often opposite definitions of similar behavioural codes. And yet both spaces are accommodated within the same world – and the world they both are part of is the world of vulnerability and precariousness.
>
> (Bauman, 2000: 160)

In liquid modernity the 'solid' conventions of the 'reality principle' are replaced by a 'precarised' hybrid existence far more pervasive, a reality which is paradoxically more intense but at the same time much less sure, less precise than its predecessor – something indefinite, cut into a series of episodes, which is none the less sublime in its ephemerality. And what this hybrid world does not share with the imagined worlds of either the 'reality principle' or the 'pleasure principle' is a distinctive singular feel. With the emergence of this hybrid world people begin to realise that their most desirable desires are sometimes risks worth taking, worth paying the consequences for. No where is this hybrid relationship better illustrated than in the world of sport. On the one hand, sport – and particularly team sport – is still imagined as that bastion of Corinthian spirit, muscular Christianity and 'rational recreation'. By contrast, for many people today 'individualised' sports, from the more conventional 'new' sporting forms such as base-jumping and snowboarding to the more unconventional sporting forms such as sadomasochism, provide the time and space to live out some of their most dangerous wishes.

Conclusions

In developing Foucault, Bauman and others' more critical insights in the final part of this book we shall argue that with the synopticon and the 'precarised' hybrid existence of the 'reality principle' and the 'pleasure principle' the ways and means of developing docile minds and bodies has shifted to a more subtle set of 'tactics' and 'techniques' which coalesce more comfortably with the 'new needs' of consumer capitalism in its 'liquid' stage. As we show, the more intimately individualised life is colonised, the more it becomes illuminated by the light of the 'gaze' and one key effect of this shift is the explosion of an 'excess' of synoptic pleasure-seeking discourses, which intersperse with the 'normative' regulation associated with panopticon surveillance and the 'reality principle'. Indeed, in relation to this analysis we draw on one of the great achievements of Bauman's sociology, which is its alertness to the ambivalence of liquid modern life where the slipperiness of contemporary social formations is evidenced between the panopticon and the synopticon, between the 'reality principle' and the 'pleasure principle', between the 'abnormal' and 'deviant'.

We began this chapter by suggesting that to be able to explore 'deviance' in sport in an effective way we needed a social theory ready-made for the task in hand. It is from Bauman and Baudrillard that our own social theory has in the main been developed, and in the process we have learned from the former that synopticon-style surveillance is, at least 'on the surface', more democratic than its predecessor with the ubiquitous 'liquid' modern frontierland (Bauman, 2002a) characterised by variety and choice replacing the closed secure confinement of yesteryear.

Focusing specifically on how this relates to sport and our fetishisms for 'deviant' otherness, in the final part of this book we attempt to ground this theory and argue that when the 'pleasure principle' comes to the fore it is individual autonomy and self-reflexivity that both facilitates and centralises this 'new' gaze. The implication that runs as a thread throughout this discussion will be that this hybrid form of surveillance is not merely a technique of power and domination, but an aesthetic, connected to much wider cultural tendencies. It is a source of confession, scopophilia, voyeurism, fetishisms, of *Enkrateia* – what Foucault referred to as the principle of 'self-mastery' in the process of assuring pleasure – and other matters that he variously located in the politics of 'self-government' and 'self-fashioning', and which we suggest all relate to the freedoms, social distinctions and regulation found in the realm in sport. As we show, following the later Foucault, this *'care of the self'* emerges underpinned by an aesthetical principle (McNay, 1994), that leads the individual to work him or herself, to not only improve his or her inner character, but to do so in a manner that is conducive to the 'cultivation of the self' through an *aesthetics of existence* made to the measure of what Foucault himself never really anticipated: the omnipresent centrality of a consumer culture.

Indeed, in this chapter we have suggested time and again that because individuals' emotional engagement with consumer culture is now so pervasive it is not surprising that the 'deviance' in sport it spawns tends to be a fascination with the consumption of a style of 'deviance' – of sex, perversity, sickness, filth and violence of a 'consumer' kind; so much so that the 'performativity' it encourages might best be termed consumptive 'deviance'. And it is with our idea of consumptive 'deviance' and sport that Chapter 6 is concerned. First of all, however, we need to address both the metaphysics and mechanics of the methodology underpinning our own research approach and it is this topic that we take up in the next chapter.

5 'Talking tactics'

Representing 'deviance' in sport

Only descriptions of the world can be true or false. The world on its own –unaided by the describing activities of human beings – cannot.

(Richard Rorty)

Introduction

This chapter is about both the actual social practice and the metaphysics of the research process. What this entails more specifically involves us making a case for our own critical understanding of ethnography in the sociology of sport, which breaks with essentialist methodological approaches in order to explore the complex social interaction that characterises the discursively constituted social formations of sport. The interpretation of ethnography we flesh out in this chapter suggests that, if we are to cultivate some suggestive and insightful understandings of the problematic of 'deviance' in sport, the sort of social enquiry we must develop is one that places a premium on the contingency of local and historically specific social practices. Our analysis in this chapter demonstrates the point that attempting to abstract 'deviance' from the quotidian of its context is an unconvincing cure for this contingency.

While acknowledging that performance and surveillance are ubiquitous today, our approach follows Richard Rorty (1991) in insisting that 'there are people out there whom society has failed to notice'. The aim of our approach to ethnography is then to make the social worlds we investigate 'visible' through a coherent intellectual framework, which at the same time elucidates those worlds as they are perceived by their incumbents. What this entails is the formation of what we describe as an alternative epistemic method of investigation for 'ethnography' – a form of tactics rather than a methodology as such – which works for 'good and assignable reasons' (Jenkins, 1995) and which we believe tells the reader something about 'deviance' in sport in new and better ways than do extant approaches in the sociology of sport. In this chapter we also call into question conventional characterisations of methodology to deal with that which should be central to any critical exploration of 'deviance' in sport: this of the unthinkable and that of the unmentionable.

The way we go about our task is as follows. In a recent article in the *International Review For the Sociology of Sport*, 'Digging the Dirt and Staying Clean', John Sugden and Alan Tomlinson (1999b) set out a research agenda that attempted to re-establish a way of doing empirical work which gives critical sociology of sport a more thoroughgoing ethico-political substance than is presently the case. In exploring the 'deviancy' associated with ticket touting in football, Sugden and Tomlinson attempt to establish, through an ethnographic approach which draws on the rhetorical strategies of the gonzo approach to journalistic enquiry, a passionate element in critical social enquiry. They do so by recognising that an affective quality should be recognised explicitly in the writing of ethnographic accounts.

As one of us has argued elsewhere (Blackshaw, 2003), although Sugden and Tomlinson continue, with authors such as Hobbs (1988), to evoke the type of ethnography developed by the Chicago school, their article provides us with a model of ethnographic writing, which is more appropriate for contemporary sociology of sport. They align this model with the popular gonzo journalistic writing pioneered by Hunter S. Thompson. In that Sugden and Tomlinson offer what they believe to be both a critical and ethically responsible way of doing ethnographic research on 'deviance' in sport and in that they anchor themselves within a coalition, which merges the sort of depth ethnography practised by Douglas (1976) with the anti-postmodern position promulgated by Ward (1997), it is particularly useful to critique their work. Evidence will suggest that it is not so much Sugden and Tomlinson's use of Douglas that is problematic – although we do provide a thoroughgoing critique of some of the tacit assumptions made by practitioners of depth ethnography – but the immense importance that Sugden and Tomlinson appear to attach to Ward's (1997) metaphysics (for a critical discussion, see Blackshaw, 2002).

This latter criticism notwithstanding, in relation to fleshing out our own way of going about research, Sugden and Tomlinson not only provide an appropriate starting point to the metaphysics of ethnography in sport, they also provide the interpretive framework against which we are able to develop our own position in this chapter. To this extent the reader will see that our relationship with Sugden and Tomlinson is an ambivalent one, because, for us, there is a central paradox at the very heart of their sociology. On the one hand, there is the strong feeling of domesticity: an elegy for the sort of depth analysis associated with the Chicago school; a wistful yearning, if you like, for home comforts, for snug routine. On the other hand, there is an urge to explore the exotic, combined with a sense of wanting to confront the world of sport in ways that sociologists are not usually prepared to admit they do. It is against the backcloth of this paradox that the central crux of our own research is in the main developed.

We would like to stress at the outset that with Sugden and Tomlinson there is more to hone and develop than there is to oppose, and in the main we use their article, not to pick holes, but to demonstrate how their work has stimulated our own thoughts and our own 'method' of ethnography. In suggesting their own sociology of sport, Sugden and Tomlinson invoke a sort of amalgam of the library-based sociology of Anthony Giddens and the ethnographic work of Paul Willis as a model of good practice, which they use to augment the project of C. Wright Mills, by stirring the critical imagination in the sociology of sport. The first section of our critique is concerned then with Sugden and Tomlinson's interpretation of C. Wright Mills' (1959) conception of the 'sociological imagination'. In the two sections that follow we deal with two dichotomies, unambiguously identified by Sugden and Tomlinson, which continue to exasperate the 'synthetic' tradition (Mestrovic, 1998) in sociology: this of involvement and detachment and that of surface and depth. We then go on to build on this critique by discussing ethnographic writing and the 'gonzo' style, that turns out to be the most significant quality of Sugden and Tomlinson's methodology. This discussion explains by example and in so doing it also draws on Foucault's genealogical approach, which breaks with essentialist methodological approaches to illustrate, with reference to the actual process of 'doing' ethnography, the complex social interaction that characterises the discursively constituted social formations of the 'field' of ethnography. The concluding section fleshes out some of the 'tactics' associated with our own research approach and returns to some of the key ideas developed previously in order to problematise the role of ethnographer of 'deviance' in sport.

Sociological imagination

Sugden and Tomlinson break with the meta-theoretical tradition in the sociology of sport in which a purportedly objective, detached way of 'doing' sociology appears to be regarded as normative (see, for example, Brohm, 1978; Coakley, 1998; Dunning, 1999; Dunning and Rojek, 1992; Maguire, 1999). In evoking Mills' (1959) concept of the sociological imagination – 'that realm which creatively might connect the self and the other, private worries and social issues, individual identity and the public good' (Beilharz, 2000: 159–60) – they illustrate that just as sport is 'real life' driven by an energising imagination, so is sociology. Sugden and Tomlinson plainly recognise that the world of sport has changed and that the usefulness of some of the still dominant theories and concepts in the sociology of sport have deteriorated to such an extent that they no longer work as well as they once did.

Their own critical contribution and particularly their gonzo method of writing, gives a much-needed boost to the sociology of sport in a number of key ways. The authors themselves prefer to stress their contribution to the critical and political aspects of Mills' project. Just as importantly, however, their writing helps us to reconceive the sociology of sport itself.

Indeed, in much 'traditional' sport sociology there are not many connections that suggest a link between what is happening in the contemporary world of sport, on the one hand, and in the everyday lives of the students we teach and public we reach on the other. We want to argue here that Sugden and Tomlinson's methodology, but particularly their gonzo style, with its rich battery of rhetorical devices and effervescent dialogue with both sociological and sporting conventions, is an indispensable way of awakening and then encapsulating the sociological imaginations of our students. In one critical sense, their approach is straightforward: it deals with the familiar, as Sugden and Tomlinson point out, 'where and how humans live out their lives in particular times and places' (1999b: 388). It also deals with the exciting realism of contemporary sport which students already relate to. In our own teaching, we have found that people have ready-made theories about sport, structuring the quotidian of their daily lives, and the gonzo approach confirms rather than refutes these, making sport sociology inclusive to them. On another level, the theories and methods associated with Sugden and Tomlinson's approach are not well-defined. Consequently, they subvert, interrupt and disrupt which in turn invites student curiosity and leads to critical engagement with the literature.

These two elements, we want to argue, suggest that Sugden and Tomlinson's critical methodology prefigures a shift from a sociological imagination as Mills conceived it to a hermeneutic way of 'thinking sociologically' (Bauman, 1987) – a phenomenological hermeneutics to be more precise – which supposes that there are new emerging sensibilities with which to think and understand sociologically. The major stumbling block to developing hermeneutics in sociology has traditionally been in the complexity of the writing of its practitioners such as Heidegger and Ricoeur. Be that as it may our own approach follows Bauman in as much as we take up the challenge of making hermeneutics more *sociological* by extending the 'sociological imagination' (Bauman, 2002c). It does this by insisting that the sociological imagination is uncomplicatedly a demonstration of the interdependence between the imaginary and the 'real', analogous if you like to the epiphanies that characterise the world of sports through its attendant glory and emotional pull.

When reading 'Digging the Dirt and Staying Clean' one gets the feeling that Sugden and Tomlinson very much want to embrace the possibilities provided by this hermeneutic turn in sociology, but the sociology and methodological framework which they have inherited from Giddens/Willis and the Chicago school demands that this desire should be made subservient and secondary to pursuing the representation of the 'real'. This is strange because implicit in Sugden and Tomlinson's invocation of Hunter S. Thompson is the recognition that their own empirical findings will always remain partial and that the rhetorical strategy of gonzo allows them to fill a gap. As such we would contend that rhetorical devices are not used to replace the real, but to clarify, reinforce and enhance it. Misjudging this contingency amounts to a failure to engage with Mills' own critical project, which was not averse to pursuing the enchanting aspects of the intellectual imagination.

Striking similarities can be discerned between this methodological legacy and Sugden and Tomlinson's interpretation of metaphysics, which castigates what they understand as the 'postmodern' imagination for its turn away from ontology and by implication its refusal to pursue the 'real' in sociology. However, they find a target here which is itself an abstraction. In a much cited quote, Rorty (1982: 166) argues that '[r]elativism' is the view that every belief on a certain topic, or perhaps about *any* topic, is as good as every other'. But as he goes on to point out, 'no one holds this view', except perhaps the most naïve and inexperienced of individuals.

Our own approach, as we have already indicated, is relativistic granted that it does not try to make any absolute truth claims, but neither do we claim that ontological questions are not relevant to the sociological enterprise, as Sugden and

Tomlinson might suggest. Sociology is important to us because of its 'realism' and its ability to tell us our truths more plainly and deliberately than we tell them in everyday life. It is important for the reader to recognise at the outset, however, that the 'real' in this form of 'realism' is always contingent, conditional and subjective. Involvement in the 'real world' is both a desirable and a necessary requirement of our sociology. Yet interpretive accounts need to be addressed directly rather than obliquely, not least because they reflect, and in turn help to reproduce, different political environments, ideological stances and nationally defined agendas, in which sociologists themselves are implicated. In this sense, the key strength of our own sociology lies in its ability to be 'up front' about its own weaknesses and in its sensitivity to the discursive, ideological and practical contingencies involved in 'making' truth. It also insists that we examine these various ontological positions in relation to the worlds that we produce through our sociological imaginations.

Contrary to Wacquant, cited by Sugden and Tomlinson (1999b: 392), our sociology does not argue that it has arrived at 'some privileged position to produce true knowledge'. Certainly, the idea of situated or 'local' knowing is emphasised and developed in our work, in common with some variants of feminist writing. However, it is only the most naïve sort of scholarship which assumes that there is some 'real', inside-the-group, interpretation which can be accessed only by members of the group themselves. This assumption in fact rests upon an essentialist version of truth which we reject. If ours is a standpoint position in Sugden and Tomlinson's meaning, it is the way it gives emphasis to 'local' ways of knowing because it recognises that dominant cultures have a moral obligation to show consideration for oppressed groups which includes presenting them with the space and opportunity to inquire and reflect on their own situation and history. Under our phenomenological vision then, things are real only after people have agreed to sanction their realness. Happenings may occur but they are only made 'real' through observation, interpretation, debate and representation.

Our position, then, is underpinned by a conception of a moral right to respect, not a guarantee in advance that 'local' ways of knowing will always prove to be the most compelling. The 'best' written sociologies are more likely to be 'local' ways of knowing, because the 'locals' are thoroughly self-absorbed in those readings and their autobiographies intrude throughout. But ultimately the most compelling and the most rigorous sociologies will be those that have relevance and pertinence for those who are judging them, which cannot be set down in advance, nor can the criteria by which they will be assessed, for they will work for different people and in different ways. However, one thing is certain: no good scholar is going to be taken in by standpoints without substance.

Our approach is no less academically rigorous than Sugden and Tomlinson's critical position: we too interpret social interactions – even the seemingly most banal and insignificant – but always through a sociological lens. In its reappraisal of metaphysics our approach merely 'changes the subject' (Rorty, 1979) and asks the research community in the sociology of sport to temporarily suspend their own favoured positions and imagine that for now ontological questions do not apply.

What we are simply saying is this: for the time being take our word and join us in assuming certain things are 'true' and then, maybe, we can succeed in getting some good work done. And if we can inspire some critical dialogue, we will also have accomplished something along the way.

On being semi-detached

The meaning of Norbert Elias' critical distinction between 'involvement' and 'detachment' has long troubled figurationalism, which has for some time been the dominant theoretical strand within the British sociology of sport. Despite the implications of the contention that Elias used the term 'interdependence' unconditionally to mean this of independence (detachment) and that of dependence (involvement) (Scheff, 1997), numerous authors have brought to our attention the unresolved methodological and epistemological problems associated with 'doing' figurational sociology (see Layder, 1986; Rojek, 1985, 1986, 1992). On a comparable level there are questions and problems that Sugden and Tomlinson gloss over in their aspiration to attain semi-detachment which is implied in the very title 'Digging the Dirt and Staying Clean'.

In their discussion of the final part of their approach, Sugden and Tomlinson suggest a gonzo approach, which enables the researcher to get 'close to the centre of the action without ever being totally incorporated within it . . . to be part of the scene . . . *at the same time* being semi-detached from that experience' (1999b: 390). Supportive of Giddens (1991), Sugden and Tomlinson seem to be suggesting that the fusion between the knower and the known in the research process is never complete and in every epistemological relation, there is and should always be some element of detachment. This stance assumes that the modern individual perceives that they are the centre of the social world and that external subjects and objects are taken into the self to be constituted reflexively in terms of that individual's cognitive (and ethical) understanding. Indeed, for Giddens (1990, 1991), it is this existential contradiction that marks off individuals in modernity from their traditional counterparts: modern men and women reflexively understand themselves as being both part of and yet detached from the social world of others.

Yet, for Foucault (1981), this Anglo-Saxon grasping of the rational, cognitive individual at the centre of the social world represents an acute epistemological misreading, which leads to a simplistic and inadequate understanding of the complex discursive processes that connect human beings (Harland, 1987). Foucault represents the concept of agency in the sense that he theorises the agent as being at the same time both constituting of and constituted by discourse. However, for Foucault, being constituted is not the same thing as saying that the individual is determined in the structuralist meaning, quite the opposite in fact, as 'the constituted character of the [individual] is the very precondition of its agency' (Butler, 1991: 13). A tacit assumption of this approach to social enquiry is that there is no epistemological split, or subject–object relation, in the research process and that the researcher is 'already infiltrated with what is to be reached 'objectively"' (Natoli, 1997: 182).

This poststructuralist argument has an underlying metaphysic, which suggests that individuality and difference are ephemeral surface phenomena, destined to disappear as people move between discourses. This is why Foucault (1981) arrived at a point in the research process where he focused on systems of discourse and discourse as practice, not on understanding cognitive processes which place exclusive emphasis on people and what they say. Foucault breaks the distinction between involvement and detachment and shows the illusory nature of Sugden and Tomlinson's assertion that we as researchers have the ability to mark our independence, or disengage ourselves, from others through semi-detachment since we remain part of the discursive field. Foucault has perhaps an overly complex view of epistemology, but the issues he identifies are central to the research problematic.

On a practical level, of course, there is frequently a perceived need for some element of detachment in the research process. Some researchers often feel that they need to detach themselves from the field in order to make their 'data' intelligible; others attempt to detach themselves simply to make the whole process manageable. As such we are aware that it is one thing to reject something on epistemological grounds and quite another to suggest that no practical guidelines can be identified for researchers. On a day-to-day basis researchers are confronted with a range of practical issues and they require practical guidelines in order to forge an adequate basis for 'doing' empirical work. But the best that researchers can do in attempting to (semi-) detach themselves practically is to try to contemplate the field of research from an *ironic* distance, in the Rortyan (1989) sense. After all, an ironic distance is the best researchers can achieve, because, as Foucault shows us, in reality there is no magical 'buffer zone' between the knower and the known. There is no way of keeping one aspect of 'reality' from another. As Natoli (1997: 182) points out 'We cannot isolate any part of the world from any other part, just as we cannot isolate ourselves from the world'. However, in approaching the issue of involvement and detachment pragmatically to achieve an ironic distance between themselves and the field, researchers can still open themselves up to the possibility of an awareness of some of the contingencies and ambivalences within the research process. This is a reflexive task which cannot and should never be avoided.

Surface and depth in ethnographic work

Throughout their article Sugden and Tomlinson present an interpretation of ethnographic work which leads to the conclusion that ethnography can legitimately be characterised as a particular form of depth analysis for exploring culture. In shaping this quite specific vision of ethnography, Sugden and Tomlinson draw heavily on the vocabulary of the Chicago school of urban sociology, which originated from early cultural anthropology. We want to argue here that this way of understanding ethnography is not arbitrary but subsumed by a very specific discourse, which utilises very specific modes of making sense of social reality – the metaphor of *depth* in particular – which are perceived to be more adequate for revealing 'reality' than any others.

Our critique utilises what Foucault (1980a, 1980b) terms his genealogical tactics, which set out to explore what is absent in discourse as a consequence of the institutionalisation of power-knowledge. In relation to the discussion of Sugden and Tomlinson's interpretation of what constitutes 'good' ethnographic work, Foucault's genealogical approach requires us to ask how these authors come to accept certain things about ethnography as authoritative, and how they come to consent to them, to regard them as legitimate, and value them as such.

It becomes manifestly clear when you read 'Digging the Dirt and Staying Clean' that Sugden and Tomlinson pursue ethnography in a way that gives preferential treatment to the concept of 'depth'. Beyond the title itself the authors argue that to be effective ethnographic researchers, we must get 'at *deep* insider information' (1999b: 386) . . . use '*deeply* grounded, free-standing commentaries' (p. 388) . . . 'providing detailed and *deeply* situated comparative data' . . . (p. 388) . . . 'using methods which get "beyond gazing at the surface"' (p. 389) . . . [and which] 'penetrate far beneath the surface and rhetoric of international sport' (p. 389). Deep meaning is taken to be 'true', whereas *surface* meaning is considered as inadequate or misleading, if not altogether false. For Sugden and Tomlinson it is as if they perceive that ethnography more than other methodological approaches enables them to reach something more substantial, more insightful, which can only be 'found' at a 'special' level of 'depth'.

However, this all-embracing concern with 'depth' suggests a genuine problem not only for ethnography, but also for the sociology of sport more generally and our lines of enquiry in particular, and raises two key questions. To what extent does the research process become classified by its capacity to seek deep meaning? Why is it by 'depth' that ethnography gets defined here? We neither underestimate the efficacy of deeply grounded ethnographic work, nor do we reject the contribution of depth immersion studies to the sociology of sport. However, we do want briefly to consider why, and under what discursive conditions, in the Foucauldian sense, depth and surface become the salient defining features of 'good' and 'bad' ethnographic research practice.

Following Foucault, we want to argue that Sugden and Tomlinson's proclivity, in giving precedence to 'depth' over 'surface' in the research process is motivated, not by sound argumentation, but by their own values, which reflect a particular discourse of ethnography in sociology. In Derrida's (1973) terms this can be related to the role of binary oppositions within linguistic formations, such that there is always inequity in oppositions such as depth and surface with one part of the relationship seen as inferior to the other. During his genealogical period (1980a, 1980b, 1981) in an attempt to undermine conventional wisdom, Foucault set out to overturn this particular binary opposition, by giving precedence to 'surface' over 'depth' in the research process. Foucault's genealogical period marks a clear shift from, but 'follows on where his "archaeology" left off, extending into new areas of discourse the campaign against science and humanism' (Harland, 1987: 155). The published treatment of this methodological shift in Foucault's work is thorough enough that a major discussion is not required here (see Ritzer, 1997; Harland, 1987). Several important consequences follow from this turn.

As we have said already, Foucault (1981, 1986, 1987) was determined to develop an epistemological and ontological understanding which allows for the 'individual' and a 'culture of individuality', but one which also shows that it is ultimately discursive practices, not cognitive selves, that guide what individuals do. It is crucial to note also that Foucault's poststructuralist project concerns itself with signs, not concepts (Harland, 1987). It is signifiers and signifieds, such as sporting celebrities then, not cognitive forms, which establish cultural meanings. In the appendices to the book, *The Archaeology of Knowledge*, Foucault (1972) emphasises this postmodern point, when he argues that discourses should be interpreted in terms of their 'exteriority' – meaning that it is appropriate for the genealogist to analyse discourses on the basis of their 'surface values'. For Foucault, it is erroneous to attempt to interpret discourses in any 'deep' sense because everyone is discursively positioned. This is why he focused on discourse as practice instead of on people and what they say.

Foucault (1980a, 1980b) made it clear that, for him, power-knowledge is the force that transforms the cultural world and genealogy is the 'tactics' by which the researcher attempts to unearth 'local discursivities' and 'subjected knowledges'. It is through these tactics that the connections, practices and institutions that comprise discourses are revealed rather than through attempts to get beneath the surface to find the 'truth'. Rorty teaches us the lesson that we must stop imagining that 'depth' analysis can tell us anything more about 'the way things are in themselves' than can 'surface' accounts (1982, 1991). With the critical imagination of the political sketch writer and cartoonist in mind we would ask, how much *more* could Sugden and Tomlinson illustrate what they intuitively 'know' of their vital sites of research enquiry, such as the internal workings of FIFA, if they were not bounded by a reliance on observable practices and quotable sources.

In carrying out our own ethnographic research we rely on *both* surface and depth simultaneously. We both look for and avoid the sense of the said as constituting individuals and attempt to focus on discourse as practice, by exploring actual lived events relating to the field of study, their surface consumption and individuals' assumptions about others which are wrapped up in the constitution of these events. Looking for the unities of discourse in what we later describe in our ethnographies we attempt to both understand and articulate discursive events, which decentre the individuals who were engaged in them. We draw on the strategy time and again when we feel that individuals are telling us something differently to what we believe to be 'true' of their actions and beliefs. In this sense, our research approach is based on intuition and everyday knowledge, meaning it was as much pragmatically inspired, as it was empirical. We understand that there are essential aspects of the 'reality' that we deal with that we 'know' to be 'true' as knowledgeable and reflexive actors. We also admit that sometimes we feel that we do not need empirical 'data' to tell us certain things, because we perceive that we already understand certain aspects of the 'field' intuitively whilst at other times the 'data' are necessarily more prominent.

This approach not only recognises and celebrates the subjectivity of the research process, but it also understands that what we know intuitively often remains far ahead of what we can possibly 'discover' empirically. Indeed, it is our contention that in more conventional approaches the empirical is often used to justify intuition in any case. Honesty of this kind is essential to the research process. It is methodologically unethical to pretend that we always follow 'scientific' methodologies, when the theoretical insights that we develop have not been 'found' or 'grounded' in empirical 'data', just as it is illegitimate to claim that research relies completely on 'grounded theory' or empirical data alone. This recognition of the efficacy of research strategies, which draw on both 'surface' and 'depth' alerts us to the possibility of undermining binary opposites to the extent that we should be able to assign to each of them more than one understanding. Concepts, after all, are like human beings, they are not simply 'good' or 'bad', 'normal' or 'deviant', but hold both and other possibilities.

Gonzo

In this section we shall discuss Sugden and Tomlinson's understanding of the role of gonzo in ethnography. On the surface, their idea of assigning gonzo a central role in ethnography may not seem so surprising, given their commitment on the one hand to the 'pursuit of objective understanding' (1999b: 390) and on the other hand to use gonzo to 'interpenetrate agency and structure' (p. 391). From our own standpoint, however, this move appears incongruous, because the part that gonzo has to play in the type of ethnography that Sugden and Tomlinson advocate is very different to the role assigned to ethnographic writing in more 'traditional' accounts. We shall argue that gonzo in ethnography operates in very different ways to conventional 'ethnographic' approaches because it asks and answers different questions and operates with different ways of knowing the 'truth' about the social world (Rinehart, 1998a). Yet Sugden and Tomlinson make no move to develop their own views regarding this key issue. In this section, we shall argue also that Sugden and Tomlinson have essentially been obliged to adapt gonzo as an 'alternative vocabulary' of pragmatic discourse, in Rorty's (1979) sense, because existing ethnographic vocabularies cannot be used to articulate what those authors wish to express in their writing about sport.

As Rinehart shows us, 'traditional' ethnographic accounts invariably attempt to 'capture' the research experience as accurately as possible, to increase both the 'reliability' and the 'validity' of the research. Typically, this approach explains the relationship between theory and method; problems associated with gaining access to the field; techniques of social research; analysing data; and writing up the final account. Ethnographic studies of this kind contend that theory emerges from the research data and typically illustrate this by characteristic examples of data from field notes. William Foote Whyte's (1943) classic study, *Street Corner Society: The Social Structure of an Italian Slum*, exemplifies this approach to ethnographic writing.

In clarifying what more contemporary ethnographic writing essentially entails, Rinehart could be describing Sugden and Tomlinson's gonzo approach:

Authors attempt to replicate the sense of the experience. If something did not happen the way it was reported, recollection made it feel as if it did . . . Truth, in this type of writing, is not a realist narrative but rather a sensual, magical, lyrical truth. The feel of the experience – verisimilitude – is what the writer is after. Exact recordings of words said are less important than what the sayer meant to say. How does the writer know what the sayer meant to say . . . immersion in the culture, in the world portrayed, and attention to context and detail.

(Rinehart, 1998a: 204)

Indeed, in an analogous way, in the following excerpt from their 'Digging the Dirt', Sugden and Tomlinson attempt, and succeed in our view, to 'reach' the audience and immerse it in the world of ticket touting, so that the audience can 'feel' and 'inhabit' that world:

It was one of those hard swallow moments. For more than an hour he had been sitting on the beach, the researcher in him hoping that the touts (scalpers) would turn up, the private person hoping that they wouldn't. He had just about resigned himself to sunbathing away a wasted research day when the French chatter and laughter was cut by broad Manchester accents. Fat Tony and his gang of ticket touts had arrived. They made camp further along the beach. The researcher came to life and studied them from afar. Cockney Joe was with them.

He had first met Cockney Joe in the buffet bar of the train between Nantes and Marseilles two weeks earlier en route to England v Tunisia. Then he thought Joe was just another fan, but the researcher had noted the extra interest that Joe had taken in his media pass. It was only when he bumped into him again last night and watched him ply his trade in an Irish bar in Marseilles that it dawned on the researcher that fat Joe was one of a gang of ticket touts. Tickets and touts were a big part of the France 98 story and the researcher desperately wanted an insider account of the ticket black market. Several pints of Guinness later Joe had let it slip that the next day he and the rest of the gang were having a day off, planning to spend some time on a small island in the bay of Marseilles. The researcher plotted to stake out the island in hope that he could make contact.

And here they were, but what to do next? They were big boys, engaged in an illegal operation and, so the researcher thought, probably wouldn't take too kindly to being spied upon, particularly on their day off, by someone who carried a press pass. But investigative research demands risks – some calculated others not. The researcher took his hard swallow, a deep breath and plunged into the still Mediterranean. He swam out to sea and arched round to come out of the water below Fat Tony's gang. 'Hi Joe I bet you think I'm following you!' He said, reading the thought's behind Cockney Joe's suspicious eyes. Fat Tony took a pull from his beer can. 'Who's this?' he barked. Joe explained that the stranger was a writer who he'd met on the train and that he was an 'all right geezer'. The researcher hurriedly explained that he wasn't a journalist, but was writing a book in which he wanted to tell the tout's story 'from the inside looking out'. Fortunately business had been good and Tony was in an expansive mood. 'I don't give a fuck if you're a journalist or not', he said, 'do you want a beer?' The researcher was in.

(1999b: 385–6)

Their use of gonzo essentially deploys the rhetorical strategies used by authors of popular fiction. 'Digging the Dirt' both problematises and reveals a world that 'feels' very real to the reader, because Sugden and Tomlinson are able to elucidate a sense of the verisimilitude, which constitutes their experience of ticket touting. The excerpt 'reveals' a sense of the ambivalence the ethnographer feels about the other (the ticket tout) in the way that he is constituted in the text. Whilst we are reliant on the authors' representation of the process of gaining access, the excerpt also 'reveals' how the researcher's presence came to be accepted by the touts and how, once this was achieved, the rest of his initiation seemed to slot very easily into place. The depth immersal suggested is itself revealed then as an ephemeral, fleeting and uncertain surface phenomenon, which articulates with the performativity of the discursively constituted world of ticket touting.

All in all, this approach to writing enables Sugden and Tomlinson to describe the 'cultural imaginary' (Castoriadis, 1987) of the world they are exploring; that is the whole realm of actions, feelings and desires of the ticket touts in a discourse that they themselves have constructed and has constructed them. This approach works best, because at the end of the research process what Sugden and Tomlinson have is not a set of 'raw' data, in the conventional sense, but a form of 'tactics', in the Foucauldian sense, for revealing the 'realism' of the unities of discourse in the population of discursive events of the world of the ticket touts. They also have a means by which to give a voice to those whose story they are set to uncover. This approach to writing allows the culture of the 'field' to 'reveal itself' to the reader, to represent the 'self-evidential reality' of the world it reflects. Gonzo lets the reader know a time and a place and the people involved much better than traditional ethnographic accounts. Quite simply it enables the reader to *see* more.

Sugden and Tomlinson's gonzo approach to ethnographic writing has clearly moved beyond the more 'traditional' form of academic reportage. However, we want to suggest that as it currently stands this element of Sugden and Tomlinson's methodology comes across as an ambivalent eccentricity because it is at odds with their own quest to uncover 'objective' truth, in the essentialist meaning (1999b: 390, 392). As we argued above, gonzo texts do not speak for themselves. Like all other narratives, they are ideologically positioned and it is nonsense to suggest otherwise, but this issue is never resolved in Sugden and Tomlinson's article.

What is also clear is that the problem of involvement and detachment resurfaces again in relation to gonzo. As we have argued, the ontological position that Sugden and Tomlinson adopt implies the acceptance of 'an underpinning objective truth that it is our duty as social scientists to discover and reveal' (ibid.: 392). They simply refuse to abandon the idea that their ethnographic work can open up for them connections to objective reality.

These criticisms notwithstanding, Sugden and Tomlinson's work on gonzo does provide a point of leverage where their own sociological thinking can open itself to embrace and perhaps affirm an alternative sociological imagination. Indeed, it would seem that Sugden and Tomlinson's gonzo writing reveals a style comparable in important ways to that writing being shaped in postmodern thought. On the other hand, there are problems with some of Sugden and Tomlinson's ontological assumptions which point to areas in which the concepts of 'truth' and 'reality' enter into sharp conflict with the gonzo style of writing. For us this implies a need for a transformation of some specific taken-for-granted metaphysical constructs within Sugden and Tomlinson's sociology. Put simply they should stop insisting that reality take a particular form and simply accept that what emerges in their writing is to all intents and purposes an autobiographical interpretation.

In the final analysis, their gonzo writing, more than anything else, illustrates Foucault's point that, how we classify and explain away social phenomena 'tells more about us, about our stance on how things are, than it does about any truth . . . It tells more about that which is true to the namer' (Rinehart, 1998a: 201). For a gonzo approach to enquiry is a way of 'making' culture, recognising the performative aspects of 'doing' research, which is contingent upon personal frames of reference. In the end, Sugden and Tomlinson's work on ticket touts represents their own fixed centre-myth, established in their own inimitable way, which is unique to the 'Brighton School'. In this sense, the world of the ticket touts presented is their own personal narrative, their own form of discourse. It is a 'true' fiction (Reinhart, 1998a), which seeks to reveal verisimilitude, but which ultimately remains an (inevitably) imperfect story that is never completed.

For us gonzo writings are better understood, not as objective accounts, but as *subjective* readings of the social world which recognise the limits of ethnography. Gonzo is best described as the world illuminating its sense of history and culture through an interpreter's reading; meaning that a piece of ethnographic work of this kind is not about the world out there in the positivist sense, rather it is something in itself: a 'true' narrative fiction. The gonzo approach is certainly systematic and it is rigorous. But it is a form of interpretive intellectual work which understands that ethnography is better understood not as some direct correspondence to reality, but pragmatically and intuitively through its *application*. The rhetorical devices used in this form of ethnographic writing are not used to replace reality, but to enhance it. As the reader will see in the final part of this book, we too are not afraid to borrow from popular culture and we are self-consciously chutzpah writers. This brings us on to the last dimension of our critique.

Towards the establishment of an alternative 'epistemic community' for the sociology of sport

An understanding of the ethnographic process as shaped by a sociological hermeneutics recognises that research must no longer try to proceed on the basis of dualistic separations, either in its understandings of involvement and detachment, or in its attempts to grapple with 'meaning' in the field. As we have argued, just as efforts to separate us as individuals from the field of research are fated to failure, within the fabric of the discourses that link selves to one another, so the concept of individual sovereignty becomes unsure. Equally, our analysis has shown that researchers must problematise the binary opposition that ethnography has constructed between surface and depth. Whilst 'deep immersion in the culture, in the world portrayed, and attention to context and detail' (Rinehart, 1998a: 204) tell us a great deal, the lure of what remains on the surface should never be underestimated.

What we are suggesting then is the possibility of decentring the conventional bias towards the communication of deep and secure meaning in the research process and the advancement of a form of tactics that deals with the 'depth' *and* 'surface' of 'deviance' in sport without legitimating 'normalcy' or 'deviance'. Surrounding the issue of what it is to be an ethically responsible researcher, we have suggested that, in liquid modernity, there really are no constitutional guarantees about what is going to be acceptable ethical behaviour in every research situation. For this very reason researchers must always be prepared to strive to question fixed notions about research 'know-how', proficiency and responsibility. Nowhere is this more relevant than in the study of 'deviance' in sport.

In relation to our own empirical work, we recognise that ethnography can evidence a powerful sense of the exoticism associated with 'deviancy' research and of us as ethnographers, being participants who share experiences with those in the field. As a result there emerges a shadow subject that requires us as responsible sociologists to examine the problematic issue of truth and power/knowledge in the research process. In the event we treat as problematic what other research approaches take for granted when we contemplate our critical concern that we may think that we know what is going on 'in the field' but conceivably we know only the gestures, the faces and the bodies we see. Of issue here is the extent to which what we chart are merely the objects of our own narcissistic inventions; our own desires for a bit of the 'deviant' sporting other.

Ultimately though, we are arguing that there is no such thing as a typical or right way of doing sociology. The best sociology is that driven by the sociologist's reflections of their experiences of the social worlds which they explore. As such research practice must be reshaped to reflect the sociological imagination based not on objectivity and detachment, but on subjectivity, involvement, enchantment, pragmatism and intuition. Our discussion of Sugden and Tomlinson's position has nevertheless suggested that the idea that sociology is rhetorical as well as empirical is far from being widely accepted. Yet our approach, following Rorty, collapses the distinction between realism and idealism to suggest that sure enough there is a 'real', material world 'out there', but we can only know that world through the contingency of our own representations of it, which can be found in all manner of descriptions, images and metaphors. We, in common with Sugden and Tomlinson, invoke gonzo tactics. But gonzo tactics for portraying 'deviance' in sport introduce a paradox into the realm of sociology, because the truth of its suggestiveness is more important than its theory, with the very implication that sociology itself is a form of fiction.

Ethnography like Sugden and Tomlinson's gonzo deserves to be read, not for the reason that those authors have found a 'new' way to uncover objective understanding in sport, but quite simply because others will find *more* 'truth' in this type of sociology. As was discussed in relation to Rorty's pragmatic philosophy, truth is something that is *made* rather than found. And for truth to be of any use value to sociology it must work, it must be able to tell us 'things' about the world in new, better ways. The sociology of sport should be about 'the power of re-describing, the power of language to make new and different things possible and important – an appreciation which becomes possible only when one's aim becomes an expanding repertoire of alternative descriptions rather than The One Right Description' (Rorty, 1989: 39–40). In this sense, both our own and Sugden and Tomlinson's versions of sociology do not involve detached presentations of 'deviance'. They involve representations and we are their representatives – sociologists, like any other people, cannot be immunised against developing their own ideologies.

Only on the basis of this understanding of ethnography can a sociological hermeneutics emerge which will do fair justice to the complexity of the contemporary world of sport. The best that sociology today can offer is not originality as such, but more the act of an evocation, which constitutes the responsibility of proselytising extant theories, ideas and concepts (Blackshaw, 2002). The task of exploring and understanding 'deviance' in sport today, then, is to keep in mind any number of interpretations – even the ones which appear on the face of it to be antithetical to each other – without diminishing the position of any of them; a task which is all the more challenging when dealing with acts of 'deviance' – even those that are considered to be 'universally' repugnant. Indeed, these ethnographies must always be prepared to examine the connections between 'deviance', power and social control. They must take into account events, on the one hand, that involve damage, heartbreak and despair and, on the other, those enactments of 'deviance' which merely emerge as a form of aspirational marketing of something else in the form of what we have called consumptive 'deviance'.

In sum, anyone who writes as we do – hermeneutically, subjectively, autobiographically, reflectively, reflexively and offering numerous interpretations of small ethnographic moments in time and space which tell their own stories and produce their own moving epiphanies – should on the face of it be reconciled to the assumption that their analyses are always going to be suggestive rather than conclusive. But whilst our analyses, like Bauman's, may be modest enough to recognise that the challenges of sociology today are subtle ones (Blackshaw, 2003), they are also suffused with the knowledge that responsibility should be at the heart of the ethnographic imagination. As such the vignettes offered in the final section of this book aim to share our subjectivity with the reader, in order that they can suspend their own ontological assumptions for the time being and *see* the relationships at stake and the implications of these for what is imagined as 'deviance' and the production of power and social control in sport.

We have chosen to write the book interchangeably through the use of a single authorial voice and through the collective 'we' as befits the particular narrative styles that we present. We do so in respect of Pierre Bourdieu's assertion that writing ethnography involves reconciling the complications and nuances in the research process with the desire to produce a readable narrative which is accessible to its potential readers (1999: 622). This is all the more vital given our commitment to developing a writing style which seeks to engage the reader by revealing the verisimilitude of the social worlds that we have contingently inhabited. Before we present those worlds however we should like to reflect briefly on the sources of our stories and inspirations for our writing in each of the three chapters in Part III of the book

Research tactics

In the midst of the intellectual, procedural and physical chaos that surrounds the final stages of pulling a book together – seeking inspiration for a conclusion, searching out the reference that you cast aside 6 months previously because you then knew where it was, tidying up the methodology and so on – I decide to check up on my emails. Ignoring the multitude of give away titles indicating requests for donations for departing colleagues you've never met and the latest never to be read School newsletter I spot something more interesting. Opening it up it reads simply, 'One word, *********'. Of course I knew what it meant but one club's name was never going to be enough. I wanted names, faces. After all there were mates to wind up and my fantasy football team to think of, which reminded me I needed to check my points tally from the weekend. Of course I went to the 'gossip' board first where the messages were already flowing, prompting the web masters to post one of their own:

> Following the recent rape allegations against Premiership players we would like to advise you that postings on your bulletin are your own responsibility. Therefore you should delete existing or future postings that could be construed as libellous.

Not that it stopped the banter:

> So libellous does exist on the noticeboard. I must be owed a f*cking fortune. As for goals coming my way with players like **** . . . . and *******
> in my team im sure they will score at weekend! Browny can i get in trouble for that? if so delete this message.

My mobile phone starts to vibrate on the desk and the text messages reveal the latest speculation . . . A new episode of football's never-ending story is underway. It reminded me that this is a story that I have been a part of for just about as long as I can remember, and certainly for the 30 years that I have been watching football matches. From the very start I was always as fascinated by the strange characters and gossip that the games seemed to attract as what went on on the pitch: Peter Taylor with his distinctive warm-up run across the pitch, as striking and diagonal as the red and blue sash across his Palace shirt; the rumours of collections to pay off Kenny Sansom's failed venture into bookmaking; the invading fans from strange sounding northern towns; the TV commentaries that somehow found their way into our playground replays; and 'that' kick by the Frenchman.

At once these events have always seemed compelling and yet normal and routine to me, underscored as they were by kindred souls whose own voracious appetite for football generates the gossip which hurtles back and forth on the back of ever-widening technological capability. In this swirl of publicity football has become ubiquitous, hard to avoid and in need of superfluous stories to maintain its hold on the public consciousness. Whether seeking them out, merely passive consumers or active agents in their production, it is increasingly hard to find those that are not touched by the tales of footballers' 'deviance' emanating from television screens, newspapers, radio and internet sites.

It is this everydayness which we seek to evoke in Chapter 6, through the materials which football has made readily available to us in the media, through our everyday interactions and history of personal experiences, in order to elucidate our concept of consumptive 'deviance'. Football is presented through the metaphor of the soap opera, and our writing draws on some of the vernacular styles associated with that genre on the basis of subjective interpretive accounts which derive from a life surrounded by football's stories. Whilst we hope that the stories we tell will reveal the verisimilitude of this discourse, we make no grand claims to depth analysis here, regardless of the degree and longevity of our immersal within the field, for our concern is with the surface consumption of football's 'deviance'. This demands no familiarity, only a desire for titilation and entertainment. The challenge is then to read directly off the screen and the page *rather* than to reveal some hidden 'truth' about the 'deviant' world of football through the 'depth' immersal which has, in its time, taken one of us to the heart of Sky television's football production and the decision-making forums of the football authorities. For our concern is with the consumption of the 'story' of that 'deviance', which we argue is not much more than that.

*   *   *

There I was at a family get-together at my cousin's home and little did I think about it at the time but my nephew Wayne was going to open the door to a life-world whose treasures I would in the following weeks be exploring in more detail. I wasn't always conscious of the fact, but I am often in my most sociological frame of mind in the kinds of social situations that are parties and nights out at the pub – the food and drink tend to flow and there always seems to be something interesting to talk about. I already knew that Wayne and his brother Des had an interest in just about any motorised vehicle – this they had inherited from their dad who himself is a keen motorcyclist. The major basis of Wayne's spare time is buying and selling cars, but here he was talking about his escapades at something called the 'cruise'. As the evening progressed his enthusiasm became infectious and it was hastily provoking my sociological curiosity. He told a group of us a story about cruising and the different ways in which he and his mates performed their cars at these events – the mock fights, the gesticulating and the violent bouts of driving. He went on to tell us about his mate who calls his motor the 'fuckmobile' – 'cos he's "had" tons of birds in the back'. And how the other night he, Wayne that is, had stood on the outside of his mate's car looking in through the offside passenger window, watching him 'aving it away' with some bird inside. It was just at the point when Wayne was finishing his story that I knew that my latest sociological odyssey had just begun.

In the following weeks I was to develop my acquaintance with the cruising scene. I'd never been to a cruise before, never been driven in anything faster than a Ford Capri 2.8 GT, never approached B & Q at such a speed, never seen an empty car park turn so quickly into such a panoply of human activity – exotic names, smooth clutch plate, the nitrous blue squirt of purge kit, skirts, spoilers, burning rubber and petrol fumes. At the offset, it felt like being in a parallel universe, being able to move around, watch others who were engaged in a fantasy of sorts, but not wanting to join in. But over a period of 4 weeks I watched young men and women, and their cars sewing together a memorable string of spectacles – each one of them the instinct of a showman, allied with a desire to be a centre-stage celebrity.

As usual one of the most important questions I had to ask myself at this decisive point in the research process was what understanding of who I am was best equipped to explore what phenomenologists would call the 'already existing reality' of cruise culture. Different to my research with 'the lads' in Leeds (Blackshaw, 2003) I was not positioned to illuminate this life-world through an emic account (Pike, 1967), from an 'insider' perspective – cruising is working-class, but it is a young man and woman's 'sporting' activity. So I tried to observe without being obtrusive. This metaphorical sense of distance however bothered me because the task of sociology is to understand the social world not from a distance but as a felt reality. Yet with researching cruising I quickly learned that what counts is not really what happens in the eyes and minds of its participants, but what takes place on the surface of things, centre-stage. With cruising, it is the performance that is everything, not the perception of it. I also found out that in this process, cruising has little to do with moderation. It is always excessive, it is always much too much. Even so I tried to pay close attention to the epistemological and ontological frames underpinning the life-world of those whom I was observing and in the process tried to give as much respect as I could to their otherness (Sennett, 2003).

The marvel of cruising is to reduce the uncertainties and anxieties that pervade everyday life, making its hold over its participants seem so happy, euphoric, even. And it is the good fortune of cruisers that they can endure its symbolic power at the level of their imaginations, rather than like this researcher, who had to endure it in its full 'glory'. The reader will learn from Chapter 7 that cruising does not really hold this researcher in its thrall. The suspension of time and place cruising involves proves to be much like everything else associated with it: illusory. As the researcher I felt as if I was engaged in a fantasy of sorts, but not wanting to join in a world that was a pretext for uncomplicated fun with exotic cars, sound affects, a modicum of alcohol consumption and a wish for lots of gratuitous sex. I learned a great deal but was glad when the research finished. Not really to my surprise, the research concluded with a swift end: the 'death' of a cruiser. The personnel just like the fashions change quickly in cruising culture. Wayne announced one day that he simply had had enough of 'fuckin' about with those wanker's down at t'carpark' and, at the drop of a hat, my short sociological adventure was over.

*   *   *

Our final 'story' draws upon a quite different sensibility which is much more closely related to conventional depth ethnography (Hammersley and Atkinson, 1995). The engagement which forms the basis of our analysis of community sport and social control and which we present in Chapter 8, extends back over 8 years of evaluative work on the various social interventions of a community sports programme linked to a third division professional football club in the East End of London. Small-scale evaluative work in a number of settings and engagement with the project's staff on programmes of policy development and dissemination of practice developed into a full-scale 3-year qualitative research programme[1] focused on the municipal housing estate-based projects supported by the Home Office Positive Futures social inclusion initiative. This research has involved intermittent life history interviews with participants and with project staff; participant observation in the office, 'the café', on the estates, at training sessions, matches and at competitive tournaments in other parts of the UK and abroad. It has also involved engagement with the policy agendas and policy-making forums guiding the government agenda on community sport.

However, rather than report on the full findings of this research here (see Crabbe and Slaughter, 2004), our concern in Chapter 8 is to reveal something of the shift in the style and approach to using sport as a mechanism of social control in the age of 'liquid modernity'. In this light a 'realist' representation of life on one of the deprived estates targeted and the 'cool' respect (Sennett, 2003) that the community sports coaches earn there, is presented in contrast to the fictional representation of physical education in 'solid' modernity associated with the book *A Kestrel for a Knave*. Conscious that, as outsiders, researchers will always be closest to the gatekeepers whose work frames their enquiry, our objective is not to reveal life on the estates from the inside and for its own sake but rather to illustrate how sport has come to find a place within the more seductive armoury of state interventions targeted at the 'disruptive elements' at the social margins.

Part III

'Watching the game'

Evoking the new aesthetics of sport and 'deviance'

6 *The Premiership*

Sporting soap opera and consumptive 'deviance'

The shit hits the fan

By all accounts it's been running for donkeys' years and the old story lines still get dragged up from time to time – Munich and the 'Busby Babes', 'Pickles' and the World Cup, 'The Hand of God', 'Harry the Dog' and Hillsborough are some of the all-time favourites. I don't remember my first episode exactly. I think it must have been screened on ITV in those days and was called *The Big Match* or something, but I always liked to go down to one of the sets back then, where you could see the actors for real. It was probably Big Mal that got me hooked. Seeing him strut around Selhurst Park with his gangster's fedora, fur coat, cigar and cheeky grin only whetted the appetite. You couldn't get enough. Thankfully he seemed to be appearing in every episode at the time as he mouthed off cockily to the cameras, whilst the *News of the World* splashed pictures of him in the bath with the Palace players and porn queen Fiona Richmond all over their front page. Then came Venables and his 'Team of the Eighties' before Terry moved on and was eventually recast as El Tel in a Spanish spin off series called *Barcelona*.

The viewing figures seemed to go down hill for a while after that when *Dallas* and *Dynasty* were followed by *Neighbours* as the nation's soaps of choice. That is until Rupert Murdoch stepped in and jazzed things up on his Sky satellite channel. He spruced up the sets and the camera work, brought in some talented new foreign stars and introduced plenty of money and glamour with his new show, *The Premiership*. It seemed like over-night that we went from one episode a week to three with weekend bonanzas, *Big Brother* style daily updates and front to back coverage in the tabloids. All we needed now was a really good story line to get things buzzing again.

There had been a few popular episodes, mostly Man United winning things as well as all the usual extra marital affairs, drug scandals, dust ups and dodgy deals but no real classics. Like any good script that would need a new star, goodies and baddies, romance, rows and fights, farewells and returns, intrigue, mystery and suspense and, more than anything else, a shocking cliff hanger to keep us hooked.

When Eric Cantona walked onto the set, cast as a mysterious and fiery Frenchman who had signed for Leeds United none of us could have predicted what the writers had in store. There was everything: rows with former bosses, dressing room bust ups and sexual intrigue, all sub-plots to Leeds winning their first League title since 1974 before it culminated in the ultimate act of betrayal as Eric upped and left for Leeds' great rivals Manchester United on the other side of the Pennine hills. There were plenty more tantrums as well as celebrations, as the story lines got us mesmerised and spitting fire in equal measure as the 'Gallic genius' strut his stuff. They even started using Selhurst as one of the sets again. In fact that's where they filmed one of the classics one Wednesday evening back in late January 1995.

Palace, cast as the struggling south London family club, were playing host to the cosmopolitan glamour of Manchester United. A David and Goliath match-up that was sure to provoke a row. It was a nippy evening and filming was done under the muffled glow of floodlights, the packed studio audience of fans being kept warm by their passionate singing and chanting. I was in a familiar spot for this one, in the Arthur Wait stand, right up against the away end where you could see into the whites of the visitors' eyes. We glared, sneered, sang and made gestures to one another in between giving it to Cantona, who we booed and mocked whilst he got some special 'close attention' on the field from the stirrer in the Palace pack, centre back Richard Shaw. And then all of a sudden in the 57th minute Eric kicked out at Shaw following a clumsy challenge.

We were back at the pantomime as boos and chants of 'off, off, off' quickly enveloped the set, before the referee produced a red card and the crowd erupted, cheers from Palace fans, cries of disbelief and despair from the United fans. As Cantona made his theatrical exit from the field, indignant, sullen and vengeful, his boss Alex Ferguson, cast as the iron father figure, avoided eye contact, showing no emotion. Eric turned towards the tunnel, walking alongside the pitch within ear shot of mocking Palace fans in the main stand. The villain of the peace was getting a hard time from those closest to him, whilst all around people were waving and maliciously chanting 'cheerio, cheerio, cheerio', wanting, *pleading* for a reaction . . . That's when they let it happen.

Time seemed to stand still as Cantona launched himself, kung fu style, at a spectator and then fell prostrate onto an advertising hoarding before regaining his feet and exchanging punches with his tormentor, a Palace fan who had been dispatched from the back of the stand. This was bigger than JR or Dirty Den getting shot! I didn't know whether to laugh or scream as the whole set stood collectively, mouths open, in a state of absolute shock and disbelief before we adopted our roles and anger erupted. The volume of abuse increased as plastic cups of tea and other improvised missiles were projected in Cantona's direction as he disappeared off set and down the tunnel. The match went on to finish in a 1–1 draw but that was just a backcloth. We had a new story to gossip about. Was this the end for Eric? What would the punishment be? Who was the fan? What did he say? What would this do to United's title challenge? What did the boys make of it back in the studio? All will be revealed in the next episode of *The Premiership* . . . We couldn't wait.

It was all good stuff for a while. No holds barred as the storyline kept on running for months. I'm not sure we ever really got to the bottom of it but who cared. After all, we all got to feel better about ourselves by sympathising with the West girls and the other children sat nearby who witnessed the villainous act. Then we got to feast on the rows and the trial in Croydon. That was one of the best. A jail sentence and Eric going on about sardines and trawlers! We all thought he'd lost his mind, but it was all part of the script. I mean what a character, 'nitro-glycerine in human form', 'Darth Vader', 'the son of a gypsy family for whom home was a cave' the tabloids told us in amongst the tales of his artistic love of poetry, painting and philosophy. A 'real' Jekyll and Hyde. Then there was Matthew Simmons. They soon wiped away the butter wouldn't melt image of the respectable suited and booted executive season ticket holder. Suddenly we were faced with a violent, fascist criminal who was sent to prison for attacking his lawyer before being stalked by vengeful United fans! We even got Eric's comeback, because they always bring the big stars back and of course that meant we could have the re-runs, over and over again . . .

Of course no one was really 'writing' this script but what we want to suggest is that it is through the everyday living narrative form of the soap opera that football, sport and indeed wider social formations create a context in which we can safely consume the excitement and *frisson* of crime and 'deviance' without facing the consequences that accompany its practice. We are drawn to the metaphor of soap opera since it exemplifies the consumerist influence within mediated representations of 'reality' in a way which makes criminal and 'deviant' behaviour palatable to the mass market. For us this is achieved through the use of particular stylistic and narrative forms which are shared with contemporary representations of sport. As such, through our own ethnographic narratives – 'true fictions' and rhetorical devices – we are seeking to reveal the ways in which football players, fans and officials become actors in a wider discursive field in which modernist truth claims are cast to the side by mediated reality plays.

Without wishing to provide a fully fledged theorisation of sport as soap opera here (see O'Connor and Boyle, 1993; Watkins, 2002) it is necessary to provide some theoretical consideration of the narrative structure of the soap form and its association with sport in order to clarify our position, before we consider the implication of this understanding for our central concern to theorise the notion of consumptive 'deviance' in sport. In Abercrombie's terms soaps 'do not have a beginning and end like most novels or films. They are instead continuous serials composed of several different stories told simultaneously' in which 'soap characters build up experience, acquire a history, which is shared with the audience'. While soaps adhere to the conventions of realism 'to persuade the viewer that this is everyday life . . . soaps are not totally immersed in the realist form, since they often flirt with other forms' including caricature and melodrama, through which characters and action are presented in exaggerated and excessive ways (1996: 48–50). These structural forms traditionally combine with a thematic focus on the everyday world associated with personal and emotional life which is considered through the spheres of 'family', 'household' and 'community'.

Whilst not fictional in the conventional sense it is clear that 'the story' of football and sport more generally shares this same basic structural and thematic format as a means of articulating the key narratives of particular seasons and events. As such, whilst several writers have utilised the conventional framework of analysis of soap opera as a predominantly female genre (see Ang, 1985; Brunsdon, 1981; Geraghty, 1991; Hobson, 1982; Mumford, 1995) by theorising sport as a male *version* of it (O'Connor and Boyle, 1993; Rose and Friedman, 1997) we would argue that such distinctions are not useful since, for us, sport – or at least mediated versions of it – *is* soap opera, without the need for gender qualification. In Eco's terms:

> A present-day sport . . . is essentially a discussion of the sports press. At several removes there remains the actual sport, which might as well not even exist . . . So sport as practice, as activity, no longer exists, or exists for economic reasons (for it is easier to make an athlete run than to invent a film with actors who pretend to run); and there exists only chatter about chatter about sport.
> (1986: 162)

Multiple story lines with historical reference points are mobilised around particular individual characters and their families in the metaphorical shape of football 'clubs'. 'Events' are then consumed through the dissection of the 'relationships, feelings and motivations of individuals, on the one hand, and the commentary that others make on these features, on the other' (Abercrombie, 1996: 51). For us this observation enables a move beyond the work of content analysts who might see soap operas as: 'pseudo-realities that present curiously distorted reflections of empirical social reality . . . [which are] more violent than the real world . . . more concerned with sex and parentage, suffer [. . .] more from amnesia, mental illness, and coma-producing maladies' (Allen, 1983 [2001]: 235).

The dichotomies between the 'real' and the 'fictional' even within the broadening genre of televised 'soap opera' appear superfluous in an era of 'reality TV', fly on the wall documentaries and *Big Brother*-style living soaps. For today whilst we are increasingly obsessed with the search for the 'real' and the authentic – and sport provides one of the key sites for this pursuit – our reliance on mediated forms of dialogue and communication increasingly takes us away from the possibility of uncovering some basic hidden 'reality' or 'truth'.

For us, the soap opera, like football – or at least representations of it – 'consciously walks the line between texts that can be read as fiction and those which, for various reasons, constantly spill over into the experiential world of the viewer' (Allen, 2001: 241). There is no 'clear distinction between actors and their characters' as Mumford suggests (1995: 125), nor between the televisual genre of soap opera and lived 'reality', as the very consumption of the soap opera necessitates the implosion of the discourse of soap opera into everyday life, as Ritzer states, 'TV is dissolving into life and life is dissolving into TV' (1997: 98). In Watkins' terms then:

> it is important to recognise that understanding and theorising contemporary sport is not simply about the spectacle but more importantly about the way

[sports] have become story plot driven and how the media facilitate this, and how like the plots in soap opera's the plots in sport have no definite authors . . . Our grasp of something known as 'reality' is weakened as soaps become more 'real' and sport less 'real'. Like opposite poles of a magnet the two cultural forms attract each other, closer and closer until they begin to implode and collapse into each other.

(2002: 37)

For Baudrillard the erosion of this distinction between the 'real' and the 'illusion' means that 'every contemporary event is a mixture of the real and the imaginary' (Ritzer, 1997: 95) since 'actual events', such as Eric Cantona's altercation with Matthew Simmons, cannot be understood in isolation from the media discourse through which we consume them. Furthermore, this hyperreality offers us simulations that are 'more real than real, more beautiful than beautiful, truer than true' (Ritzer, 1997: 96), or in this case, more shocking than shocking: such that we consumed not only the actions of Cantona but the terrified expressions of the young children looking on, the menace in the eyes of the players running to join the mêlée, the hysteria of rival fans and revelled in the moral indignation of media commentators. The shock itself is anaesthetised though as we consume from afar, sat in our living-rooms, reading the papers over a morning cup of coffee. Indeed, this kind of 'deviance', consumptive 'deviance', is 'designed' for consumption by the armchair fan, to be replayed from every angle, experienced through the eyes of every participant.

Whilst Rojek, echoing earlier critiques offered by Frankfurt school theorists, takes issue with Baudrillard's ideas for being 'less than fair to the critical and interpretative capacities of the audience' (1990: 8), we would suggest that it is the very exaggerated nature of the medium which draws the audience in, since it is so much more seductive and exciting than the unmediated experiences of everyday life which fail to live up to the expectations we create through our consumption of the televised version. As Horkheimer and Adorno argued decades earlier, the culture industry is so seductive that we have to live it out, with the 'whole world . . . made to pass through [its] filter' (1993). Non-mediated interpretations are somehow seen as less complete and explicit.

It is for this reason that even the academic literature on sport is replete with references to the media reporting of scandals. Baker and Boyd in particular consider examples involving O. J. Simpson, Nancy Kerrigan, Tonya Harding and Mike Tyson to illustrate 'the power of sport ['deviance'] stories to occupy the public mind' (1997: ix). As researchers and educators we are ourselves implicated through the design of courses, selection of stimulus material and authorship of this book, each of which entices through the deployment of ringside accounts, images and reminiscences of the shocking, the dirty and the foul. Our capacity to make judgements on the appropriateness of these materials inevitably relates to our own fascinations, proximity and consumption of them.

Indeed, beyond the academy this is why 'everyday life' experiences are themselves increasingly saturated by intertextual references to mediated examples of the spectacular, exotic and 'deviant'. As such, even those of us who 'were there' to witness Cantona's extraordinary reaction on 25 January 1995 were robbed of any sense of authenticity as we were enveloped by the wider media discourse and 'reality' play. Forced to share our feelings and invited to embellish on them as journalists, friends and colleagues asked 'do you know the fan?', 'I bet you couldn't believe your eyes?' 'Wasn't it awful?' as their eyes pleaded for more and more explicit detail, that our singular interpretation could not satisfy.

Ultimately of course, as we suggested in Chapter 4, this consumption of and fascination with 'deviance' involves its protagonists in a process of self-identification with the 'real' perpetrators and invokes gratuitous pleasures and aesthetic thrills as they watch . . . again and again; such that Umberto Eco was compelled to reveal his own approval not of 'football' but of:

> those crowds of fans, cut down by heart attacks in the grandstands, those referees who pay for a Sunday of fame by personal exposure to grievous bodily harm, those excursionists who climb, bloodstained, from the buses, wounded by shattered glass from windows smashed by stones, those celebrating young men who speed drunkenly through the streets in the evening, their banner poking from the overloaded Fiat Cinquecento, until they crash into a juggernaut truck, those athletes physically ruined by piercing sexual abstinences, those families financially destroyed after succumbing to insane scalpers, those enthusiasts whose cannon-crackers explode and blind them: They fill my heart with joy. I am in favour of soccer passion as I am in favour of drag racing, of competition between motorcycles on the edge of a cliff, and of wild parachute jumping, mystical mountain climbing, crossing oceans in rubber dinghies, Russian roulette, and the use of narcotics.
>
> (1986: 168–9)

One might summarise the focus of this polemic through the use of the term sporting 'deviance', but what is most important is the allure of the idea of these activities. Eco does not desire to be *in* the Fiat Cinquecento as it crashes into a juggernaut truck, to pull the trigger to his *own* head in a game of Russian roulette or to *face* the consequences of financial destruction at the hands of the ticket tout. His joy is informed by the safe knowledge of a continuing human capacity for such activity; his consumption of it a comforting hand on the shoulder, an expression of all our desires for a bit of the 'deviant' other and the self-expression it implies. In this context anything becomes possible such that Cantona can be *re*-imagined as people's hero, an island of unrestrained freedom who, in Baudrillard's terms, faces his destiny head on, escaping the 'cleanliness' and 'morality' of sporting convention. It is he who faced up to his tormentors whilst others might cow down in the face of potential repercussions, he who, invoking the slogan of his Nike sponsors, 'just did it'. As a letter writer to the local newspaper in the neighbourhood of Crystal Palace's Selhurst Park stadium, the *Croydon Advertiser*, put it:

> Eric Cantona only did what most of us wish we had the courage and athleticism to do when confronted by the kind of foul-mouthed, hate filled trouble makers

who are still making football grounds unpleasant places to be. He should be lauded, not vilified.

(*Croydon Advertiser*, 3 February 1995: 8)

Similarly for the former England player John Barnes who commented at the time of the launch of the officially sanctioned 'Let's kick racism – Respect all fans' initiative later that year:

> To be honest with you in the long run, some good may come out of [Cantona's assault] because that really brought it home that because mostly where [racial abuse] is actually done, black players have not responded to it, so people just make light of it because it can't be that bad because nothing has happened. Now he has actually responded to it they have actually seen how important the issue is because until something like that happens people don't realise how important it is because if someone was to call me a black bastard I will laugh it off and walk off and people would say well it is not that important because he hasn't said anything about it.
>
> (Interview, 28 September 1995[1])

For Eco such transformations of guilt and innocence are possible because football substitutes or symbolises political interests. Eco describes the sign of football as:

> A sign that leads to other signs and back again . . . a trap of openings and closures in which infinite conjecture and infinite possibility rule over certainty and structure to destabilise the notion of a fixed truth waiting somewhere out there to be discovered.
>
> (in Trifonas, 2001: 11)

However, such undecidables may only relate to the celebrity, whose status is elevated above and beyond the 'ordinary' citizen even when they are propelled into the headlights of the media gaze, since it is the celebrity that can hold the audience's attention as stories are dragged out in new directions. By contrast, for Simmons, the future was to be spent in exile from football, a walk-on part, or 'celetoid' (Rojek, 2001), whose celebrity has no meaning outside of Cantona's fame despite the more profound impact upon his life. For whilst Cantona's actions are now celebrated and have reinforced his iconic celebrity status, Simmons was later to reveal how the incident continued to haunt his work, personal and social life beyond the initial media scramble to write the 'story':

> I stayed in prison for one night of my sentence. The chef at Highdown Prison cooked an excellent curry, and I had a good night's sleep because there was no press around me for the first time in a long time. I wish I could have stayed a bit longer.
>
> The man I was working for as a double-glazing fitter let me go, and it was very hard to get more work. I'm good at my job, but that was irrelevant because

of what happened. A few months after the court case, a friend said his company was looking for someone to do odd jobs, so I thought, even though it might not be the best of jobs, it would give me a chance to get my life back in order. I think I fooled myself into thinking I could work my way up the ladder, even slowly, but it didn't happen. My bosses were sending everyone on courses and I was the only one who was asking and not going . . . No one said anything to my face about the incident; I suppose they didn't want people talking about it, but I would prefer it if people did say it to my face. Instead, they would arrange things to do together without telling me, and I felt they were talking about me behind my back. My life was a little bit miserable at the time . . .

I started going out with a new girlfriend not long after the case, and we had a baby about a year later. Unfortunately, things didn't work out between us. I don't know if the incident was the only reason we broke up, but it certainly put a lot of pressure on her . . . A lot of friends and some members of my family haven't spoken to me since the incident. It doesn't upset me, because it's good to know who's going to be there for you when it matters, and who's not. They just haven't made any contact, and that's fine by me.

I had a season ticket at Crystal Palace and they asked me to give it back . . . I've been back a few times since with a friend, but I'd rather stay away from there [now].

(*The Observer*, 29 September 2002)

It is the absence of such stories which is as significant as the dramatic presence of celebrity in the consumption of sporting 'deviance'. For whilst Cantona's 'character' was defined in this moment, prompting his elevation into the consciousness of a global audience beyond football, Simmons played, and could only play, the marginal supporting roles of innocent victim or provocative thug. Wheeled in, like Katie's kidnappers in Coronation Street, to generate a storyline before being dispatched back to Everyday Street. Ultimately, after the fact, we don't care what happened to him other than in fleeting memories of his encounter with Cantona every time a new biography, movie or sporting story involving the former Manchester United player breaks out.

The trial

Mr White, the next big thing in English football, is sat around a table in the *Square on the Lane* with Mr Blonde, Mr Brown and two other friends from his home town, where they are joined by reserve team striker Mr Blue and his own birthday celebrating entourage. It's a far cry from the days of Norman Hunter and Jackie Charlton. There is no spit and sawdust, aroma of woodbines or pints of mild to be supped over a game of cards or dominoes, a time when a punch might settle a dispute or put an end to a drama rather than set one up. Nor is it *Stringfellows* though, despite the smartly dressed doormen, big collared open neck shirts and Prada-designed leather jackets. The footballers are vying with the Wednesday night gelled haired student crowd to be the loudest and brashest as they down alcopop cocktails of Mule with Bacardi Breezers in the three floored once trendy cattle market on Boar Lane. It's the sort of place where you want to be seen, where the girls watch the boys watch the girls go by in ever more erotic fashion as the music drowns conversation. A stage where even stoicism is a performance of presence. A place where you feel the buzz not of what you are doing but what the night might bring. Endless, burdenless possibilities for laughter, comradeship and 'action', giving rise to a warm, zestful sense of invulnerability and an escape from introspection and fear.

As the group move on they stagger around town, the visitors revelling in the stares and fleeting glances from passers by as they bask in the reflected celebrity of Mr White. The normally anonymous former amateur boxer Mr Blonde now every inch the prize fighter with Mr Brown and the others larging it in the face of onlookers, oblivious to the chill night air as they glide along, carefree, beyond restraint, impervious to the cold. You don't feel the cold when you're the star of the show on the set of metropolitan night life but doormen were already on their guard as the alcohol suffocates the responsibilities and burdens of celebrity and gives rise to an intoxicating glow, an aura of presence, as they kick cars on the way to DV8, the aptly named lap dancing club, before necking a few more with the plebs in Yates' Wine Lodge and The Observatory on Boar Lane and finally the student club night at the Majestyk. Riding on a tide of arrogance directly to the VIP lounge it was there that they met up with Mr White's team mates including Mr Pink and Mr Orange, sharing stories, taking the piss and eyeing up the talent. A lads' night out like any other.

There's always one to spoil the party though, who has too many, tries to start a fight, gets kicked out and ends up turning the whole night on its head. It was classic Tarrantino from then, timelines inverted as we witnessed the evening's events being played out through different lenses in the post-event midst of a court room drama. A feast of detail was up for consumption as we got to know the characters and the plot thickened. Dressed immaculately in their dark suits Messer's White, Blonde, Brown, Blue, Orange and Pink sat in the dock at Hull Crown Court as daily episodes of the soap focused on the trial for 2 months and were relayed to an eager national audience. You couldn't get a ringside seat for love nor money. The script writers from the tabloids had grabbed them all, spare a few which were saved for significant observers, oh, and of course, a couple of seats for the family of the victim.

Back to 'reality' . . .

On the evening of the 12 January 2000 Sarfraz Najeib, who was studying at Leeds Metropolitan University, had been at the Majestyk night-club in Leeds' City Square with his brother Shahzad and three friends. They left shortly after midnight and whilst standing outside the club became involved in a verbal exchange with an aggressive drunken man who had just been asked to leave the club. When he took offence at their amusement with his condition an altercation took place and punches were exchanged. Fearing a beating, the five students then fled and were chased across City Square, along Boar Lane and down Mill Lane where Sarfraz tripped and was beaten unconscious by a group of white men who had apparently been in the club with the aggrieved man. By all accounts Sarfraz was repeatedly kicked, stamped on, punched and bitten on his face and left in a pool of blood, seemingly lifeless, before his friends and brother were able to tend to him and find an ambulance to take him away. He spent 2 days in a coma and needed 12 stitches to his head, suffered cranial and facial swelling, a broken nose, a fractured bone between the eyes, a broken cheekbone and a broken leg.

. . . Of course we were far more interested in what was going to happen to 'the lads' than the victim, and Mr White and Mr Pink in particular, for these were two of *The Premiership's* star performers and had been charged with the assault. Almost in recognition of his bit-part status at the local football club Mr Blue was soon written out of the story, acquitted of the charge of affray and causing grievous bodily harm with intent. His place was to be taken by Mr Orange, Mr White's best mate at the club, who was up on a charge of conspiracy to pervert the course of justice following his efforts to protect the others after their evening out had ended in the ignominious drunken disarray of eviction from the club, a street brawl and puke splattered luxury cars, clothes and white leather furniture.

As we thought about the implications of the affray and GBH charges against the young England footballers it was Mr Orange who provided the first twist in the tale. Having nervously agonised in the court room for days we were stunned when he changed his statement and contradicted the testimony of the others by revealing that Mr White had confessed to him on the night of the incidents that he and some friends 'had just had a fight with some Asians' and that Mr Blonde had bitten the victim. Orange then bowed his head and wiped tears from his eyes as his fellow conspirators trooped out of the courtroom, their anxiety revealed as they ignored his gaze, leaving us eager to tune in the next day.

Without resolving the previous episode's turn of events the theme of betrayal continued when Orange, warming to his task, dragged the mastermind of the defence into the affair and took us behind the scenes of one of the country's leading football clubs by claiming that it was the law firm of one of his club's directors which had led a deliberate and concerted attempt to save the players' skins by encouraging them to tell lies. It was all over the press, 'Lawyer told me to lie', 'sensation in Hull's court four', 'My lies to police to save a mate', as we gossiped about the moralities of grassing, corruption at the club and what would happen to the players' friendship, the *Daily Mirror* leading with Mr Orange's claim that 'My great pal begged me not to say the truth'.

As usual it was not the lawyer who was on trial though and he wriggled out of any further unwarranted media interest in the manner of *Dallas's* devious but cunning JR Ewing as our fascination with celebrity ensured a focus on the two key characters rather than a dull unfamiliar solicitor. By now Mr White's increasingly furrowed brow and nervous demeanour spoke volumes of contrition, regret and frustration with the sordid outcome of a night out with friends that went horribly wrong. Meanwhile, the loudmouthed, cocky Mr Pink was everywhere, the focus of all the sub plots as we heard of him batting off unwanted delving by barristers before flying down the M62 motorway on the opening day of the trial to score the winning goal in a Champions League match to secure passage to the Quarter Finals. In the courtroom, dressed all in black he was cast as the villain. The swagger, contemptuous and convoluted denials accompanied by tabloid tales of racist abuse, teenage thuggery, drug use and an East End council estate upbringing which painted a picture of white trash dressed in designer clothes. On the field, featured in the all white strip of Leeds United, he was the talismanic, inspirational midfield player who emerged as a Roy of the Rovers style hero after scoring the winning goal. His goal celebrations pictured in the *Daily Mirror* above the caption 'Take a bow' whilst his barrister declared to the jury in his final speech 'One day the dream he spoke of – the dream of seeing England to victory by him scoring the winning goal in a future World Cup – I hope comes true'.

Just as it was all set to be resolved though, in the final episode of the ten week series, the judge called a re-trial, setting up the prospect of a sequel . . .

Another dose of reality

Whilst the prosecuting QC had said in the Hull courtroom, which heard the trial of those accused of the assault on Sarfraz Najeib, that the crux of the case lay in 'what took place off-camera' in recognition of the inconclusive video evidence, it was soon clear that the case was itself actually being played out, in real-time, on the television and in the newspapers. Ultimately, the 'trial', in a judicial sense, as much as the assault itself, disappeared as it was taken over by a media soap opera, leaving Sarfraz to live with the physical and mental horrors which prompted his father to express his mind to the press before being let down by the *Sunday Mirror* who carried his story despite written undertakings that it would not be printed until all the verdicts were returned.

The *Sunday Mirror* reporters who had been working on the story and had been primed to publish in the wake of an anticipated Friday afternoon verdict were devastated when the jury did not play to the *Big Brother* script, in which contestants on the reality TV show are voted out by the public on a Friday night just in time to reveal all to the Sunday tabloids. Whilst British contempt laws dictate that when a court is still sitting nothing prejudicial can be published that has not been heard by the jury in case their deliberations are unduly influenced, a Monday verdict would mean the paper having to wait 6 days for a chance to publish its 'exclusive', by which time the storyline would have been exhausted by rival daily papers. Rather than face the loss of the story they ran with a two page exclusive interview and pictures under the headline 'Leeds United Trial – The Victim's Father', in which the claim that the Leeds United players, Jonathon Woodgate and Lee Bowyer had been involved in the assault and that it had been racially motivated was reasserted (*Sunday Mirror*, 8 April 2001).

On Monday 9 April 2001 the jury was asked whether any of them had read or seen the story. After a tense 10-minute adjournment the foreman returned to answer yes before the jury was discharged and a trial which had cost eight million pounds of taxpayers money collapsed, since in the judge's opinion the article carried a 'clear and substantial' risk of prejudice.

> . . . They kept the episodes flowing for a while of course with club fines, fall outs at the club, transfer listings and a series of lurid tales of the players' former indiscretions but in the end the culmination of the second series in December 2001 was a bit of a flop despite Mr White being found guilty of affray along with Mr Brown and the sentence of 100 hours community service. Indeed the judge seemed to positively empathise with the players' trauma which it was suggested in Mr White's case had been 'etched upon your face'. It was the less familiar face of Mr Blond who really took the rap though, getting 6 years for affray and GBH whilst it was no surprise when Mr Pink walked free without a blemish on his character, other than the judge's recognition that his police interviews were 'littered with lies'.
>
> Of course the possibility of a third series was left open with the student victim of the attack indicating that a civil action would be brought against both the players and the club who it is alleged were involved in a cover up. In fact proceedings were brought against Mr Pink the following spring but by then no one was paying too much attention to the Najeibs. Other more central figures were asserting their presence once again.

Grabbing a piece of the action

David O'Leary's book *Leeds United on Trial*, was serialised in the *News of the World* on the Sunday after the conclusion of the trial (*News of the World*, 16 December 2001). The mass circulation tabloid featured exclusive coverage on the front page and six inside pages, in which O'Leary preferred to focus on the poison pen letters that his own family had received rather than the suffering of the Najeibs. Whilst he claimed to have kept the news from his wife and children for over a year in order not to frighten them, the prospect of bringing added publicity to the book appears to have been the overriding factor in releasing the details at a moment that cynically upstaged the continuing sense of injustice amongst the victim's family.

Aware of the intense interest there would be in his insider account but also the need to protect fragile celebrity egos within his faltering team O'Leary chose to celebrate the performances of his star midfield player Lee Bowyer in the wake of his not guilty verdict, suggesting in an interview in the *Sunday People* that 'Lee's attitude throughout this ordeal has been unbelievable. His performances have shown him to be a wonderfully gifted player and his character has shown him to be a remarkable young man' (*Sunday People*, 16 December 2001).

O'Leary's capacity to 're-present' Lee Bowyer did not relate to a more sophisticated understanding of the intricacies of the British legal system than the tabloid 'script writers' had managed to develop. Rather it is tied up with the ways in which the 'deviance' of this incident was consumed and contingently interpreted. In the context of a narrativised representation of events, 'characters' become absolutes such that Bowyer was theatrically cast as the absolute embodiment of evil, the racist white thug, the epitome of white working-class masculine thuggery in the manner of the pantomime baddie. Outside of the spectacle of the trial, however, an alternative discourse prevails, a sporting discourse in which Bowyer the player can be reclaimed by the football community and celebrated as one of 'ours'. A palimpsest figure emerges as Lee Bowyer the player is celebrated on the back pages and in the sports news for his barnstorming on-pitch performances whilst news reporters and anti-racist campaigners present a monolithic contrast, neither of which can claim to represent the more complicated and difficult to read jumble of contradictions that is Lee Bowyer and indeed our liquid modern condition.

Equally within the ritualised performative theatre of the football stadium Bowyer became a key symbolic focus for supporter rivalry and the performative consumption of 'deviance' within the game such that Leeds United fans sang in playful, 'kinky' recognition of the player's acknowledgement in court that he was wearing no underwear:

> He's here, he's there
> He wear's no underwear
> Lee Bowyer, Lee Bowyer.

By contrast, Chelsea fans invoked the prospect of incarceration during a match between the two sides on 1 April 2000, when the trial was drawing towards its conclusion, with:

> He's going down
> He's going down
> Bowyer's going down.

More significantly, the stadium setting also provided a context in which the racial undertones within the trial, which ultimately led to its collapse, could be performed for wider consumption in unrestrained ritualistic fashion, denying the possibility of marking off the judicial process from wider populist imaginings. As such, during a subsequent match played between Leeds and Liverpool on 13 April 2001, whilst Liverpool fans mocked Bowyer with cries of 'There's only one racist bastard'. Playing to the villainous casting, sections of the terrace culture at Leeds were then able to further antagonise opponents and revel in the horror of liberal sentiment by demonstrating a racialised ordering of normative preferences with chants of:

> Johnny Woodgate is our friend
> Is our friend, is our friend
> Johnny Woodgate is our friend
> HE HATES PAKIS.

Such renditions are themselves intimately tied up with the performative construction of identity in a specific localised context. As one of us has argued elsewhere:

> football clubs provide a key ritual and cultural mannequin onto which the clothes of identity, locality and regionalism are tailored and paraded . . . a context in which urban cultural change and uncertainty are diluted through the renewal of the sense of place and belonging that is captured as fans move towards and through the turnstiles on matchdays.
>
> (Back et al., 2001: 41–2)

Yet these identity claims are themselves highly contingent upon the roles that supporters play out and their own desires to celebrate and insert 'deviance' into the discourse of the wider soap opera. As such, during their match with Leeds in April 2000, before Bowyer had left the club, Chelsea fans also drew sardonic parallels with the image of Leeds as the site of the horrific crimes of Peter Sutcliffe, the 'Yorkshire Ripper', declaring 'He's going down with the ripper'. The Chelsea supporters in this context were not literally suggesting that the crimes were on a par with those of Sutcliffe but were engaged in playful performance, attempting to ridicule supporters of their opponents through association with what is presumed to be a universally villifiable 'deviant'. Following Bateson, in such contexts verbal comments, practices and actions can be subverted and inverted by the shared performance to the extent that they constitute a kind of 'fiction' (1978: 155). The context of the football stadium is an exemplary arena where the temporary suspension of conventional patterns of communication produces this kind of 'play'. Ironically, in this context, a 'deviant' identity can also become a prized possession which can be proclaimed in the face of hostility as a mark of invulnerability, a means of disarming those who would side against you. As such, a favoured chant of an overwhelmingly male section of Leeds United supporters during the 1980s, when the club's fans carried a fearsome reputation for football hooliganism, celebrated and internalised a whole catalogue of deviant and sexually perverted identifications and the horrific crimes of the 'Yorkshire Ripper' in particular:

> My brothers in borstal,
> my sister suck's cocks,
> my mothers a whore down the Battersea docks,
> my uncles a pervert,
> my aunties a slag,
> The Yorkshire Ripper's my dad lalala
> LALALALALA LALALALA LEEDS!
> LALALALALA LALALALA LEEDS!

In some respects this 'playing' with 'deviance' invokes Roland Barthes' discussion of wrestling in his collection of essays in the book *Mythologies* (1957), where he articulates the view that sport is not so much seen as a 'sport', but more as a drama which draws the attention of the audience to the emotional entanglement surrounding the narrative and the characters rather than the physical contest. In this work Barthes pre-empts Baudrillard by theorising wrestling as 'hyperreal' through a discussion of the excessiveness of the suffering of wrestlers which is what compels the audience to watch it, in much the same way that it is the excessiveness and dramatic emotional struggles between characters that underpins the soap opera form. In conveying this idea, Barthes suggests that the 'real' of the pain exhibited by wrestlers must be understood in an alternative way.

However, just as recent events in the overtly staged environment of WWF wrestling have demonstrated the real physical dangers associated with the sport, which have led to serious injuries and even death (Dube, 2000), no one can deny the injuries and pain suffered by Sarfraz Najeib. However, we cannot feel that pain or suffer that pain. Equally, we have no desire to experience his victimhood, to be like him or to hear about the intimate details of his life and family or sources of his being. So the experiences of victims like Sarfraz Najeib become redundant, merely subject matter for more 'significant', saleable and extendable narratives in which we are invited to take sides with characters whose *lack* of depth enables them to be reconstructed at a moment's notice.

This point relates to Baudrillard's infamous discussion of the first Gulf War which the title of his book implies 'did not take place' (1991). Despite the near-hysterical reaction that this work has prompted in some quarters, Baudrillard was not denying there was a 'real' physical war resulting in death and destruction on a horrific scale, but that from a western vantage point the war only occurred and could only occur through the media discourse emanating from TV sets which presented nothing more than their own tele-visual imaginings. Similarly, the sheer volume of deliberation over the Sarfraz Najeib case swamps, suffocates and leads to the disappearance of any notion of the 'truth' that the trial set out to uncover. In Baudrillard's sense, language and the swirl of publicity breaks free from its moorings in the manner of a tornado. The story becomes bigger than the details from which it emerges, picking up detritus along the way in order to satisfy our own insatiable demand to be titillated by the intricate details of a 'deviant' celebrity life style.

The column inches and our consumption of them do not relate to concerns for Sarfraz Najeib – despite the media-projected insistence of his father and solicitor – nor to the violence that occurs on a nightly basis in our city centres or the moral rectitude of sports celebrities. Rather, they provide a means to develop new story lines for the *Premiership* soap opera. In turn, these stories provide new armoury with which to vilify or celebrate Leeds United and its players; new reference points for discursively constructed binary boundaries between notions of inclusion–exclusion, normality–deviance, racism–anti-racism which are grounded in our own subjectivities rather than some uncoverable 'facts'. Just as Bowyer becomes a metaphor for both white working-class thuggery and the persistence of its indefatigable spirit in the face of its deconstruction, so Sarfraz Najeib can coexist as both the innocent 'black' victim and the provocative 'Paki' who was asking for it.

Bring on the Rhinos

Outside of the tornado of football's Premiership media events other harsher realities also come to bear in sport. Indeed, if the absence of any 'real' evidence enabled the Bowyer/Woodgate soap opera to take its own course, in the case of a more recent incidence of violence – also in Leeds and involving three players from Leeds Rhinos and one player from Rochdale Hornets rugby league clubs, the 'real' – the spectacle of 'caught on CCTV' video evidence *was* used to confirm the 'truth' about what 'actually' happened on the evening in question. Further, it was also used to play out discursively constructed notions of violence through a nexus of 'racial' and social class ideologies that led to three of the men receiving severe custodial sentences. After an incident involving a fight between four players, Paul Owen (Rochdale Hornets), 24 years old, was jailed for 15 months, Ryan Bailey, 19 years old, was sent to a young offender's institute for 9 months whilst Chev Walker was also sent to a young offender's institute for 18 months.

Indeed, it was generally thought by the local media (see *Yorkshire Evening Post*, 30 July 2003), the rugby league press (see *Leaguer and League Express* and *League Weekly*, both 4 August 2003), rugby league fans and by each of the clubs in question that these sentences were out of all proportion to the offences committed. The shadow of the events surrounding the Bowyer/Woodgate incident obviously played a key role in the drama that ensued and in Derrida's terminology that particular case could be recognised by its 'absence of presence'. As the Rochdale Hornets' chairman, Ray Taylor, put it:

> Without doubt, the Leeds Rhinos lads and [Owen] have been made to carry the can as an example of punishment now to be handed out by the courts in Leeds following the non-custodial sentences of the former Leeds United players, Jonathon Woodgate and Lee Bowyer after their well publicised court case.
>
> (*League Weekly*, 30 July 2003)

Judge Paul Batty QC intimated as much when he remarked in his summing up of the trial that such violence had become an 'all too frequent occurrence in this city and cities when nightclubs close' (*The Guardian*, 30 July 2003).

The incident involved a fight among the three men and another Leeds Rhinos player, Dwayne Barker, outside Creation night-club in Leeds. Why the fight started is not altogether clear, but it involved an argument after Owen had been tricked into handing his mobile phone over to an unidentified young woman. As the *Guardian* report (29 July 2003) explained, as he tried to recover his phone, 'the Leeds players thought she was being assaulted and set about Owen' and a fight ensued lasting 4 minutes. During the incident, Dwayne Barker had his jaw broken – we are assuming by Owen – and both Bailey and Walker subsequently attacked Owen. The CCTV evidence showed that the three players who received custodial sentences used their feet in the ensuing mêlée. That Barker escaped a custodial sentence was due to the fact that, he had not, in the words of the judge, 'put the boot in'.

Whilst not wanting to condone what occurred during this incident, there are a number of issues raised by the case. In marked contrast to the Leeds United case, none of the rugby league players received any financial or legal support from their clubs and each immediately pleaded guilty – so in effect what was presented through the CCTV evidence was taken for granted to be the 'truth' of what happened. There is another issue which connects this case to the trial involving the Leeds United players. Obviously making comparisons with the salaries of top-flight footballers, the judge suggested that 'sporting heroes, often paid the kind of salaries their fans can only dream of, have a duty to behave in an exemplary way' (*Yorkshire Post*, 30 July 2003). Both Bailey and Walker are first-team players with Leeds Rhinos and at the time of the incident had just been selected for the Great Britain squad (even so, their salaries are likely to be not much more than the average national wage). However, despite these connections there is an obvious difference between this case and the Leeds United case. The rugby league incident was a fight 'between friends' rather than an apparently 'racialised' attack. Yet although there was not one reference to 'race' in relation to the Leeds Rhinos incident, as we have already said, the issue of 'race' – as well as social class – was conversely, in our view central to the custodial sentences meted out.

In relation to the issue of 'race' we are not referring to the context of the argument which led to a fight between the three Leeds Rhinos players, who are each of mixed racial appearance and Owen who is 'white'. Rather we are concerned with the way in which the 'truth' of the players' actions was played out through what Gubrium and Holstein (1994) would call the 'present-time enactment' of the court case, which was in our view informed by ready-made ideologies underpinning both the 'racial' and social class backgrounds of the players involved.

As Lawrence (1982) has argued, common sense racist stereotypes about the behaviour and the size of black people are often used to operationalise racist ideologies in the process of 'pathologising' black culture, acting as they do, in Stuart Hall's (1981) terms through a 'grammar of race'. Indeed, John Hoberman has argued that representations of black sportsmen have reinforced broader notions of black criminality

> by merging the black athlete and the black criminal into a single threatening figure . . . first, by dramatizing two physically dynamic black male types which are often presumed to be both culturally and biologically deviant; and second, by putting the violent or otherwise deviant behaviour of black athletes on constant public display so as to reinforce the idea of the black male's characterological instability.
>
> (1997: 208)

That the three Leeds Rhinos players were of mixed racial appearance rather than black made no difference in this particular case and the discursively constructed binary boundaries of 'black' and 'white' were forced to hold good.

As Back *et al.* (2001) have argued, such forms of contingent racialisation are always articulated to other lines of social division, and we would add that social class stereotypes played an equally important role in this process, particularly in relation to the tacit acceptance of the players' culpability. The 'performativity' of all this was evidenced most particularly in relation to the discursive construction of Walker who received the harshest sentence. The judge was told by the prosecution that '16 stone (101.6 kg) Walker was the principal party in the violence' (*The Guardian*, 30 July 2003) and the judge himself, in summing up, told the court that 'Walker was seen kicking Owen, while he was on the floor, and then dancing about "like a boxer"' (*League Weekly*, 30 July 2003).

Ultimately, the rugby league players' embodied racial and social biographies denied them access to the glamorised celebrity show trial of their sporting contemporaries from across the city, who have since moved on in search of greater glories at Newcastle United, their actions, appearance and status revealing their 'guilt' and the inevitability of a custodial sentence. Such racial constructions remain contingent, however, and can remain on the sidelines when isolated from the 'cinematic' form and disguised by institutional authority. For on Tuesday, 26 November 2002, the black Bradford Bulls rugby league player Leon Pryce was himself arrested and charged with assault occasioning grievous bodily harm with intent, following an attack on his club's former fitness conditioner Eddie McGuinness, which took place at the Walkabout pub in Bradford city centre on 14 September that year. The attack occurred during an argument involving McGuinness, Pryce and Pryce's father, Dennis. McGuinness needed 48 stitches to ten separate injuries to his face after Pryce hit him with a glass he was holding. The court was told that Pryce lashed out when McGuinness grabbed him by the throat and threw him backwards during the argument.

Without the spectacle of video evidence or victims from outside of the rugby league 'family', and with the club's backing, Pryce at first pleaded not guilty and continued to deny the charge, but later he admitted a guilty plea on a lesser charge of unlawful wounding in self-defence. He told the court he believed that McGuinness was going to attack him and that he over-reacted in self-defence and eventually received the more modest sentence of 120 hours community service.

Yet, in both cases, outside of the contingent community of rugby league enthusiasts the public's interest was ephemeral, fleeting, attracted only by the voyeuristic fascination with the awesome force, power and physicality of sporting performers whose appearance and behaviour is characterised by images of an altogether more grimy, harsh environment: no significant protests to organise, no retribution, miscarriages of justice, or even terrace chants, just familiar storylines and a turn of the page in the quest for more excitement.

In bed with the Beckhams at Beckingham Palace

'David' strolls into his hotel room casually peeling off his jacket to reveal a flamboyant open necked white shirt as his mobile phone rings. He picks up the phone answering inappropriately 'Pronta', before relaxing into a conversation in which we are party only to his words.

'Oh alwigh' Victoria. Cor wo' a wacket. Is that li'll Romeo in the background there wailing away?'

. . .

[surprised] 'It's your new demo tape?'

. . .

[defensively] 'Nah nah nah, I like it, I like it.'
David climbs onto the bed as his wife talks.
'Yeah, yeah, we got "ere alwigh". Lo' a turbalence over de Alps but then they give Roy Keane a sedative an' 'e calmed down after tha'.'

. . .

'Yeah I miss you too babe.'

. . .

[speaking more softly] 'Yeah?! Victoria what are you wearing?'

. . .

'Are you? What with a Gucci?'

. . .

'*Nice*. Those autumnal shades will really set off the old Eastern look won't they?'

. . .

'Yeah? and . . . wo' abawt . . . underneaf?'

. . .

'Oh. I was thinking more of a Dolce & Gabbana vibe meself as it goes'

. . .

[whispering] 'Eh . . . take it off.'

. . .

'Yeah . . . butterfly clips on a silk bodice . . . phwooarr . . . That's like 'omage to early Lagerfelt that is . . . yeah.'

. . .

[whispering] 'Slip it off then.'

. . .

[looking quizzical] 'Slowly?'

. . .

[Relieved] 'Nah nah nah, just take it off. They don't go agether a' all.'

. . .

'Yeah call you back later on when you've changed. Yeah alwigh' then, alwigh'.'
Putting his head back on the pillow David picks up a croissant from his plate and takes a bite as he switches on the television to watch some daytime Italian TV.

This scene is taken from a satirical comedy sketch in which impressionist Alistair McGowan plays the role of the football star David Beckham who moved in the summer of 2003 in a drawn-out £25 million transfer from the world's richest club side, Manchester United, to the most successful football team in the world, Real Madrid. The humour of the sketch is however unrelated to football. It is tied up with Beckham's marriage to the former Spice Girl, Victoria Adams, and public fascination with the most intimate aspects of their relationship and their sexuality, a titillation of our desire to witness what goes on behind the bedroom doors of an apparently idyllic fairy-tale marriage which is ultimately reduced to depthless consumerist mundanity.

Of course, if the Premiership is a soap opera, then 'The Beckhams' might be considered a spin-off series which is premised upon a carefully constructed celebrity presence which has an infinite capacity for the deployment of 'deviant' story-lines. Through a range of modes of consumption the Beckhams' celebrity is able to titillate and humour us, gladden and sadden us, evoke sentiments of possession and rejection, desire and jealousy.

Celebrities are seen by Rojek (2001) as cultural fabrications, carefully mediated and worked upon by cultural intermediaries who operate to stage-manage their presence in the eyes of the public. At the same time, the market is seen to turn the public face of the celebrity into a commodity in the sense that consumers desire to possess them whilst their ability to do so is tied into the modern phenomenon of mass-circulation newspapers, TV, radio and film. In poststructuralist terms, however, the celebrity image is inflected and modified by the mass media and the audience. Celebrity is seen as an evolving field of intertextual representation in which meaning is assembled in infinite variety by agents, press officers, columnists, satirists and fans, which confirms the importance of understanding celebrity as a developing, relational field of power characterised by the versatility and contradictions of the 'public face'.

It is the infinite variety of discourses that 'the Beckhams' can be constructed within which allows them to be read through the metaphor of a soap opera. At the heart of this adaptability is David Beckham, whose identity cannot be tied down in the modernist sense for he is the embodiment of the polysemic self who transcends the conventional demarcations of gender, sexuality, social class, 'race' and, indeed, sports celebrity. Whilst he was once sent off for kicking out petulantly at Diego Simeone in a 1998 World Cup second round match between England and Argentina and blamed for England's subsequent exit from the competition, his is more often the 'deviance' of an intimate, domestic variety. Rather than tales of pitch-side rucks and night-club brawls the story-lines surrounding David Beckham are more likely to focus on the transgressions associated with his sartorial preferences, sexual practices, ambiguous gender and indeed rumoured infidelity.

Depicted in a *Face* magazine fashion photo shoot as a blood-drenched victim of violence he is referred to sympathetically as 'the biggest woman in the entire history of sport', comfortably declaring, 'I'm not scared of my feminine side and I think quite a lot of the things I do come from that side of my character' (July 2001). The point emphasised again and again as he was pictured wearing a sarong, prompting the *Sun* front page headline 'Beckham has got his posh frock on'; with fingernails painted pink at the christening of fellow celebrity Liz Hurley's baby; and, most tantalisingly of all, as willing to wear his wife's underwear, Victoria revealing on Channel 4's *Big Breakfast* in January 2000 that 'He likes to borrow my knickers'. But it does not stop there as Beckham plays to many audiences, as a gay icon pumping iron, doused in baby oil and with painted nails on the front cover of *GQ* magazine (June 2002), as a black icon and even a 'black' man trapped in a 'white' man's body (Channel 4, 25 April 2003). In truth his is a body without foundation. It is a canvas on to which we can paint any number of pictures but which is underscored by his erotic sex appeal. As Peter Conrad (2003) suggests, echoing the implications of the narrative style adopted in Alastair McGowan's satire at the outset of this section:

> [Beckham] is available for interactive fantasising, like your other half during phone sex: that is the deal the celebrity makes with us, and Beckham solemnises the transaction with that shy, dazed, long suffering smile of his – a promise of surrender, compliance, infinite availability.

In this sense 'the Beckhams' provide a basis for transcendence and the sanctioned liberation of sexual desire and fantasy in the age of consumer capitalism. With every confessional and every performative demonstration of their own excess we are encouraged to wonder a little bit more about what goes on in the one area of their life where the camera doesn't wander. Ultimately it is the comic format, with its freedom to delve into the realms of the unspeakable and unmentionable in the name of humour, which takes us closest.[2] In his interview with the couple for the British television charity fundraiser *Comic Relief*, Ali G, the spoof 'gangsta' rapper created by Sacha Baron Cohen plays to the audience's desire to get into the Beckhams' bedroom relentlessly:

> (Ali enters the lavish set clad in burgundy leather shell-suit and trademark shades and cap. Dry ice rises up around him as he turns his back to the camera to strike a pose, proudly displaying the glittering 'SAVE AFRICA' emblazoned across his back; just above a map of Italy) . . .
>
> *Ali*: Now really big it up for me guests tonight – every boy wants to be in his boots and every man wants to be in his missus. Big up for none other than Victoria and David Beckham!
>
> (The couple appear on the stage and join Ali on the plush white sofas. Hand-shakes and greetings follow)
>
> *Ali*: So what does you two do together on a night in?
>
> *Victoria*: We're pretty normal. We like sort of getting in and you know, watching a video, a take-away, that kind of thing – your video actually!
>
> *Ali*: Aiii, For real! Now does you go to watch him play football?
>
> *Victoria*: Yeah I do. Whenever I can. I like watching him play.
>
> *Ali*: Now there's a really insulting song that they [opposing fans] sing about you. Have you heard it? What is the words?
>
> *Victoria*: I can't repeat that really, it's pretty insulting.
>
> *Ali*: (to Beckham) But have you heard it?
>
> *Beckham*: No I haven't heard it.
>
> *Victoria*: Well what is it?
>
> *Ali*: Well I heard something, is it about you taking it up . . .

Victoria: Oh yeah yeah, ok? It's Posh Spice? (leans forward and silently mouths 'takes it up the arse')

Ali: (loudly) So you take it up the arse!

Victoria: No!

Ali: That ain't an insult, that is the biggest compliment you can get!

Victoria: Your just saying that cos you're a bit of a batty boy yourself.

Ali: (leaning back in his chair) You is crossing dangerous territory! All I can say is that I wish they would sing that about me Julie. Nah but serious, do you take it up the arse?

Victoria: Of course I don't.

Ali: (to Beckham) So you telling me you ain't never been caught offside?

Beckham: No!

Ali: Cos I heard you was well good at getting round the back and bending your balls in . . .

Ali: What do you think it is that makes a girl posh? . . . Me always feel that a posh girl was one that won't go all the way on the first night. You know, only gives you the top half. (Turning to Beckham) So tell me exactly how posh was she on the first night?

Beckham: She was posh for about four months.

Ali: Four months? I tell you, me Julie started off well posh, but after about half an hour, she was well common! Now David, if I can call you that, cos I never met you before, David, they say posh people talk like they've got a plum in their mouth. Does your missus sound posh when she's got your plums in her mouth?

(Crowd erupts and Beckham chokes with laughter)

Ali: What was you coughing up then?

(Beckham can only silently stare and meets Ali's eyes for a couple of seconds)

Ali: Ahh, you were trying to communicate something then to me, I think (does 'psychic look' as he touches his temples).

Victoria: He was gonna say that you're not actually meant to speak when you've got your mouthful so you wouldn't actually have that problem . . .

Ali: Now why do you think you is a pin-up for so many gaylords? I'm not gonna call them batty boys now cos me is politically correct. I mean just because you wear skirts, have a suntan and a skinhead, talk like a girl and hang out with Elton John. So how does it feel about being the picture for batty men?

Beckham: You tell me . . .

. . . *Ali*: (to Beckham) Well, if I had to do it with a man, it might as well be you! Like, if someone said dey was gonna nuke the whole of Staines, unless you, you know, ball Beckham? It's Staines man, you know, like me nan as well. But you to me, right! If you had to ball a man, who would it be?

Beckham: Ummmm, probably you!

Ali: You can only say that when you is so confident about your sexuality . . . Now me gotta say, the obvious thing for the rest of the audience here and the country, is that we would love to see you to ball each other. How's about right now for comic relief?

Victoria: I'm posh, I don't do that kind of thing!

Ali: Come on, let's see your red nose. You ain't doin' it?

Victoria: Why don't you get your Julie out here and you know, you?

Ali: (To Beckham) Can I ball your missus?

Beckham: (blushing) No.

Ali: (To Beckham) Can I ball you?

Beckham: Course you can.

Ali: Somehow I don't think the BBC would allow that to go on the Telly – me going into your danger area. Anyway, we just wanna say good luck with everything – being parents, being the footballer, being the singer. Respect to both of you for coming along. You both is looking fine! I gotta say, Please! Big it up for the main couple in England – POSH AND BECKS!!

Here, celebrity sex becomes family entertainment in a manner which extends beyond the conventions of the sports star interview and which gives playful licence to each and every one of our own fantasies and sexual gaze. The format enables the male sporting body and persona to be made available for consumption beyond the sports arena, where O'Connor and Boyle had earlier recognised its seductive potential as a means of wooing a female audience (1993: 116). Indeed, the ironic misogyny and homophobia of the interviewing style opens up the forbidden zones of popular discourse and invites us to visualise and contemplate the unimaginable and unspeakable. Sporting 'deviance' here is wrapped up not in the certainty and comfort of rule books, the sports ethic and Corinthian values but in our quest for freedom from constraint and the excitement of our voyeuristic desire for a bit of the 'deviant' other.

However, the conduit for this voyeurism, Ali G, has attracted considerable criticism since for Felix Dexter, of *The Real McCoy* black comedy series

a lot of the humour is laughing at black street culture and it is being celebrated because it allows the liberal middle classes to laugh at that culture in a safe context where they can retain their sense of political correctness.

(Gibson, 2000)

Whilst this may be so, the Ali G character is more commonly said to have been inspired by the white Radio 1 DJ Tim Westwood, who it is suggested has feigned a 'black' street accent for his hip-hop show. Cohen is reported to have become so irritated by white, middle-class listeners phoning in to request dedications to the 'the Staines Massive' and espousing their own stereotypical representations of LA gang members that he created the Ali G character, not to poke fun at black people but at 'wiggers' – white (and Asian) people who want to be, or even think they are, 'black'. The identity of Ali G then remains a matter of conjecture. In the manner of the mediated persona of David Beckham himself, through Cohen's refusal to give interviews, the character has taken on a life of its own, whose identity is open to limitless individual interpretation. As Gary Younge suggests, ultimately 'he is breaking taboos and ridiculing vanity. The less his interviewee gets the joke, the funnier the joke is' (Younge, 2000).

The Beckhams' appeal then is also tied to their willingness to laugh along with the joke, with a further irony provided by David's own association with black culture and the controversial suggestion in a recent television documentary, *Black like Beckham*, that he might *be* 'black' as a consequence of his consumer preferences for fast cars, smart jewellery, 'urban' music and cornrows in his hair (Channel 4, 25 April 2003). Whilst Tony Shaw has argued that 'Suggesting that splashing shed loads of cash in an extravagant, "bling-bling" manner is sufficient to be regarded as a black icon demonstrates an extremely narrow perception of what black culture represents' (Snow, 2003), this surely misses the point.

Even if it is possible to establish such a category, it is clear that David Beckham is certainly *not* 'black', but is better understood as a floating signifier, in Stuart Hall's (1996) terms. Brought to the market through an endless array of carefully constructed story-lines, he can be contingently consumed as such, just as is Cohen's alter ego, Ali G. As with other celebrity icons before him he can 'be' anything and transmit any message since, for the everyday consumer, he does not 'exist' outside of the commercial imperatives of the mediated discourses in which he is produced, as a 'brand'. The pursuit of global recognition for this brand inevitably leads to the creation of more and more characters – black, gay, feminine, hard, stalked, royal, innocent, sexy, gifted, vacuous, spiritual – which whilst being more and more sensational are required to be packaged in marketable, imitatable formats.

Rather than the DIY product of punk-inspired teenage rebellion then, his Mohican haircut is derived from a celebrity stylist, prompting parental approval for 5-year-old copycats in barber shops nation-wide and Japanese women to have their pubic hair styled in the same fashion. His own sartorial transgressions are ignored by the range of Marks & Spencer's sporty boys clothing which carries his name. The alleged plot to kidnap Victoria and his children Romeo and Brooklyn is averted by a *News of the World* tip off in return for exclusive rights to the story and pictures of the arrest of the Balkan gang against whom the case was later dismissed. His multi-million pound transfer to Real Madrid the subject of power games involving intrigue, dirty dealing, acrimony, double-crossing and mind games which all added to the glamour of the Beckhams' life style.

Conclusions

This is consumptive 'deviance'. The 'deviance' that we introduced in Chapter 4, which authenticates a style, a fashion, a thrill. A performance with the appearance of 'deviance' and all its unpredictability and dangerousness but which is scripted and ready-made for consumption through its provocation of media attention: entertaining at the same time as 'feeling' like the real thing. Its distance leaving us unable to question its authenticity whilst leaving us safe from its consequences and responsibility for those who are caught up in the media whirlwind which surrounds it. In the internet age, it prompts consumers to seek out, embellish and generate rumours, speculation and gossip in defiance of the conventional protocols of justice and legal process. As the 'celebrity' solicitor Mark Stephens commented in the wake of speculation surrounding the names of eight Premiership footballers linked with the alleged rape of a teenager in September 2003:

> Sex, violence and celebrity hits all the buttons with the public's curiosity. No longer do members of the public wait for information to be published or broadcast, they are actively seeking it out . . . which is leading to the spread of e-mails, texts and scurrilous websites.
>
> (PA, 2003)

As we suggested earlier, following Rojek, new technology has presented people with even more opportunities for 'wild leisure' in the form of pictures and video clips of anything from sexually depraved acts to genocide, which present individuals with the vicarious 'delight of being deviant' (Katz, 1988):

> The expansion of network society lays the foundation for the enlargement of wild leisure patterns. For, it renders rational-legal limits permeable and simultaneously neutralizes the identity of the viewer. The opportunities for voyeuristic and vicarious experience are significantly enlarged.
>
> (Rojek, 2001: 191)

As televised sport becomes ubiquitous, motor sport relies on the prospect of crashes, the winter Olympics on downhill skiing smashes, ice hockey and rugby league on mass brawls to entice new viewers, new consumers. Indeed, Tomlinson's critical engagement with Guy Debord's situationist polemic on consumerism, *The Society of the Spectacle*, manifestly illustrates the contemporary ordinariness, 'normality' and popular embracement of sporting 'spectacle' (2002) and the consumptive 'deviance' that goes with it.

7 Cruising and the performativity of consumptive 'deviance'

> The deepest thing in man is his skin.
> (Paul Valéry)

Nursing his unease like a time-bomb waiting to explode Jonty was ensconced in the driver's seat, impatient, waiting, biting his nails, smiling and nodding, but not listening to what was going on around him. Then all of a sudden someone gave him the nod: 'That's it, come on then, push us. Push us harder you cunts. Come on, push us . . . Verooom . . . Verooom . . . 'Go on push. Push harder'. Verooom . . . Vrrrrrrrrroooom . . . 'They're pushin' now'. Verrrooooooooom . . . Vrooooooooom . . . Screeeechin'.

The tarmac soon started to devour the rubber of the two tyres on the front wheels of Jonty's motor and they began to burn. The sound of rubber on tarmac screeched until it disturbed; and within seconds the smell of the burning rubber began to pervade deeper, into the nose, the head, the lungs, omnipresent. Heaven waiting for an angel: tyres squealing and smoke filling the air. 'Can you smell her? Surely they can smell her, now? . . . Push harder you cunts' . . . Verroom . . . verroom . . . Verrrrooooom . . . 'See that. She's burnin'. Watch me burn this baby. Burnnnninnn' . . . Drippin' . . . Burn baby burn, disco inferno, burn baby burn . . . . Shred the fuckin' tread, man' . . . People cheering . . . 'Look at me burn. Look how I burn . . . Full on ICE mixed with shred smoke. This is betta than head. Watch me shred the tread. Are you lookin'? Are you lookin' at me?' Verrrrrrrrrooooom . . . Vrooooooooooooooooooooom . . . Vrooooooooommmmmmm . . . Vrooooooooommmmmmmmmm . . . 'Gunna blow. Fuckin' blow baby . . . . BANG! . . . BANG! . . . 'Look at us. Look at mee. I'm Jonty . . . Look at meeee. Look at meeee . . . Look at Jonty go go go goooooo!!!!'

Just over two hours before Jonty had to rapturous ovation 'shredded the tread' on the front two tyres of his modified Vauxhall Corsa, a drive of motor cars had begun to amass in a car park in the non-place (Augé, 1995) or *nowhereville* (Bauman, 2003) just beyond Wakefield town centre. It has been argued by Augé (1995: 78) that in marked contrast to places (those topographical sites loaded with substance), *nowherevilles* are merely repositories of liquid flows – what George Ritzer has called nullities – 'which cannot be defined as relational, or historical, or concerned with identity'. However, this sense of nothingness was lost on Jonty and his fellow cruisers – we say lost for the simple reason that *nowherevilles* abound with tarmac and tarmac is the bit of the city cruisers are most interested in – who could be seen on this early August evening, pouring into this particular *nowhereville* which lies trapped between the centre of Wakefield and its suburbs to the south of the town which bifurcates towards Barnsley and Doncaster.

With all respect to the cruisers it is clearly evident to most other observers that this Wakefield *nowhereville* doesn't have an existence to speak of. Even on the street map it is no more than a series of blank criss-crossing white lines emptied of their once powerful significance. You are in Wakefield, but you could just as easily be in one of the *nowherevilles* of Leeds, Bradford, Barnsley or Sheffield and would be inundated with the same shops and stores and the same current advertisement hoardings that are here: the ubiquitous B & Q, McDonalds, Staples, Burger King, Currys and the rest. This *nowhereville* is in the deindustrialising desert of a once culturally thriving Wakefield in which retail warehouses and stores have taken over abandoned factories, disused railways yards and derelict churches, schools and workers' homes. The remnants of once vibrant and living industrial worlds superseded by death-in-life zombie terrains: industrial, working communities in terminal decay replaced, not by anything utopian, but by globalised nullities (Ritzer, 2004) built for nothing else but consumption: ubiquitous consumer palaces which cater for the appetites of voracious consumers. Bereft of any 'solid' substance *nowherevilles* are destined to be made conspicuous only by fleeting internal landscapes – trajectories of the mind and geographies of the soul – whose liquid contours ebb and flow like the consequences of that which they reflect. 'Things' to be consumed – 'things' which are often consumed in deeply affectual ways – but 'things' which always flow ephemeral, not lingering, through time and space. As a result the lived experience of the *nowhereville* reflects the temporariness of this liquid flow. Each *nowhereville* encounter is always experienced as a detached kind of existence, of 'being "in" but not "of" the space' temporarily occupied, to the extent that it offers its incumbents nothing more than the 'transience as a facility chosen at will' (Bauman, 2003: 142).

At 6pm-ish on this Monday evening the Wakefield *nowhereville* seemed to be occupied by two temporary realities in crossover: two different ontological flows intruding upon each other, not in an altogether negative way – after all they were both consumer cultures of sorts – but definitely in a way external to one another, not generated from the same yolk, but from different elsewheres, alien to one another. Yet they almost came together, practically in touching distance and then the first was gone in a puff of disappearance. All that was left of this reality flow – still bright and breezy only minutes before – was the last scrub of shoppers and day-time retail workers leaving, heading for home or somewhere else. The second, on the other hand, was still an embryonic reality, which in a short time and for a short time only, would be an exemplary conversion of an ordinary life into a form of theatre.

Burger King had knowingly cordoned off its car park entrance, but by 7.30pm the smaller car park immediately attached to the B & Q and Staples warehouses had started to fill. Outside the gateless entrance to the retail park the road coming south from the town had become a warm-up track, and the traffic lights went through a now unmeaning performance of changing colour as modified cars could be seen pouring into the car park like visitors from outer space. This outpost of the *nowhereville* would soon be packed to overflowing and its tidy unawares would soon take the form of a pretend arena. The high-spirited theatricality of the cruise is always vivid; and so much of it is about play-acting. And what better arena to demonstrate this than the B & Q car park where a quick-appearing, lively audience is always eager to become part of the action.

Very soon the B & Q car park looked the same as it did on any Bank Holiday afternoon. The sense of occasion was increased by queues waiting to get in and you could hardly find a parking space. As ever a starling-busy retail park it was. But this evening its function was being redefined, and at this moment it was in the throes of the completeness of ephemeral change. What was only a short time ago familiar launched itself at you, transformed. The cruise vehicles had metamorphosed the car park into an arena of impressively modified motors, most 'blinged-up' to the nines. Not even the buildings were exempt from change: everything was palimpsest. The chronology of regular time and the landscape of regular space – 8a.m. to 8p.m. at Staples and B & Q – had been reinvented as an alternate form of fantasy and desire. It was impossible not to be immediately domesticated by the time and place, the attention at once arrested by all those insignificant and discernable changes produced by the emergence of the cruise. The August weather helped. There was little vapour in the sky above – barely any to qualify as cloud anyway – only exhaust fumes which floated intense against the backdrop of the intense blue dusk.

In marked contrast to the cars, the warehouses and retail outlets now looked bleak; design-and-build monoliths locked and shuttered, warehouses for a set of commodities that had just gone out of fashion. In fact, the whole vicinity had given way to a hermeneutic of an altogether different kind of consumption: the performativity of 'modded' kit with flashing lights, the resounding sound of smooth clutch plate, purring 24-valve engines, the nitrous blue squirt of purge kit, skirts, spoilers, six-speed gear boxes, alloys and the burning rubber. Even the interiors of the cars were instruments of performativity: chrome floor plates, leather seats, bucket seats, and chain-mail steering wheels, wicked ICE with speakers blasting out drum and bass. The miscellany of last week's event, some scraps of metal – bits and pieces of an exhaust, a coil and some nuts and bolts – and the indelible scars of rubber still messed up one corner of the car park and added to the authenticity. It was a hive of activity. Drivers intermittently rattled about at full pelt. Groups and couples assessed each other and each other's cars, admiringly, ears pricking up and eyes lifting only at the sound of a noisy 'Shaguar' zooming into the arena, whence a queue of attentive onlookers instantly formed, buzzing over the open bonnet. This cruise was quickly turning into a great river of an event and everybody seemed irresistibly carried away with its flow.

Wacky races

> [In] our time, a mythic time, we are all chimeras, theorized and fabricated hybrids of machine and organism; in short, we are all cyborgs
>
> (Donna Harraway)

These establishing scenes were a prelude to the cruise's dramatic core which was soon to kick in. In place of the small talk that emerged at the offset there now began to develop more visual and violent methods of exchanging ideas and emotions. There were two main specialities on offer: burning, or 'shreddin' the tread', and street racing. If burning calls for no amount of skill on the part of its participants street racing is a different matter. And what happened next was hardly a surprise. In a matter of seconds what had been a throw-away remark about a 'shit lookin' shed of a souped-up Nova' had become a dromological challenge between two individuals and their cars, apparently both new to the scene. This was no serious score to be settled, just a race up to the first roundabout after the exit and back to prove that the 'shed' could beat the arse off an ostentatious two-tone silver-cherry Punto, which had been posed dramatically against the backdrop of the red, shepherd-delightful sky by its owner: its juxtaposition an assertion within the informal structure of the cruise which seemed to be the hallmark of its owner: at once confident and intensely charged.

The Punto driver woke up the engine and the small but powerful beast roared. The speed of the engine revs extending with the music emanating from the beat box in the boot: plasmatic rhythms pumping out on drum beats and electric bass kicking things into motion. The Nova, like its driver, looked and sounded like a religious ecstatic, a manic skinny mannequin jerking about in his seat, psychotic, punishing his pride and joy, his fringe down over his eyes. All of this prevaricating drew huge cheers from the crowd, adding to the beautiful mess of revs: the purring Punto adding oomph to the dirty squall of the Nova.

The Nova was quickest away. A sense of excitement rose like the exhaust fumes from the two cars and a race with a metaphorical death had begun. Responding, the Punto moved up from first, second, third and fourth in a matter of seconds, then fifth, the outside body of the motor pulsing with the noise of the engine and the vibration from the ICE box. The two racing cars soon got out of focus because they were concentrated in the smoky haze of the road-cum-racetrack, but you could see them racing as they started to move swiftly out of the car park on to the empty road, heading for the roundabout.

Not unsurprisingly, the Punto 'pissed the race' and was back in a matter of a couple of minutes leaving the Nova in its trail. In many ways the race was superfluous and what happened next went way beyond the schoolboy machismo of the two racers; it became a passionate competition between two tribes of cheering observers – but tribes without a centre, a core, a leader – all the same this was a reality play that was thriving in the midst of being unrelentingly adversarial.

Cruisers perform their manoeuvres, not simply to win races, but also to reproduce them for the *sake* of reproducing them, in order to expose each other for lack, for ridicule. The driver of the Nova misjudged the corner coming back into the car park and the audience laughed without mercy. As he prepared to swing the car back on track they could be heard willing him to 'fuck up' again. He obliged by crashing around into kerbs and bollards, searching for some sort of recognition, trying his utmost not to fade out of the limelight and into the shadows, but now he was largely ignored. You could see the embarrassment painting his cheeks as he pulled up. Only a little earlier he had surged into the memory with the recklessness of a new criminal. He had been inflated with energy one minute, punctured the next. His stature was palimpsest and had had change forced upon it: he had bloated like a giant, but had been forced to shrink back to a nothing, a small insignificance, merely a hyperactive 'boy racer' in a shit shed of a motor.

What knits cruisers together is the way that the celebrity of the performance emerges as an almost pathological need for recognition and attention. Cruisers do not want to be an ephemeral part of some ephemeral experience of stardom, but they accept the truth that cruising celebrity is destined to be experienced only in an individually existential and fleeting way. But this has not prevented celebrity so conventionalising itself in this cruising scene that anonymity is felt to be a pain worse than the worst death.

Winning the race and taking his own temporary place on the centre stage, the driver of the Punto had given his Nova counterpart not only a confrontational performance but a lesson in aesthetics. It was said by someone that the engine in the Punto had not been working as it should be. None the less, its limping rhythms had worked well enough, conveying its driver's journey upwards and onwards to his own ephemeral stardom. The engine might have been lacking but the Punto driver's performance had still served as an unambiguous symbol for the best way to do things, and that is why his reputation had been sedimented. In Harraway's (1991) meaning, he had cyborg-like, deconstructed the distinction between machine and human being and had succeeded in becoming an extension of his motor. Virillio (1997: 110) is much less sanguine and sees little enchantment in the technological hybridisation of machine and humankind. Contrary to Harraway he suggests this technologisation is more accurately understood as 'instrumental' and 'automatic' than intuitive and brings about instead, not a hybridisation as such, but 'the loss of contact with the body of that voluptuous "speed machine"', to the extent that 'putting on' one's 'racing car' is destined to become merely a 'cybernetic steering of disunited lovers'.

Connected with his voluptuous 'speed machine' or not, the Punto driver had with accelerator and clutch pedal beneath his feet, not only won the race, but fixed on a note here, a chord there, performing a tune with which his audience had celebrated. His movements had been very fast and delicately articulated, and his knowing hands had handled his motor as if he were playing a musical instrument that only he could hear. He had risen magnificently to the occasion. Yet his performance was less exotic than he himself imagined, simply redolent of Wakefield and its intricate West Yorkshire socio-cultural dance. He had simply exploited the ridiculousness of this cultural game as an incongruous foil to his own momentary celebrity and stardom. He had become instantly legendary, the centre of a mythology he had shrewdly encouraged and over which he exercised a modicum of control. What no one, including himself, could possibly have imagined at that very moment was what would no doubt be the ephemerality of his reign.

The aftermath of the race soon became routine, as it always does at cruises. Without a doubt, cruising is not a leisure activity that is intractably difficult to understand. This is because there is no profound truth associated with it: cruising is all surfaces and no depth; and every cruise blurs into the next one. Predictably, the start of the rest of the evening drifted past in the repetitive fragments of meaningless repetitive performances. Not unsurprisingly, the attention quickly drifted away from the cars and began to absorb itself in the social interaction, which was transformed by a small group of young women moving around the motors, eager to please. Flashing your breasts and thong-clad bum crack is not only cool for young women at cruises, it is virtually compulsory – and this group was not going to be denied its moment of glory.

Before long a display of hyper-sexualised behaviours settled like a spellbinding shroud over more young women who were there. All manner of characters moved in and out of vision, performing their own version of this gendered 'deviance'. After closely watching the behaviours of one, two, three, and then four young women in the immediate vicinity, it seemed that to be a young woman at a cruise you *had* to be involved in the machinate elements of the unfolding of a kind of semi-pornographic performance. A red-haired young woman dubbed 'ginger minge' by four young men cheering from the inside of their 'modded' Peugeot could be seen lifting up her top to display her breasts as the group yelled 'get your tits out for the lads'; two dark-haired young women, were also jumping in unison while baring their buttock cheeks and pulling up their thongs; and then there was the more restrained young blonde woman sitting on her boyfriend's motor, waist twisted so that her breasts and nipples were more pronounced, trying to make men desire her or because she simply knew what was required, it was difficult to discern. Either way, the young blonde woman, just like the others, seemed to be revelling in the gendered hyper-feminine performativity that constitutes this crucial part of cruise culture.

Cruising is a mode of performativity dedicated to wild, hedonistic pleasure in a number of guises. Indeed, the cruisers generate the heat of their own culture, both within and without their motors, checking out the performativity of each other's work, as well as parading, revving, skidding, burning and dancing, gossiping, performing for each other. Hyper-feminine performativity merely adds to this criss-cross and fluid continuum that gets more and more intense until it implodes inside itself – put on hold until further notice. However, on this particular evening the final act in the event of this performativity was forced to draw to a close before it peaked, through the entrance of the police helicopter, flying in, low, performing through its own performativity one of the most spectacular variations of the decentred excesses of liquid modern state surveillance,[1] to bring out a kind of mimetic fracturing, dissolving all that went before into a dash for exits. The world of the cruise and the 'real' world escaped now ran into each other. Instantaneously the cruise was no more.

Understanding cruising culture

There is a platitude in sociology that suggests that to understand any aspect of the social world we need to have a grasp of its historical context. However, cruising is a 'deviant' leisure activity as much without a history as it is one without a future. It limits itself to the present, to the 'here' and 'now'. What Bruce Bégout said of that 'nowhereville of all nowherevilles' Las Vegas, applies to cruise culture. In his words:

> [cruising] confines itself to the fleeting moment and no more, cramming it, like a sausage skin filled to bursting, with all its latest technological inventions, with the stars currently in vogue, with whatever is all the rage. In breaking down duration, it experiences itself as a kind of instantaneousness that stands for time in all its tenses, a *nunc stans* that releases all those who live there from any future horizons and from any mooring to the past.
>
> (Bégout, 2003: 20–1)

Cruising is merely a *performative community*, whose inspiration springs from the performativity of individual cruisers: it is both an event for consumption and something to be consumed by.[2]

Cruises: the ultimate performative communities

The ephemeral *performative communities* associated with cruising culture are reminiscent of Michel Maffesoli's (1996) *neo-tribus* and Scott Lash's (2002: 27) 'post-traditional' *Gemeinschaften*: they are 'mobile and flexible groupings – sometimes enduring, often easy dissoluble – formed with an intensive affective bonding'. Their affiliation is not really one of friendship, or of a community proper, but one of symbiosis, and their only glue is their incumbents' *individually constituted*, though insatiable appetites to connect with others. Indeed, cruising is unequivocally *not* about community in the orthodox sociological meaning, and its narrative structure is sustained by a reflexive individualism. Cruisers are simply '*operators* who are willing to forego a secure source of fruit for a chance to connect more of the world' (Wellman *et al.*, 1988: 134). That individual cruisers may have shared experiences and friendships with one another and others in a different context is neither here nor there; cruising is the self-constitution of a 'community' which takes place between autonomy and fragmentation (Delanty, 1999). To paraphrase Bauman (2002c: 176), cruising is but one more 'peg' community which bears many markings of the 'real stuff' – it offers the *experience* of belonging, of that quality of life which communities are deemed to deliver and for which they are coveted. It, however, lacks the traits which define the 'real stuff': durability, a life expectation longer than that of any of its members, and being 'a whole greater than the sum of its parts'.

If cruises are not the 'real stuff' of communities, neither are they institutions, nor even organisations. They are what Scott Lash (2002: 40) has called disorganisations.

According to Lash, disorganisations are not only overwhelmingly *cultural* pre-organisations, but they also presume a 'non-utilitarian, non-strategic and non-self-identical mode of individualization'. Simmel would have called them examples of 'sociation', while Durkheim would have understood them as 'elementary forms'. Both theorists would have suggested that cruising is one of those more 'trivial' forms of social interaction, which is constantly coming into being and being broken off, maintained 'until further notice', fated to exist against the backdrop of a life of undecidability.

Nevertheless – as Durkheim would also no doubt have commented – disorganisations do exist with their own sum of 'collective representations'. Indeed, cruising has its own ready-made archive, a shared lexicon of words, ideas and images. Restless, in some ways gifted, but always erratic, cruising operates this DIY lexicon with its own intense 'collective representation' which holds the imaginations of its participants and audience in thrall. Consequently, the spirit of the imaginary togetherness it creates is much more important to its incumbents than its actuality. To paraphrase Maffesoli (1996: 49):

> By 'pretending' they are participating magically in a collective game . . . it reminds cruisers that something like the 'community' has existed, does exist or will exist. Cruising is a question of aestheticism, derision, participation and reticence all at once. It is above all through this mythical affirmation that its incumbents are its source of power. This aesthetic game or sentiment is collectively produced just as much for individual cruisers as for the power which orchestrates it. At the same time, it allows one to remind this power that it is only a game, and that there are limits which must not be breached.

As such, the disorganisation of cruising is made to the measure of liquid modern times: a momentary stopping place more for gestures than consequences, of uncomplicated surface lives manufactured only for the time being, paraded as a *performative community* aching to be credible.

The 'real' of cruising culture: it's all about 'playing' the game

Cruising is merely about performing modified cars, performing bodies. Yet despite its apparent simplicity cruising is, like a butterfly, hard to catch, in a number of senses. First, the culture of cruising is quite literally difficult to pin down precisely because it is a disorganisation dislocated in no place in particular; it is always on the move and the theatre for its performativity is always at an improvised stage set. What is more, cruising represents the ambivalence associated with liquid modernity. In marked contrast to those leisure theorists (e.g. Rojek, 1995) who stress the deconstruction of boundaries that differentatiate 'work' and 'leisure' in liquid modernity, Lash (2002: 174) suggests that the 'playing' associated with games such as cruising must be understood in contrast to 'working', which still relates to 'leisure', but not in the hegemonic way it manifested itself in the moribund representational culture of solid modernity. He elucidates:

The worker uses implements, tools, instruments; the player uses equipment, 'gear', 'kit' . . . The player is also different than the spectator and the worker in that he plays *games*. Games, which are paradigmatic for the technological culture [of liquid modernity], are spatialized in the sense that the representational-culture relationships between viewer and painting, between reader and text are not. The latter relations are two points outside a concrete space – a subject and object. The representational culture speaks the idiom of the symbolic and the imaginary. You play games in neither the symbolic, nor the imaginary, but the 'real'.

However, the 'real' of the cruise needs to be understood in marked contrast to the solidly embedded and localised 'real' as it is conventionally understood. As Scott Lash explains, the 'real' of games such as cruising

is disembedded and generic – whether in the digital space of electronic form of life or the 'non-place' of international airports, or brand environments . . . To be in the real is not to relate to other subjects and objects in a distanciated and monological way, as do the reader/viewer: it is to engage with subjects and objects dialogically and interactively . . . [The cruiser] operates less from [his] conscious mind than [his] *habitus*. [He] is oriented to [his] environment less through *mémoire voluntaire* than *mémoire involuntaire*.

(Lash, 2002: 174)

Lash is suggesting that in games, such as cruising, communication may be paramount, but it is through individual reflexivity and the intuition of the *habitus* of the 'field', rather than through individual conscious reflection, that games operate. This is how cruise culture is played out. Lash never identifies the work of Michel Maffesoli in respect of the arguments he is making. However, what he is alluding to is a Maffesolian perspective, which is explicitly taken up by that author in *The Time of the Tribes*. For Maffesoli (1996), the *élan vital* – the 'creative impulse' or 'living energy' – is the basis of all life. Maffesoli establishes 'intuition' as a critical concept for understanding leisure in the contemporary social world. Lash's work is also reminiscent of Maffesoli when he is suggesting that time and space are not merely 'real' in the everyday understanding of the word but that they are contingent on time and context. However, what Lash does add to Maffesoli's perspective is the important point that 'surfaces' become crucial to understanding the way games such as cruising operate in what he describes as the new technological culture of liquid modernity – as opposed to the representational culture of solid modernity: in the chaotic world of cruising an 'intuition of appearances' rather than 'intuition of essences' prevails. Basically, for the player, in the technological culture of games, there is nothing deep as such, 'only things, as they appear to interested actors' (Lash, 2002: 174). And the surface life of cruising appears to provide a permit for any interested player to do as they wish; it gives the impression that it is valid for 'everybody'.

Cruising and the performativity of difference

Yet for all its surface accessibility, cruising is also difficult to pin down because it takes a number of forms. There are 'official' cruises and 'unofficial' cruises and the latter tend to be more raucous than the former. Be that as it may *all* cruises seem to be characterised by their predictability. They tend more or less to take on the same attributes from one cruise to another and what goes on at cruises tends to be governed by the same principles. Indeed, all cruising is about performing the right 'look', the right 'style', which is defined by the coded and ever-shifting parameters of 'kroozin' kool', the constant balancing act of being able to read and perform how cars, clothes, driving, walking, talking, should be. On the one hand, cruising is about the mundane rituals of displaying and checking out each other's motor cars and bodies, and on the other hand, it is centred on street racing. However, both these activities are closely related in the sense that each is about performance and performativity: a hybrid world where the mundane quotidian of performativity – display, gossip and tittle-tattle – collides with the apocalyptic and spectacular performativity of burning and street racing. This contrast of significance and absurdity, of the spectacular and the mundane, is what, for its followers, makes the whole event worth pursuing.

The majority of cruisers are young men who are players who play out their own kind of magic, which they find with cars and women. Indeed, despite the fact that its own vernacular is central to cruising 'identity', the lay observer can very quickly get a grasp of most of what is being said because it always relates in some way or another to cars, women and sex – even motor car accessories are described in terms of their pornography. This is confirmed by the pure barbarity of the misogynist and sexist language that explodes between the individual male cruisers, which destroys any moral expectations the lay observer might anticipate.

As well as being sexist and fraternal, cruising is also a childhood feeling of freedom and irresponsibility. Cruisers come to cruises in search of a familiar truth, nothing mysterious as such, just something which can be made tangible with something on four wheels. Indeed, the discursive field in which cruising constitutes itself allows for the deconstruction of taken for granted hegemonic norms. It is in this process that individual cruisers are able to perform not only an augmentation of their existential capacities for the affectual and the imaginative, but also experience an atmosphere of intensified engagement with other like-minded people. However, the majority of what happens does not take place within an 'inner-circle' because there does not appear to be an 'in-crowd'. That said this does not prevent the majority trying to penetrate the vapid edges of what barriers exist in order to have their own brush with celebrity.

On the face of it then cruising has no apparent hierarchies, only aesthetics, everyone included, nothing excluded, not even the fumes from the engines and burning tyres, which pervade the cruise scene as surely as a security blanket; just the amazing reality of an ephemerally flowing magical world played out with a creative intervention. Yet when you begin to look a little closer cruising begins to resemble the cultural desert of the geography of the physical *nowhereville*: flat and featureless, with few distinguishing characteristics or points of difference, a harsh mechanical environment in which it is easy for men to be sexist and obtuse towards women. Cruising is an ephemeral optative leisure life style, which is, on the face of it, determined by choice, but is to all intents and purposes dictated largely by gender, age and ability to afford the right performance kit. Cruising is also a mode of performance that swaggers with an uncomplicated capitalistic atmosphere: a cultural mix of heady marketeering combined with trappy commercialism and personal aspiration; it is mass similitude dressed up as individual preferences and everywhere advertisements for anything and everything are performed: from car logos to beat box ICE (sound systems) to Calvin Klein underwear carefully displayed above pants without waist bands.

This commodification of cruising reveals the unrelenting nature of capitalism, its vitality and vigor, and the opportunities it presents for individuals to live out their most imaginative fantasies of consumptive 'deviance'. In so doing it brings to our attention the most cherished commodity available to liquid men and women: the palimpsest desire for personal transformation, but one whose sensibility is inescapably attuned to a marketised private world. And the actions and behaviours of cruisers provide intimations of what the consequences of a fully privatised existence might bear a resemblance to. The key difference though is that this version of 'pure' capitalism is much like the anarchy and chaos found at cruises: it is staged and ephemeral rather than absolute.

Eye lust

As has been intimated already, to know what happens at cruises the researcher does not really need a good grasp of what has gone before; it is all too predictable. Take the cruise audience's faces; these too always seem staged rather than authentic. Going by 'appearances', their audiences are the best reviews cruises could have: all smiles and cheer. But looking closer, they always seem to react as one; their faces change together as if they all know what is going to happen. The results are entertaining, but also serious – serious because they are not about thinking, but accepted wisdom. Cruising seems to be a passion which possesses its incumbents so completely as to lift them out of the realm of choice and individual decision-making. They look as if they believe in the present moment as if it has a special genius. And as a consequence all measure of critique disappears and at the same time displaces the possibility of different, singular experiences for the ephemeral representation of a fantasy which is collectively desired. Cruising is a habit-driven appreciation and what cruisers see is not what there is, but what they want to see. To this extent cruising is for the most part a passion faked.

Virillio (1997: 91) would describe this process as a manifestation of the growing *industrialisation of vision*, which he calls *eye lust*. Virillio suggests that *eye lust* is a 'perceptual disorder' which must be understood as a kind of mad 'eye training', brought about by 'the wild acceleration of ordinary, everyday representations'. For Virillio, *eye lust* amounts to nothing less than a 'subliminally *optically correct* conformism' that manages a 'conjuration of the visible'. Basically, the ocular representations to which cruisers are so committed seems to bring about the impoverishment of their 'collective' vision.

Cruising transformations

If cruisers are characterised by their predictability, they are also people of performativity. The cruise is a place more for gestures than consequences, of uncomplicated surface lives manufactured only for the time being, paraded as performances aching to be credible. Cruising people are not made of anything substantial as such. Cruising 'identities' are not really identities at all, but merely palimpsests which tend to be of the temporary adhesive kind. Cruising identity-making is concentrated on performing rather than building anything solid as such and in this way it thrives on its ambivalence; it is always about performing 'identity' rather than expressing who you are. To this end, cruising sustains the liquid modern individual's predilection for the palimpsest reinvention of him or herself; that is, the capacity of individuals to erase traces of the past and assume new ready-made identities.

As Lyotard might say of it, there really is no such thing as a 'deep' or 'solid' cruising *identity*, only a performative cruising *transformation*. This is because cruising takes place in what Lyotard calls *open space-time*, in which the selves of the individual cruisers are but ephemerally transformed. And in the process – to paraphrase Bauman (1992b: 184) – the one thing lost is 'being' itself: cruising has no solid roots in time. This is because the cruising sort of 'being' 'is always escaping determination and arriving both too soon and too late' (Lyotard, 1988). Cruising space-time is that of the perpetual present and ubiquitous 'here'. And cruisers are merely the conjurors of a site-specific style of performativity which is made to-the-measure of the cruise itself. Indeed, the cruising sort of 'being' is always conducted in a performative mode, as part of a bigger drama that has:

> a stiff scenario closely followed by the actors, but [this] stiffest of scenarios remains a scenario, a contrived text scripted in this rather than that way, and a text which could well have been scripted in that way rather than this; and even the most disciplined actors remain actors, playing their parts, this part rather than some other which they could play instead with the same flourish and dedication.
>
> (Bauman, 1992b: 184)

There is a meta-discourse of individualism that predominates in cruise culture, but at the same time there is no attempt to find 'true' selves; cruising transformative 'identities' are merely defined in the performativity of cruising. Yet this performance of 'identity' is always a transaction with others and what does run as a thread through each and every performative cruising transformation, every twist and turn, every screech of a tyre, is the continual wish, the desire, the search for a language, a voice with which to speak, not to be understood, but to be desired; a form of communication that each of them hopes will give them a transformation marked by the contingency of a route to stardom, to celebrity.

The seriously wild cruising zone

In his discussion of the deterritorialisation and reterritorialisation of urban areas Lash (2002) also analyses this displacement of fixed identities through the idea of 'zones' and he suggests too that the sorts of identities found in wild zones are indeterminate identities. Lash (p. 28) also argues that patterns of social differentiation in the contemporary city and other urban spaces are reflected in processes which entail the waning of social structures and their concomitant substitution by a configuration of global flows – flows of money, information, images, books and any number of cultural products. Drawing on the work of Luke (1995), he goes on to argue that, where global flows are particularly 'heavy', cities witness the emergence of 'live zones', literally the social, cultural and economic 'happening' places. Conversely, where flows are 'light', they see the emergence of 'dead zones', which are socially, culturally and economically lacking. For this reason Lash suggests that social class today has become less a matter of location and more a matter of location in space, and for this reason, social differentiation must be understood in relation to the spatialisation of zones.

Following Luke, Lash identifies two other types of zone: wild and tame. He suggests that, generally speaking, 'tame zones' are often found in 'live zones' and 'wild zones' in 'dead zones', but not necessarily always. According to Lash, the 'live and tame zones' are inhabited by the 'utilitarian wing' of the new bourgeoisie, while the 'live and wild zones', or new gentrified cultural spaces with their myriad choice of entertainment including cinemas, clubs and restaurants, are inhabited by the 'new-media cultural intellectuals'. Dead zones on the other hand tend to be either moribund or 'dead and wild zones'. In the latter, 'identities are fluid, disintegrated, social disorganisation is the rule. These zones, in comparison with those of the expressive middle classes . . . are *seriously* wild' (Lash, 2002: 29).

In Lash's understanding, cruising is seriously wild and it allows cruisers to explode beyond the quotidian to explore the limits of self-indulgent aestheticism. Yet the 'seriously wild' acts of 'deviance' performed here are less the works of monsters or statements of 'deviant' identities than ways in which the individuals involved choose to accessorise themselves in their performativity of 'kruizin' kool'. Cruisers do not have any political ambitions nor a clearly defined ideology as such, but these are amply compensated for with sheer energy and a delight for the most inane rituals. Cruisers are instinctively against any kind of politics because these would literalise their cultural space, which as it is, unfettered, allows them simply to perform themselves in 'wild' ways.

Presdee (2000) suggests that the kind of leisure associated with 'wild' zones, such as street racing with cars, incorporates some of the important features of Bakhtin's classic carnival, including pleasure seeking relating to edgework and its oppositional status and the subversion of the dominant hegemony. As he puts it with street racing the:

> reworking of the streets is important, the event contests and, symbolically at least, takes control of a public domain. The performing on the streets of

theatre with cars is, at least part, a celebration of the occupation of the streets in opposition to a municipal ownership, although of course this control is contested between two rival reams. Most importantly, and this is referred to by those interviewed about the events, the hotting was about identity, demonstrating that one belonged to a group through communal display, thereby constructing an identity of excitement and opposition.

(Presdee, 2000: 51)

In common with a number of other theorists, we want to suggest that Presdee overemphasises the oppositional nature of activities such as street racing and joyriding and in so doing presumes too much about their political nature. Our research suggests that cruising deconstructs such normative truth claims about the ways in which politics are today played out in popular culture. Cruising may be 'seriously wild' in the ways that it exceeds and disrupts what most people describe as 'normality', but this is performed not to oppose and resist anything as such. If crusing is relational, it is relational only to itself. In this sense cruising exceeds the limits of dualistic understandings of it by performing itself. Cruising is not oppositional, it is simply excessive.

This leads us to suggest too that cruising reflects neither the 'carnival we know' nor the 'exploding carnival in post-modern culture' (Presdee, 2000). Instead, cruising must be understood as not only performatively constructed, but also performatively consolidated in the discourse that creates it. Cruising is nothing more than a celebration of the values of a discursive formation underpinned by the aesthetic of liquid modern capitalism. What is more, it is as much about the performativity of the quotidian of this hegemony as it is about the performativity of its more 'wild' activities. In the words of one of our respondents: 'mostly it is just hangin' about and checkin' out each others' motors and eyein' up t'birds as it is about racing and burnin'. In this sense, cruising hangs on a thread between the mundane and the spectacular (Blackshaw, 2003), which, for us, better than the idea of the carnivalesque, illuminates its 'affective feel' and its 'cognitive 'truth' (Rinehart, 1998a: 204).

Performing gender, performing 'deviance'?

Yet if cruising, as Baudrillard (2001: 73) might say, has been 'divested of ideology, of the class struggle, of history', it still appears to be founded on a myth that is to all intents and purposes patriarchal and which is founded on a nostalgia for a time and a place when masculine superiority was ubiquitous. And for all its apparent 'fluidity' cruising seems to be underpinned by the image of the solid modern discourse of hegemonic masculinity and within its culture the motor car and its accessories – including women – seem to symbolise powerful metaphors for the supremacy of phallic strength.

In Gubrium and Holstein's meaning it would appear that the cruising culture attempts to elucidate the 'here' and 'now' of young women, in order to make its ready-made versions of women's *'biographies'* a 'present-time enactment' (Gubrium and Holstein, 1994: 697). In this process it could be said that what is being acted out is 'artful, a complement to the play of difference' (Derrida, 1978), an artistic ruse which is both locally informed and organised. This would lead us to conclude that there is no hypostatised woman assumed behind the young women's performativity of what it means to be a cruise 'bird'. This is because women's performances seem to be staged both *for* and *of* the cruise; that is the performativity of the young women is scripted in the more complete performance of a heteroglossia (Bakhtin, 1981).

Drawing on the idea of a heteroglossic performance might lead us to articulate a particular view of cruising culture, which suggests that it is scripted *for* the other rather than *of* the other. From this perspective, it might lead us to conclude that young women involved are 'volunteered' to perform in dialogic concordance with the 'truth' and 'knowledge' about women promulgated in the life-world of cruising: the 'up-for-it cruise birds who blow meat whistle', the 'dirty birds', the 'slappers', the 'cellulited whores', the 'cum drippers', 'the spunk swallowers'. Indeed, it would seem that the discourse surrounding cruise culture attempts to inculcate the 'truth' that women are highly sexually charged and it is only men they desire and it is only men who can release their sexual fantasies in order to bring them pleasure; leading us to conclude that the 'subject' woman is a specific kind of *transformation* (Lyotard, 1988), rather than an identity as such, that is controlled through cruising's own ready-made discourse – a discourse in the making of which women play a pivotal and active role.

Understanding gendered 'deviance' ready-made cruise style

As we have already indicated, cruising is as much a product of mundane rituals as it is of spectacular or dramatic experience. Many of these rituals of performativity are tacit and seem to lack any sense of direction or focus, other than being patriarchal.[3] However, we want to argue below that although the rituals of cruising always invariably relate in some way to the subject of the other and that in cruise culture no group is more exotic than young women – who are incidentally so other that they are never simply young women – that performing performativity here is also a passion for an exotic life, which is celebrated by *both* the men *and* young women.

Freud would no doubt have understood this kind of gendered performativity as merely a repository for private singularities; that is a kind of defence mechanism or a fantasy which allows male cruisers to project their desires on to the object of otherness (women). Yet this Freudian-inspired observation is lacking in the sense that it imagines that cruising is a kind of essentially sexist 'deviant' activity that exists out of time – but nothing could be further from the 'truth'. As we have already seen cruising appears to lift its incumbents into a contingently outlandish and mythical world of unfettered sexism and misogyny where every extreme is allowed to unfold.

From an orthodox feminist position it would seem that young women at cruises must be either indoctrinated or at the very least self-deluded by cruise culture, and/or have got to be secretly punishing themselves for their misdemeanours. Yet this explanation is lacking too because it fails to take into account women's reflexivity. What is also an over-simplistic understanding is the one which suggests that the young women's actions must be somehow detached from their identities proper, from the 'real' women who they are, as is often conventionally said of strippers and prostitutes (McKeganey and Barnard, 1996), two groups who sell themselves in one way or another. On the contrary, the young women we observed seemed to be enjoying themselves, to the extent that the essential dynamic of what was being performed seemed to be something from within, rather than without, and their individual enthusiasm seemed to spur one another's. Indeed, the young women we observed simply seemed to have their own gift for hyper-performativity; that is their own need to perform intermittently in excessive ways, which is made-to-the-measure of the palimpsest demands of a liquid modern patriarchal society.

There is also another way in which the young women's role in the making of cruise culture might be understood. That most astute cultural interpreter Herbert Marcuse a long time ago observed resentfully the way in which capitalism maintains its hegemony through a process of 'resistance through incorporation'. Basically, Marcuse argued that one of the major reasons that capitalism flourishes is that it readily incorporates from dissenting movements and institutions those aspects which dovetail with its *modus operandi* – but resists the remainder. In the self-same way it might be argued that cruise culture incorporates women at different levels of its contingent social order – from their roles as mere 'accessories' to fully-fledged cruisers – at the same time as dispensing with any challenge to the patriarchal heterosexist hegemony which prevails.

Yet Marcuse's explanation is also found wanting. In common with more recent poststructuralist feminist accounts (see, for example, Irigaray, 1985, and Kristeva, 1986), which suggest that women more often than not tend to be constituted through discourses as the inassimilable other, which enables them to operate by virtue of their very exclusion, it fails to take into account young women's own investment in the making of cruise culture. We want to argue below that the young women who attend and participate in cruise culture cannot simply be read off as the objects of men's narcissistic inventions. Our argument is that they have a pivotal role to play in what is in effect a *pretend* game of social domination.

We can begin to understand this counter argument by considering the aesthetics of gender performativity at cruises. Showing off one's body parts at cruises is not confined to women, and men often go to extensive – and bizarre – extremes to make their own mark in the strip stakes. Be that as it may, from what we observed nobody really pays any attention to men taking off their clothes at cruises – especially the young women. In the poststructuralist meaning – from Lacan (1977) to Irigaray (1985) and Kristeva (1986) – it would no doubt be argued that this is not unsurprising precisely because the scopophilic male gaze of cruising culture maintains its pleasurability precisely because it cannot be returned. Yet, what we want to argue is that at cruises the production of this scopophilic male gaze appears to be the work of the *imaginary institution* (Castoriadis, 1987) of cruise culture rather than of some essentialist dialectic operation of gendered power already constituted in 'society'. This is because the imaginary institution of cruise culture is not really oppositional. That is, it 'does not come from the image in the mirror or from the gaze of the other. Instead, the "mirror" itself and its possibility, and the other as mirror, are the works of the imaginary, which is [it's] creation *ex nihilo*' (Castoriadis, 1987: 3). Drawing on the consumer principles which act as the guidelines for a liquid life worth living, the young women at cruises perform as much for themselves and each other as they perform for the men.

What is more, the 'fate' of young women in cruise culture must be understood as representative rather than postulated. They may be the ones who actively advertise features relating to the subjectivity of what 'young women' should be in cruise culture, which *appear* to be fixed and inescapable parts of 'young women's' 'identities'. However, these cruising transformations are merely contingent labels of self-manufacture, in the making of which the young women themselves collude; what Butler would call 'a set of repeated acts within a highly rigid regulatory frame that congeal over time to produce the appearance of substance, a natural sort of being' (1990: 33).

Our findings confirm Butler's argument that the performativity of gender is an 'effect' rather than a 'solid' ontological status. These findings also relate to Butler's work in the way that they imply that the performativity of young women's transformations are discursively determined, rather than being a matter of agency or individual choice. This is not the same as saying that cruising emerges in a cultural vacuum, in which its members are confined as unreflexive agents. On the contrary, cruise culture is simply performed through the repetition of its own ready-made discourse, its own code of intelligibility, which is never mechanical. Through the performativity of the discourse of cruising 'the appearance of power shifts from the condition of its subjects to it effects, [and] the conditions of power (prior and external) assume a present and futural form' (Butler, 1997: 16). Yet in what we observed if there was a move from 'parody' to 'politics', it was in a way contrary to what Butler suggests in her work, because the young women involved seemed to be attempting to confirm rather than disrupt essentialist assumptions about what it is to be a woman.

Indeed, cruising is largely an apolitical zombie world (Beck, 2002) in which everyday commonsensical understandings of women's emancipation have been put on temporary hold and in which Norbert Elias's civilising process appears to be running backwards as humankind sheds its unnecessary frills. Mapping a worn out version of a solid modern patriarchal reality on to a leisure activity is a fine conceit in which the young women as well as the men here collude and it provides a way of holding back a wider reality which in its 'political correctness' has become wearisome. To this extent the outside world is never allowed to seep through the perimeter fence that envelops the cruise culture. Cruise culture is very much a discourse adept at controlling the flow of freedoms and it keeps its own version of what is 'ordinary' and 'tacit' moving briskly along – which is a discourse pervasively reflected throughout much of contemporary-mediated popular culture – there is no looking 'outside' or 'forward' to future gender emancipation.

Young women's complicity is central to the 'making' of the discourse of cruising and they happily collude in ignoring other 'truths' of the world outside cruising culture with a 'surface' act that reflects a kind of radiating tolerance. Indeed, the young women appear to take great pleasure in playing with the style of this inequity and adapt it to their own uses – teasing, ridiculing and controlling men through what Jones and Stephenson (1997) describe as an *invested* kind of performativity. The observer can witness the truth of this invested performativity at any cruise. We observed it time and again through the myriad ways young women would draw men in through their sexuality simply to tease or to ridicule them – most often not in any hurtful ways – before 'letting' them struggle away. The trigger for this invested performativity being like anything else at cruises: simply the events involving the mundane and spectacular of cruise culture.

The pirate flag of truth-making in which cruising is wrapped makes the gendered disparities performed look much more 'deviant' than they actually are. The consumptive 'deviance' associated with cruising is more a world of convention than of anything dangerous and out of the ordinary. Cruisers are merely disciples of mainstream consumer culture, who through their interest in cars have reinvented a discourse underpinned by two ancient myths – the myth of rebellion and the myth that women are men's sex objects – to *supposedly* exclusive male ends. Shorn of all its surface bravado, what goes on at cruises is nothing more than what is performed. Cruising is a triumph of form over content, of surface over depth, of putting off until later what is presently being denied. Nothing is transformed, yet at the same time nothing remains the same: everything merely performs what it is, just at that moment, in the 'here' and the 'now'. Instead of – dare we say it – genuine pernicious sexism, male cruisers exert a sort of surface nuisance; instead of genuine misogyny, a parodic bathos. It is pertinent to conclude then that difference is not so much unwelcomed in cruise culture as simply inadmissible. The life-world of cruising is simply built on an entire aesthetic dedicated to the surface strategy of being theatrically atrocious to the very young women its culture in actual fact not only adores but performatively celebrates.

This is what leads us to conclude that the performativity of cruising for young women is an invested kind of patriarchal performativity. This is a game of 'surface' social domination which is guided by a mythic reality and the young women involved are the chief myth-makers. Yet invested performativity is not merely attributable to the young women, it is implicit to all actions and behaviours associated with cruising, which, in Paul Ricoeur's (1992) understanding, confirms the self-serving epistemology of 'attestation' underpinning cruise culture, which enables it to operate its own contingent patriarchal 'truth' about the 'world'. However, the straightforward truth is that, in the performativity of gender stakes, the young women simply outclass their male counterparts. As for the men – who in their other lives are unable to escape the strictures of a specific class *habitus* – in Bourdieu's meaning – they perform themselves in a cruise culture likewise entrapped as figures unable to exist other than as mere palimpsest performances in a pre-programmed narrative scene. At cruising events a surface patrician world meets a culture of motor cars which is carnivalesque in as much as everything is approved in bad taste. Within the confines of this determined uncertainty everything that is performed is subject to strict formulae; the performers perform what is expected of them and, as we saw, even the audience is subject to well-defined codes of conduct. The cruiser's world view is a sensibility attuned to the imaginary institution (Castoriadis, 1987) of a patriarchal world. However, the actions and behaviours of the men and young women involved in that world are merely intimations of what the consequences of a tacitly accepted patriarchal existence might bear a resemblance to – *might*, because here gendered difference is staged and ephemeral rather than absolute.

Conclusions

Yet we have seen that it is much more than gendered difference at cruises that is staged and performed. It is as if the whole of cruise culture is cast through a plot that has an air of excess and excitement, but one which never really offers any surprises. Indeed, we saw that cruising is a performance that always glides and in which every excessive action is articulated as if it really means something; but most of what goes on actually means very little. Beginning with an onomatopeic introduction at the start of this chapter we saw that in terms of cruising's visual aura, the most emphatic surges of excitement came with the burns, the street races and then when young women performed their bodies. It seemed as if cruisers could stretch reality in order to experience it and we saw that hyper-performativity was used as a formidable tactic, to make what is essentially a pretend world gripped by the ordinariness of extreme excess. The more cruises you attend the more you realise that you have simply entered an uninspiring, prosaic world of ordered disorganisation. A fantasy world, but also a 'real' world, where it is impossible to distinguish whether the beauties and uglinesses played out are being parodied or merely performed through the performativity of what is in effect the excess of consumptive 'deviance', which dominates the contemporary world of sport and beyond.

8 'Jumpers for goalposts'

The community sports agenda and the search for effective social control

No other form of social control is more efficient than the spectre of insecurity hanging over the heads of the controlled.

(Zygmunt Bauman)

'Get in goal lad!': Kes, physical education and solid modernity

Mr Sugden was passing slowly across one end of the room, looking down the corridors and counting the boys as they changed. He was wearing a violet tracksuit. The top was embellished with cloth badges depicting numerous crests and qualifications, and on the breast a white athlete carried the Olympic torch. The legs were tucked into new white football socks, neatly folded at his ankles, and his football boots were polished as black and shiny as the bombs used by assassins in comic strips. The laces binding them had been scrubbed white, and both boots had been fastened identically: two loops of the foot and one of the ankle, and tied in a neat bow under the tab at the back . . .

[Sugden] opened the door and led the [boys] down the corridor and out into the yard . . .

'Come on, you lot! Hurry up! . . . Line up on the halfway line and let's get two sides picked!'

They lined up, jumping and running on the spot, those with long sleeves clutching the cuffs in their hands, those without massaging their goosey arms.

'Tibbut, come out here and be the other captain.'

Tibbut walked out and stood facing the line, away from Mr Sugden.

'I'll have first pick, Tibbut.'

'That's not right, Sir.'

'Why isn't it?'

''Cos you'll get all the best players.'

'Rubbish, lad.'

'Course you will, Sir. It's not fair.'

'Tibbut. Do you want to play football? Or do you want to get dressed and go and do some maths?'

'Play football, Sir.'

'Right then, stop moaning and start picking. I'll have Anderson.'

. . . Tibbut scanned the line, considering his choice.

'I'll have Purdey.'

. . . [The selections continued] And then there were three [left]: Fatty, Billy, and Spotty Crew-Cut, blushing across at each other while the captains considered. Tibbut picked Crew-Cut. He dashed forward into the anonymity of his team. Fatty stood grinning. Billy stared down at the earth. After long deliberation Mr Sugden chose Billy, leaving Tibbut with Hobson's choice; but before either Billy or Ratty could move towards their teams, Mr Sugden was already turning away and shouting instructions.

'Right! We'll play down hill!'

The teams broke for their appropriate halves, and while they were arguing their claims for positions, Mr Sugden jogged by the sideline, dropped the ball, and took off his tracksuit. Underneath he was wearing a crisp red football shirt with white cuffs and a white band round the neck. A big white 9 filled most of the back, whiter than his white nylon shorts, which showed a slight fleshy tint through the material. He pulled his socks up, straightened the ribs, then took a fresh roll of half inch bandage from his tracksuit and ripped off two lengths . . . Mr Sugden used the lengths of bandage to secure his stockings just below the knees, then he folded his tracksuit neatly on the ground, looked down at himself, and walked on to the pitch carrying the ball like a plum pudding on the tray of his hand. Tibbut, standing on the centre circle, with his hands down his shorts, winked at his Left Winger and waited for Mr Sugden to approach.

'Who are you today, Sir, Liverpool?'

'Rubbish, lad! Don't you know your club colours yet?'

'Liverpool are red, aren't they, Sir?'

'Yes, but they're all red, shirts, shorts and stockings. These are Manchester United's colours.'

'Course they are Sir, I forgot. What position are you playing?'

Mr Sugden turned his back on him to show him the number 9.

'Bobby Charlton. I thought you were usually Denis Law when you were Manchester United.'

'It's too cold to play as a striker today. I'm scheming this morning, all over the field like Charlton.'

'Law plays all over, Sir. He's not only a striker.'

'He doesn't link like Charlton.'

'Better player though, Sir.'

Sugden shook his head. 'No, he's been badly off form recently.'

'Makes no odds, he's still a better player. He can settle a game in two minutes.'

'Are you trying to tell me about football, Tibbut?'

'No, Sir.'

'Well shut up then. Anyway Law's in the wash this week.'

He placed the ball on the centre spot and looked round at his team. There was only Billy out of position . . . The goal was empty . . . He levelled one arm at Billy.

'Get in goal lad!'

'O, Sir! I can't goal. I'm no good.'

'Now's your chance to learn then, isn't it?'

'I'm fed up o' goin' in goal. I go in every week.'

Billy turned round and looked at the goal as though it was the portal leading into the gladiatorial arena.

'Don't stand looking lad. Get in there!'

'Well don't blame me then, when I let 'em all through.'

'Of course I'll blame you, lad! Who do you expect me to blame?'

Billy cursed him quietly all the way back to the nets.

Sugden (commentator): 'And both teams are lined up for the kick off in this vital fifth-round cup-tie. Manchester United versus . . . ?' Sugden (teacher): 'Who are we playing, Tibbut?'

'Er . . . we'll be Liverpool, Sir.'

'You can't be Liverpool.'

'Why not, Sir?'

'I've told you once, they're too close to Manchester United's colours aren't they?'

Tibbut massaged his brow with his fingertips, and under this guise of thinking, glanced round at his team: Goalkeeper, green polo. Right Back, blue and white stripes. Left Back, green and white quarters. Right Half, white cricket. Centre Half, all blue. Left Half, all yellow. Right Wing, orange and green rugby. Inside Right, black T. Centre Forward, blue denim tab collar. Tibbut, red body white sleeves. Left wing, all blue.

'We'll be Spurs then, Sir. They'll be no clash of colours then.'

'. . . And it's Manchester United v Spurs in this vital fifth round cup-tie.'

Mr Sugden (referee) sucked his whistle and stared at his watch, waiting for the second finger to twitch back up to twelve. 5 4 3 2. He dropped his wrist and blew . . .

*   *   *

'He was slipping his jacket on when Sugden entered the changing room. Sugden watched him, then, as Billy headed for the door he stepped across and blocked his path.

'In a hurry, Casper?'

'Yes, Sir, I've to get home.'

'Really?'

'Yes, Sir.'

'Haven't you forgotten something?'

Billy looked back at the bare peg and the space beneath it.

'No, Sir.'

'Are you sure . . . What about the showers?'

. . . Billy turned back into the showers and began to scour himself with his hands . . . While he worked on his ankles and heels Sugden stationed three boys at one end of the showers and moved to the other end, where the controls fed into the pipes on the wall . . . The blunt arrow was pointing to HOT. Sugden swung it back over WARM to COLD. For a few seconds there was no visible change in the temperature, and the red slice held steady, still dominating the dial. Then it began to recede, slowly at first, then swiftly, its share of the face diminishing rapidly.

The cold water made Billy gasp. He held out his hands as though testing for rain, then ran for the end. The three guards barred the exit.

'Hey up, shift! Let me out, you rotten dogs!'

They held him easily so he swished back to the other end yelling all the way along. Sugden pushed him in the chest as he clung his way round the corner.

'Got a sweat on, Casper?'

'Let me out, Sir. Let me come.'

'I thought you'd like a cooler after your exertions in goal.'

'I'm frozen!'

'Really?'

'Gi o'er, Sir! It's not right!'

'And was it right when you let the last goal in?'

'I couldn't help it!'

'Rubbish, lad.'

Billy tried another rush. Sugden repelled it, so he tried the other end again, Every time he tried to escape the three boys bounced him back, stinging him with their snapping towels as he retreated. He tried manoeuvring the nozzles, but whichever way he twisted them the water still found him out. Until finally he gave up, and stood amongst them, tolerating the freezing spray in silence.

When Billy stopped yelling the other boys stopped laughing, and when time passed and no more was heard from him, their conversations began to peter out, and attention gradually focused on the showers . . .

The boy guards began to look uneasy, and they looked across to their captain.

'Can we let him out now, Sir?'

'No!'

'He'll get pneumonia.'

'I don't care what he gets, I'll show him! If he thinks I'm running my blood to water for ninety minutes, and then having the game deliberately thrown away at the last minute, he's another thing coming!'

(Hines, 1968: 86–108. © Barry Hines, 1968.
Reproduced by permission of Penguin Books Ltd)

This excerpt of gritty social realism from the novel A Kestrel for a Knave, upon which the award-winning film Kes (Woodfall Films, 1970) was based, provides a compelling antidote to the romanticised representations of youth sport associated with advocates of 'rational recreation' and its more contemporary incantation in the form of physical education. These movements, which emerged out of the Victorian concept of 'muscular Christianity' (Money, 1997), advocated an approval for the moral and physical value of sports and games which underpinned the rapid expansion of 'modern' sports throughout the nineteenth and twentieth centuries.

In many respects Hines' alternative interpretation might be seen to reflect the arguments of his marxist contemporaries, Rigauer (1969), Vinnai (1970) and Prokop (1971), who saw sport as reproducing social behaviour within an authoritarian regime which is functionally and normatively consistent with the needs of capitalism, whilst maintaining the illusion of its status as an autonomous liberatory domain. In similar vein, Hargreaves (1986) considered the British physical education system as a disciplinary regime which acts as a means of social control by 'schooling' bodies to reproduce specific class, gender and ethnic divisions. This work was itself indebted to Foucault's consideration (in the seminal text *Discipline and Punish* (1977)) of the role of the normalising 'gaze' in controlling and maintaining 'docile' minds and bodies to secure a stable and predictable work-force; a perspective which is easily applied to Hines' work in relation to the ridicule, infantilisation and emasculation of those subjected to 'Sugden's' gaze as a consequence of their un-interest in *his* game of football.

Whilst for Garland (1990) Foucault's more sophisticated understanding of 'deviance' is unable to identify with the irrational and counter-productive features which accompany actual processes of social control, his work does reveal the myriad ways in which people think about and know their own sense of reality. Since in Hines' novel, it is 'Billy Casper's' non-conformity with the modernist, rationalised sporting discourse which characterises physical education and the fixed notions of 'normal' behaviour that this implies for his instructor which is pertinent. As such, whilst many sporting discourses continue to emphasise sport's 'functional' role as an agent of 'normalisation', a force for 'good', Foucault's work alerts us to the fragility and contingency of such conceptualisations in the face of alternative realities such as 'Billy's'.

Yet while, in keeping with Gruneau's critique of the structural determinism of many marxist accounts (1983), there are instances of resistance to the constraining disciplinary regime of sport in Hines' work, ultimately what we are presented with is the 'legislative' authority (Bauman, 1987) of the vindictive PE teacher, 'Sugden', in the age of 'solid modernity' (Bauman, 2000) which suffocates 'Billy's' individuality. Here, sport clearly seeks to establish societal norms and reveal the 'deviance' of the minority such as 'Casper' and 'Fatty' whilst setting itself the task of facilitating conformity to a restricted set of shared values and rules within the context of an overbearingly rigid hierarchical class system. 'Fatty' is cast to the side as 'excess' waste, unfit for the 'manly' activity of football and by implication physical labour, through his lack of athleticism whilst 'Billy's' perplexing non-conformity draws only ever harsher sanctions from Sugden's iron fist.

These values, enshrined in the institutionalised 'cultural capital' (Bourdieu, 1984) associated with 'Sugden's' qualification badges and the school rules, which are denied to and deployed against 'Casper', are seen to empower the teacher as much as asserting the primacy of the hierarchical disciplinary regime of industrial capitalism. Whilst they are no more fixed than 'Sugden's' contingent preference for the performances of the 1960s English football legend Bobby Charlton over his Scottish contemporary Denis Law, they have the authority of fixity. As teacher, captain, referee, commentator and disciplinarian, 'Sugden's' authority may have many guises, but it only has one voice, one body, one fist. It is he who makes authority 'real', who monopolises all of its forms and imposes his will through the discourse of sport, demeaning those who fail to grasp its authority: 'Rubbish lad! Don't you know your club colours yet?'; 'God help us; fifteen years old and still doesn't know the positions of a football team!'; 'Are you trying to tell *me* about football?' Where imposed, there is no room for debate, no exceptions from the rules: 'You know the school rule, don't you? Any boy wishing to be excused Physical Education or showers must, AT THE TIME of the lesson, produce a sealed letter of explanation signed by one of his parents or legal guardian'.

However uncomfortable they might be with it, people generally knew where they stood in relation to this kind of legislative authority, resistance taking place only at the margins: when forgetting your kit; climbing on to the crossbar of the goal to alleviate the cold and boredom; privately mocking the teacher; letting a goal in to end the game or attempting to sneak away without having a shower. The attraction of school sport for those of the appropriate physical build and level of ability operating in spite of the 'school master' rather than through his emancipatory mission, in its provision of an opportunity to express oneself outside of the physically constrained and equally oppressive disciplinary regime of the classroom (Willis, 1977).

As we suggested earlier, in liquid modernity these arrangements of power and authority have become increasingly blurred and uncertain. As Bauman's sociology shows, in liquid modernity status and prestige are continually up for grabs and individuals, instead of being fated to an inherited place in the world with its own constricted realm of experience, are now compelled to find avenues for their own self-expression in the face of a bombardment of endless possibilities with, at the very least, the articulated prospect of realisation. Under such arrangements and from our contemporary vantage point it is the intimidatory teacher, 'Sugden', whose actions are now subjected to ridicule, whose disciplinary regime is exposed as a self-indulgent spectacle of abuse through the knowing gaze of those who read and view this work.

The Gascoigne Estate Crew: dealing with the 'deviants' in liquid modernity

If what once appeared as a blight on our capacity adequately to deal with the aspirations and inequalities faced by working-class youngsters can now be read as a vaguely comic satire at the expense of the physical education teacher, what it does not represent is any relinquishing of the social control agenda. As we argued in Chapter 4, with liquid modernity come new forms of power and control, and perhaps most significantly the relocation of the role of sport in that agenda from the school playing fields, which have in many cases quite literally been sold off (NPFA, 2003), to the market-place.

As we highlighted earlier, Garland and Sparks argue that 'late' or, in our terms 'liquid', modernity is the product of an amalgam of post-Second World War social, political and economic changes which have prompted a cultural transformation characterised by 'new freedoms, new levels of consumption and new possibilities for individual choice' (2000: 16). In the process the 'solid' certainties of the social class systems illustrated in Miles' work, with their legislative, hierarchical authority have gradually broken down and given way to a mediatised and technology-driven society of horizontal social networks (Castells, 1996). In the resultant chaos of contemporary capitalism, driven by the twin aesthetics of celebrity and consumerism, 'rules' do not carry the same burden of restraint. There are no fixed roles or type-casting, whilst the labels that we carry are imposed upon ourselves, both metaphorically and physically in the shape of designer brands, in pursuit of new identities and life styles. We live by the laws of consumer culture, which hide behind the myths of meritocracy and are reflected in the way in which, as Bauman has suggested, identity is characterised by the wearing of 'light cloaks' rather than the imprisonment of 'iron cages' (2000). The world is presented as a stage on which to write your very own reality play, on which to imprint yourself in the imagination of others, where to be unnoticed, invisible, becomes a source of degradation and self-loathing.

However, if social class is no longer seen as a restraint nor can it be used as an excuse for 'failure'. In liquid modernity, in the popular imagination, inequality and neighbourhood are products rather than ingredients on life's menu. For as Bauman has argued, today social inequality is, at least perceived as an individual matter, just as the rewards of consumer capitalism are consumed and enjoyed individually or, at best, as a contingent temporal collectivity in the manner of the consumers of the sporting spectacle. Liquid modernity is an era that tempts the sacrifice of stability, security and, by implication, collective relations, to the 'will of individual happiness' (Bauman, 1997).

. This pursuit, as Bauman has shown, is first and foremost tied to the market-place which, in turn, breeds new forms of servility in the shape of the 'flawed consumers', not only lacking the competencies for work, but the capacity to be accomplished shoppers and, for that matter, sportsmen and women. For 'in a consumer society, a "normal life" is the life of consumers, preoccupied with making their choices among the panoply of publicly displayed opportunities for pleasurable sensations and lively experiences' (1998b: 37). In such circumstances, as we saw in the last chapter the 'flawed consumers' may be tempted to create their own pleasures outside the rational conventions of the market-place but driven by the same desires and aspirations emanating from consumer society. As such, 'tempting fate by challenging the forces of law and order may itself turn into the poor man's favourite substitute for the affluent consumer's well-tempered anti-boredom adventures, in which the volume of desired and permissible risks are cautiously balanced' (ibid. p. 39).

In this respect, in their seminal critique of the Sociology of Leisure, *The Devil*

Makes Work, Clarke and Critcher recognised the widespread interpretation of sport's role in challenging 'deviant' behaviour among unoccupied working-class young men. Accordingly, they suggested that state-sponsored sports interventions, including much school sport, were organised around the perceived need to deal with the 'problem of working class youth' by keeping them 'off the street', 'under supervision' and with 'something constructive to do' (1985: 135).

As such, the funding representatives or agents of those who are legitimate members of consumer society, the socially 'included', sponsor the endeavours of community sports agencies because of their presumed capacity to 'reach' and 'manage' a constituency of the 'excluded' who have proven increasingly trouble-some for more traditional interventionist agencies. In accordance with Andrew Scull's famous essay, *Community Corrections: Panacea, Progress or Pretence* (1983) which sought to account for the fundamental shift in the basis of social control from the 1970s onwards, such agencies are also in tune with the process of *decarceration*, whereby the focus of control has shifted beyond the walls of those institutions charged with incarcerating problematic sections of the population, namely prisons and mental asylums. At the level of political rhetoric this is celebrated as progressive reform, a more humane way of doing things, the belief is that 'it increases community responsibility for the control of crime and delinquency' – and that this is something that should be applauded.

The negative vocabulary newly associated with incarceration contrasts markedly with the (supposedly) new, 'community'-based system of social control, since 'community' is a word bereft of all negative connotations. As Bauman suggests, it is a word that also has a 'feel', a good feel, 'like a fireplace at which we warm our hands on a frosty day' (2001: 1). To talk of community corrections then is to talk more fondly and optimistically of dealing with our social problems since, crucially, 'community' is a word that sells, that has a market value, particularly when put together with sport and more particularly – in the context of young, urban males – football.

On the Gazza

Driving through the de-industrialising urban sprawl of East London towards Barking in 'Terry's'[1] football laden Ford Galaxy the driver is in familiar pose, calmly chastising more aggressive fellow crawlers on the overflowing roads 'Who are these people, Tim. I ask ya. Am I drivin' a Honda Civic 'ere?' as he outmanoeuvres a black BMW with tinted windscreens to secure a place on the north circular, halting his adversary in his tracks, his calmness eliding with readiness for confrontation. Dressed casually in his office kit of canvas jeans, check shirt and 'Timberland's' 'Terry' is the sort of guy you know can look after himself but who you'd also find it hard not to get along with. A stoic master of deprecating London patter which names no victim but leaves its audience on its toes, matching a solid physical presence that belongs to his genes rather than a gym. He is taking me to the Gascoigne, a notorious sprawling housing estate in Barking where the organisation of which he is now Director has been running estate-based sports activities which spawned the successful amateur football team, the Gascoigne Estate Crew, several years ago.

Whilst physically melting into the concrete jungle that constitutes this part of London, the Gascoigne's 'problems' are announced to residents and would be interlopers by the large street sign at the gated opening to St Margaret's reading 'The Metropolitan Police working in partnership with the local community to create a safer environment'. To the network of welfare, regeneration and crime partnerships hovering over the estate like vultures, bringing scraps of comfort back to the institutions they serve, in the form of window dressing and crime statistics they can't account for,[2] the banner gives a new presence to their work, masking another reality beyond the slogans.

On the inside of this 'gated community', where the barriers are tactically deployed to keep residents in rather than trespassers out, there is little sign of the partnership which has become part of the everyday vernacular of contemporary social policy. The Baseline youth project, victim of the same problems it is there to curtail, is protected by steel doors and a secure access system that you might more readily expect at a nightclub entrance guarded by bouncers, whilst shirt sleeved police officers do the approaching, prompting the suspicion of younger residents.

The 2000, predominantly local authority owned, homes on the estate consist mostly of a mixture of inadequate low rise, low spec. balcony access flats and high rises so typical of early 1970s housing developments. They accommodate a mixed populace, less than 50 per cent of which is employed and, in contrast to the rest of the borough, a third of which is non-white. Most households do not own a vehicle and over 15 per cent have a lone parent living with dependent children (National Statistics, 2003). The estate is, if not 'liquid', then certainly flimsy and transient rather than 'solid' in the sense of the nostalgic image of the traditional East End community (Young and Willmot, 1957).

It is also, if the populist rhetoric is to be believed, pervaded by the fear of crime (Golder, 2003) which has foundation in the Gascoigne ward of the London Borough of Barking and Dagenham being in the top three wards in each category of crime statistics bar one in the Borough's most recent audit of crime and disorder (LBBD, 2001). And yet this notoriety is simultaneously a source of resentment and cause for celebration amongst its young residents. Each escalation of violence a travesty for its victims whilst adding to the stock of street gossip, local mythology and veneer of urban authenticity.

As we drive past the boarded up Abbey Arms on Ripple Road which neighbours the estate, 'Terry' comments:

'The first night I came down 'ere there was a guy lying on the floor outside that pub dead. Just lyin' there dead, on the pavement.'

This was no attempt at shock treatment, no search for respect, for 'Terry' and I have known each other and this world, which we both contingently inhabit, for many years, but it did set the context for the evening, just as it must have done for 'Terry' four years earlier when *he* was the unknown visitor.

It occurred to me that back then, arriving on the estate in his club track suit, carrying a bag of balls, the coach must have struck passers-by as looking somewhat out of place. The estate is often crowded with strollers, many of them seem to have little immediate purpose apart from passing the time, bumping into friends and standing to talk for a while. Young mothers with push-chairs walk from one side of the estate to the other and then back again without venturing out. Groups of young wannabe's huddle together outside the parade of shops. Unknown faces inevitably prompt interest here and curiosity gradually got the better of some of the youngsters as they approached the man in the tracksuit to ask what he was doing. As 'Terry' recalls:

'I'd just been going down there for a few nights and wandered round, I saw there was a hard play area that had seen better days, but you could use it. The kids started askin' who I was and I just asked them if they were interested in football and dished out a few leaflets. I told them I'd be there on Monday night, and they were like, "Yeah, yeah, all right" and I knew they were thinking I'd be gone before anything got going but there were a dozen or so there the next Monday and we started to suss each other out and then we just kept going, rain or shine, Mondays, Wednesdays, weekends.'

Since then, in the face of 'Terry's' relentless commitment, consistency and organisational thoroughness, over 200 youngsters have become involved in the project, several of whom are now employed as sessional coaches themselves and whose work he had come to monitor on this evening. His ability to connect with the young people here relates to an intuitive understanding of how the multiple discourses on crime and exclusion, which dissolve the easy distinctions between victim, offender and consumer, are woven into the very fabric of daily life.

    ... As we parked up and wondered over to the hard court play area running alongside St Margaret's 'Terry' took on the role of interloculator, commenting 'See this kid he'll have your watch off you in a moment. He's an Old Bailey trial waiting to happen. He'll be a one man TV programme in 10 years', before provocatively shouting out, 'Oi ginger!' as the kid mucked about on the far side of the court. A 10-year-old crop haired, bare chested urchin looked up defiantly before recognising his mentor and crying out 'Terry!' and running over, jumping up and hugging him as though he were a returning much missed father. His enthusiasm just as passionate as 'Billy Casper's' desire to escape from the imprisonment of Sugden's P.E. lesson. Other kids saunter over and the banter flows as those unfamiliar with 'Bob's' mate conduct their own surveillance, testing out the 'outsider'. The impossibility of a fixed identity in liquid modernity enabling this white, fair haired 1960s cockney son of an East End council estate to play with his audience and their racial stereotypes, telling them he's Albanian.

    'You're not Albanian', dismisses one kissing his teeth.

    Smirkingly indignant, 'Terry' proclaims,

'I *am*. What is this, customs? You want my passport? I'm tellin' ya I'm *Albanian*.'

Always alert he spots one of his players. A 'face' on the estate whose status he knows will settle the score and provide an opportunity to embellish.

'You know Saz?'

'Yeah.'

'Albanian yeah? 'E's my bruver.'

Unconvinced but sufficiently unsure, the young pretender moves on.

'Why you here?'

'I'm scouting. Come to see *you*.'

They turn back to the kick-about that has been going on in advance of the training session whilst we lean against the perimeter of the brick and wire enclosure. The youngsters are soon putting on a performance, half an eye on the game, half an eye on the shadowy, uncertain possibility that 'Terry' represents. As non-conformist as 'Billy', 'Bob' has climbed on top of the steel portakabin that doubles as a store room to which any pretence of security has long since been abandoned until 'Terry', unimpressed, calls him down. Soon he's back alongside us sharing tales which invert the authority of his local school's rules.

'When d'you break up for summer?'

'I've finished. Bin excluded.'

'Why were you excluded?'

'Didn't do my work innit.'

'Why not?'

'Cos then you get excluded and you don't 'ave to do no work.'

'Bob' jumps around like a circus act without a trapeze, constantly fiddling with 'Terry's' watch and lifting his keys.

'What car d'you drive 'Terry'? Is that your Merc?'

'I'm not telling you what car I drive. It'll be gone in 2 minutes.'

'Is it the Beamer. I won't nick it. I just wanna sit in it. Go on let's 'ave a drive.'

In a flash they all run off up the street after someone said something about what someone else had said. We took our cue to go off for a stroll ourselves and when we return 'Bob', 'Dean' and their mates were back hanging out beside the play area with 'Kels', who now works for the organisation and leads many of the sessions on the estate and who was dressed for action in shorts and club T-shirt but was making no move to get things going in the face of the indifference of the warm summer's evening sunshine. The organisational intensity of 'Terry's' early interventions having now given way to 'Kels' 'anti-structure' approach as he sits chatting with some of the 'kids' while his seventeen year old coaching assistant 'Paulo' is said to be cruising the estate on a Suzuki 750 motorbike. 'Terry' is not showing it yet but you know he'll be making sure things are back on track next week.

As we join them, 'Rob' claims to have just punched a boy who had a knife at the other end of the estate in the recent spat whilst his mate 'Dean' plays down his pretence as he wheels around on his mountain bike.

''E's just actin' tough innit. We just chased 'em.'

The brashness subsides as 'Terry' teases him.

''Ere's the Old Bill 'Bob'. Come to get ya.'

As three uniformed officers wander towards us 'Bob' shiftily moves to sit between 'Kels' and 'Frank', who also helps out with the coaching, prompting interest in 'Kels's' T-shirt and the ball he is bouncing.

''Ave you goh' any more of them? Can I 'ave one?'

'Terry' is prompted into tried and trusted wheeler dealer mode.

'I'll tell you what. You be good till November. Don't get excluded till November and I'll get you a T-shirt and a ball.'

'Till November, that's ages.'

'It's the summer holidays now isn't it, so you've only got to manage September and October.'

'Then you'll give me one of those T-shirts and a ball?'

'Stay in school till November.'

'Yessss.'

'Be good for your teachers, yeah.' He knows that in all likelihood he won't, but you've got to try, give everyone a chance rather than write them off.

Meanwhile 'Terry' teases 'Frank' about his fake 'Beckham' earrings and plays with notions of sexuality without recourse to homophobia in this playground of masculine performance. Onlookers fail to emulate the precision of his jousting, crying dismissively,

'Pussy.'

But 'Frank' passes the test, unperturbed and dressed immaculately in his Evisu jeans and designer trainers he responds incongruously,

'I'm blingin' man, innit,' as 'Rueben', similarly attired, walks past, acknowledging 'Terry' and stopping to chat.

'You not playing football?'

'No.'

'Who's your mate?' (who 'Terry' has not met before) 'Nice trainers. How do you afford them? You working, yeah?'

He responds proudly,

'Yeah.'

'Where you working?'

Unhesitatingly, encouraged and empowered by Grant's compliments he responds,

'McDonalds.'

'Come down next Monday if you wanna play football, yeah. Nice shoes fella.'

As we go to move on 'Terry' is looking out for 'Paulo', who had been riding up and down the estate at speed, the same 'Paulo' who at the age of 15 had once screeched past him at 110mph whilst wearing no helmet on the north circular in order that he would not be late for a training session. Now 17 he was driving his brother's bike, who is 16 and unlicensed to ride it, but as 'Terry' commented:

'At least he's got a helmet on now.'

'Bob' takes on the role of PR officer trying to get the local celebrity to stop a few times as 'Paulo', recently returned from a spell playing as a trainee with Bristol Rovers football club, ignores him until 'Terry' drives past and calls out, just once,

'PAULO.'

Instantly glancing round, sapped of his invulnerability, the driver stops and turns his bike tentatively, as 'Bob' tries to talk his way into the car with 'Terry' patiently fending him off, before 'Paulo' anticipates 'Terry's' concerns, proffering that,

'It's legal.'

'Yeah, yeah but what about you. Are you legal?' Teasing him 'the police are up there you know.'

'Are they?' queries the now concerned star performer.

Reserving judgement for now, 'Terry', eager to ensure his continued participation in the coaching sessions which he would normally help to run and which have moderated his excesses and run-ins for the past two years, tells his attentive protege:

'Turn up next Monday. You must be there. I don't care if no one's there and there's no coaching going on. You *must* be there', before we drive off thinking of 'Paulo' as we pass the exit placard declaring 'Gascoigne estate welcomes careful drivers'.

In the midst of the banality of these everyday encounters one might question The Youth Justice Board's dissemination of the organisation's work on the Gascoigne as an example of best practice amongst interventions with young people at risk of offending. Why is it the case that so many social inclusion professionals regard 'Terry's' unstructured forays[3] on to the estate as being so revolutionary? Is it not slightly perplexing that those people who are supposedly responsible for regenerating the excluded wastelands of the urban metropolis believe those very same areas are out of bounds, dangerous places where other people live and work. When considering the plethora of government and community organisations who state their purpose as positive intervention in the lives of the marginalised and at risk, why is it that a small community football programme can seemingly enter into the lives of these people in a way that very few of the others can claim to do, bridging the rapidly widening chasm that separates the world of the 'excluded' from those of the 'included'?

It is in the search for answers to these questions that we can see beyond the easy vernacular exchanges between the coaching staff and participants, towards identification of a shifting aesthetic of social control and modes of distinction within the era of liquid modernity which explains the favourability with which community interventions of this type are treated.

From legislating to interpreting: community sport, consumerism and social control

If Zygmunt Bauman draws a distinction between the intellectuals of solid modernity who wish to 'legislate' universal values in the service of state institutions, and intellectuals as 'interpreters', who deploy their specialist knowledge to explain and interpret texts, public events, and people to wider audiences (1987, 1992a), maybe we can identify similar emerging trends within the sphere of community sport practice.

In Bauman's (1987) scheme of things, in the era of solid modernity 'legislators' were the handmaidens of the State, working as social engineers to construct a rational, efficient and integrated industrial society. In this context the physical education instructor operated with the missionary zeal of the colonial imperialist, spreading the emancipatory vision of sport, on the basis of absolute cultural confidence and unfailing certainty in their way of doing things. It was the PE teacher who embodied the all-seeing, all-commanding regulatory gaze of Foucault's panoptical system of surveillance (1977), which keeps those being watched subordinate by means of uncertainty, forcing the 'watched' to act in accordance with the modernist sporting discourse, because they never know 'when' or 'who' might be watching but are fully aware of the sanctions that might follow non-compliance.

Whilst Foucault himself never mentioned its role in this process, sport is perhaps the social practice which best of all exemplifies the nature of surveillance in the modern 'disciplinary society' (Andrews, 2000). In this respect, Jean-Marie Brohm's book, *Sport: A Prison of Measured Time* (1978), argued that sport participation in capitalist societies leads athletes to become alienated from the practice of sport and ultimately their own bodies. The body becomes a mere instrument, a technical means to an end, a machine with the task of producing the maximum work and energy, focused towards the achievement of a specific task. The result is that the body ceases to be a source of pleasure, creativity and fulfilment, or a means of self-expression in the manner presented by 'Billy' in his training of the wild kestrel which provides the central narrative of Hines' book (1968); or indeed in his efforts to relieve the boredom and freezing conditions of his PE 'lesson' when he climbed on to the cross bar and began to perform to his own tune before being forced down by 'Sugden'.

'Casper! Casper, get down lad! What do you think you are, an ape?'

'No, Sir, I'm just keeping warm.'

'Well get down then, before I come and make you red hot!'

Billy grasped the bar again with both hands, adjusted his grip, and began to swing: forward and back, forward and back, increasing momentum with thrusts of his legs. Forward and back, upwards and back, legs horizontal as he swung upwards and back. Horizontal and back, horizontal both ways, hands leaving the bar at the top of each swing. Forward and back, just one more time; then a rainbow flight down, and a landing knees bent.

He needed no stops or staggering to correct his balance, but stood up straight, smiling; the cross bar quivering.

Applause broke out. Sugden silenced it.

'Right, come on then, let's get on with the GAME.'

(Hines, 1968: 97–8)

Satisfaction from sport in the era of solid modernity, even at the level of school games lessons, comes in terms of the coach's acknowledgement of competitive and precise outcomes rather than the physical experience of involvement, whilst failure and non-conformity, constructed as 'deviance', are met with repressive disciplinary action. It matters not whether at the hands of the school master or the blazered guardians of the sporting institutions which regulate the practice of sport according to globally recognised rules and disciplines.

With liquid modernity, however, comes a new celebration of diversity and relativism in which the market takes over from the state in producing willing consumers rather than obedient citizens, accomplishing its ideal the minute it 'succeeds in making consumers dependent on itself' (Bauman, 1992a: 98). Yet if, as Bauman (1992a) has argued, consumption has emerged, for the masses, as the new 'inclusionary reality' or normalising constraint, with consumers bound into the social by seduction – driven by the images of 'perfect', sexy bodies emerging from commercial gyms, the dreams of football superstardom peddled to youngsters at soccer skills summer camps, the celebrity sports stars adorning the covers of life style magazines and the safely consumed images of sporting 'deviance' – the excluded non-consumers remain subject to repression whereby as Bauman (1992a: 98) points out, 'repression stands for 'Panoptical' power'.

Ultimately, it is this repression, manifest in the form of the welfare services, which reinforces the seductive authority of consumerism. Rather than emancipation from want, disease, squalor, ignorance and idleness that underpinned the creation of the British Welfare State, the welfare services now reveal the horrors of non-participation in the consumerism of the free market, by reforging 'the unattractiveness of non-consumer existence into the unattractiveness of alternatives to market dependency' (Bauman, 1992a). In the legislative authority of state agencies such as the DSS, Benefits Agency, Probation, Connexions and others, today's welfare services constitute a repressive governmental 'gaze' that collectively 'polices' the 'flawed consumers'.

For Bauman (1995: 100), within this repressive arrangement 'distance' is of the utmost importance since it is not merely used to differentiate 'us' from 'them', it also allows 'us' to construct 'them' as 'the objective of aesthetic, not moral evaluation; as a matter of taste, not responsibility'. The estate dwellers are dismissed as 'vermin', 'scum', 'asylum seekers', 'immigrants', 'white trash', an underclass to be avoided, to escape from. This process is what Bauman describes as idiaphorisation, which essentially marks the comfortable but anxious majority's disengagement with a commitment and responsibility for the poor. As he puts it:

policy turns then from the subject matter of social policy into a problem for penology and criminal law. The poor are no longer the rejects of consumer society, defeated in the all-out competitive wars; they are the out-right enemies of society.

(1998b: 77)

Yet this dichotomy between the repressed and the seduced, like all binaries, is of limited efficacy as a basis with which to grapple with the complexities of social issues in our times. For we are hesitant to add the work of agencies such as the one we have described to the list of institutions engaged in repressive surveillance targeted at the 'flawed consumers' that Bauman so eloquently describes; since it is in the space between these arbitrary classifications that the work of 'Terry' and his colleagues finds its niche. In the development of their programme the key workers have consistently attempted to develop projects which will, in their eyes, make their work more relevant to the 'communities' that they see themselves as serving as well as attracting the funding to secure their future operations. The move on to the Gascoigne estate and others across the boroughs of East London was a consequence of a decision that their work should be taken to the very core of what was more widely perceived as the rotten heart of social exclusion, where 'the enemies of society' lived.

However, whilst, through their surveillance, the more repressive agents of the state such as Youth Offending Teams and Probation Officers had identified the 'targets', the 50 young people 'most at risk of offending', in each of the locales earmarked for such inclusionary work under the auspices of the national Positive Futures programme, the organisation's coaches had their own approach. Their capacity to connect with the 'target' group relating to their own biographies, social outlook and interpretive market savvy, which infiltrates the monologic of the one dimensional legislative authority of solid modernity.

In the domain of sport and community development work a coach who is linked to a professional football club has the kind of cultural capital, the absence of which would now be marked by 'Sugden's' badges and qualifications and their outdated 'anorak' formality. But professional football club coaches do not generally wander on to the Gascoigne; their status derived from their cool distance, their association with the celebrity, wealth, glamour and media presence of the institutions at the heart of the consumer society that they serve. Third Division football clubs do not carry the same appeal as those from the Premiership but this community programme's association with a club from the lower reaches of the professional game[4] still provides a sense of authenticity which can buy an introduction, an opportunity to engage. Beyond that introduction the capacity to achieve the aspirational goals that the organisation sets itself is reliant upon an empathy with the participants, which marks the work apart from the repressive regime of modernist physical education.

On the Gascoigne, no one is referred to as 'Sir', there is no kit to forget, nor showers to miss, no disciplinary use of violence. It is the young players, embodying a refusal to be denied access to the consumerist sensibilities of the mainstream, rather than PE teachers, who adopt the sartorial preferences of footballing icons from the Premiership and Sky TV's *Dream Team*. There is a place for everyone, with teams of all ages, sizes, abilities and gender available to those who are interested as teenage girls look on moodily at the lads practising tricks without fear of chastisement. Commentaries and banter are of the playful interactive variety rather than sneering in tone.

In this environment 'Terry' is the 'expert' interpreter *par excellence*. The embodiment of what Garry Robson calls Millwallism (2000), his own biography intrudes throughout, providing an intuitive knowing of the condition of those he works with. Constantly reading the multitude of clashing texts presented in front of him, weighing up the shifting boundaries between the need to engage with the young people he meets and the spectre of a governmental gaze which requires distance whilst placing primacy on the demands of state surveillance operations to intrude into the lives of those it fears. Picking up on the nuances of individual style and quick with a comeback 'Terry' is at ease in a way which makes those he works with comfortable. When 'Bob' tells of his sister smoking indoors, now is not the time to probe further whether he means cigarettes, spliffs or crack cocaine. The police are not tipped off about 'Paulo's' unorthodox means of arriving at training on time. 'Barry's' casual tale of a fight with 'Bob's' Dad over a mattress which flew out of a window too quickly is no reason not to encourage him to do some summer coaching. Experiences are shared, forming the basis of lasting relationships through which guidance is sought and 'Terry's' approval is prized rather than his ire. Since in his terms:

> it's about having the right people out there, week in, week out, building those relationships with the kids. Without that, it doesn't matter how much money you throw at it, or how good your intentions are, it just won't work.

As such, all kinds of contingencies are at play across the panoply of social distinctions which mark the liquid modern period as the organisation's work necessarily sets up clashes and discomforts the easy routines of a more parochial existence in its efforts to make new opportunities available to participants.

It's a London thing[5]

On the coach to Great Yarmouth for a football tournament shared by the predominantly black *Eastside* and a similarly inspired all-white team of socially marginalised young men from Portsmouth who have occupied the back seats, 'T' plays his music loudly and proudly. He plays it for *Eastside*, black London telling the yokels how it is – that's how he sees it.

'It's a London thing' is the shout every time 'T' increases the volume and the rear section mutter their displeasure.

Walking slowly and deliberately down the gauntlet, a Portsmouth lad approaches the driver and asks him to turn the volume up on the radio. Everybody heard. He had wanted them to. All of them.

'We're not mugs, never heard of the Portsmouth thing?'

He turns around and walks toward his friends. Having struck back he now had to walk back. 'T' pumped up the volume. The slow walk back to home-town friends demanded a Spaghetti Western backing track, it was too noisy to hear the competing beats, he walked like Clint Eastwood all the same.

'Pussy.'

'Pussy-man.'

He ignores it, but you can see that he is glad that he has wound them up.

No party gave way, they just played the music louder. The coach driver wasn't enjoying himself in the midst of the noisy friction.

'I don't care if you smoke lads.'

The Portsmouth lads smoked, the purists from London waved hands over noses and let it be known that they didn't want to stink like a tramp.

We arrive. It's taken forever. And now it kicked off as we waited for the bags. Bodies thrust into each other, arms stretched out.

'Come on then.'

'T' is in the middle of the melee with the gauntlet-walker.

'He called me a nigger, man.'

The head coach 'Sol', who shares his charges' racial identity, places himself in the middle of it all.

'Leave it!' We walk away.

'He called him a nigger, y'know. 'Sol', serious, he called him a nigger.'

The Portsmouth white boys head for their 'chalets'. 'Sol' calls the team together.

'Got to be more careful than usual. You've seen it already. We might get a lot of name calling but we've got to be better than them. Don't let them wind you up.'

He laughs and pauses and says 'you saw what they were like out there . . .'

Two days later, tensions amongst the two defeated semi-finalists had eased amidst south coast respect for the distinctive trademark goal celebration which invoked the garage dance hall yell: 'boo, boo!' alongside London urban dance moves and the reciprocal acknowledgement of fellow gatecrashers from the margins. On the bus home the Pompey boys sang the Pompey chimes, *Eastside* responded with a contrived offering extolling the merits of east London citizenship. 'They're alright this lot y'know' seemed to be the popular consensus of the *Eastside* team as they raised farewell salutes to westbound disciples of the football thing.

Biding time, waiting for the moment and using life as an educational tool characterises the approach as with the case of 'Jay', the captain of one of the estate teams who now has aspirations towards working for the organisation and emulating the standards set by his mentor, 'Sol'. As yet, 'Jay' is some way short of developing the professional and life skills to take on that role and was recently in court following a fight where the magistrate told him in no uncertain terms that if he came before the courts again he would be sent to prison. 'Sol' vouched for his character and potential despite his knowledge that he was already 'known' to the police because he genuinely believes that 'Jay' has a future working in this field. He believes *in* 'Jay'. He likes him: 'he's a nice lad, they're all nice lads'.

Whilst in the footballing context 'Sol' is unforgiving of 'Jay's' excesses and easy involvement in confrontations and fights he does not conceive his role as moral guardian to the players. He is non-judgemental about stories of off the field 'deviance' that filter into the dressing-room. But 'distance' is always entwined with involvement and beyond his role as a football coach 'Sol' became a central figure in 'Jay's' life and when a casual girlfriend fell pregnant and 'Jay' felt a sense of responsibility but did not believe that the relationship had a future, he turned to 'Sol' for advice on how he should proceed, apparently demonstrating the extent to which the players have trust in him. 'Sol's' approach in such situations is to outline the options as he sees them rather than to impose 'solutions'.

In this sense we can borrow from Sennett's (2003) critique of the lack of mutual respect which otherwise tends to pervade the provision of services to those who are forced to abide by or are dependent upon bureaucratic welfare organisations and their representatives. He presents what is essentially an argument for the performativity of 'respect' in a world that is not only saturated with contingent social relationships, but also pervaded by inequality, where gaining respect becomes a matter of composing the appropriate kind of 'performance'. Success here is measured not by mere acts or gestures but by the extent to which the performance embodies what it takes to generate respect between two communities of people who do not know and do not really want to know the full extent of each other's subjectivity. Here then, in maintaining a 'cool' distance, 'respect' and 'authority' is based upon an understanding of the futility of any efforts to impose it in the manner of 'Sugden'. The work of the coaches described here is not concerned with putting today's 'Billies' in their 'place', for in the face of the ubiquitous media presence, even on the Gascoigne, youngsters have learned that they are no different from anybody else and that to perform their individuality is the only game in town. In liquid modern times, gaining respect has become a matter of being accepted by the other as 'cool', as Sennett himself puts it: paying respect to the otherness of others.

As such, rather than developing sporting talent the success of the community sports intervention discussed here lies in its position as a 'cultural intermediary'. This concept has been most readily applied following Bourdieu (1984) in his book *Distinction: A Social Critique of the Judgement of Taste* and Featherstone's (1991) use of the term in his book *Consumer Culture and Postmodernism* as a way of understanding the emergence of a 'new middle class' which has helped to collapse some of the old distinctions between 'popular' and 'high' culture and opened the possibility for a broadening of access to an intellectual and artistic way of life. We use the term here in relation to a quite different cultural axis between the socially 'excluded' and the 'included', the repressed and the seduced, in relation to our contention that the community sports programme has been able to bridge what is otherwise perceived as an ever-widening gap between the excluded minority and the included majority through its appeal as somehow legitimate and authentic to individuals, groups and agencies on either side of this discursive divide.

Whilst 'from above' such interventions are regarded as innovative and offering an effective and 'fresh' approach to tackling the criminogenic consequences of exclusion, the constituencies they 'deal with' are seen to appreciate and welcome the 'intervention' because it is perceived and experienced as being of a non-interfering and non-threatening variety. The coaches are seen in different ways from many of the other agents of social control such as teachers, police officers, probation officers and youth workers. They are regarded as opening up possibilities, providing guidance and demystifying mainstream society rather than asserting some kind of repressive authority. The credibility of a sports background coupled with an empathy for the condition of those they work with has encouraged many young people on the estate to become qualified as coaches themselves, going on to work with this and other community schemes whilst many more have been influenced to go back to school, on to college or into jobs. Others may have fallen by the wayside or been identified as having little hope of escaping a life peppered with incarceration but none are ignored, demeaned or denied access.

The national and local media have even been encouraged to visit the estate, eager to hear and reproduce stories of how football has changed the lives of the Gascoigne Estate Crew's players, how the intervention has turned them away from a life of crime and prison. Whilst we remain sceptical of such one-dimensional accounts, for the comfortable 'included' society 'successful' intervention in this context necessarily implies rehabilitation and works on a model that conceives its participants as being so badly damaged by the scars of social exclusion that they have been rendered socially pathological to the extent that they are identified as being: 'most at risk of offending', 'ex-offenders', and/or having a record of 'drug dependency'. The presumed success of the intervention is then related to the evidence of their 'salvation' in the face of a reduction in crime rates and personal accounts of redemption since 'Terry's' arrival on the estate with a bag of footballs.

Primarily then, the social exclusion component of the organisation's work is regarded as legitimate because, crudely put, it is thought to stop those young people who are most at risk of causing others nuisance, loss or harm from continuing to do so rather than necessarily transforming their own lives. In this fashion redemption becomes an individual matter for those that feed the comfortable majority's fears rather than a matter of collective responsibility. To the comfortable, new jobs, degree courses, coaching qualifications and a return to school are incidentals, 'feel good' stories that reinforce belief in the capacity of individual aspiration, subservient to the headline crime statistics which might reveal a deeper malaise within consumerist social arrangements.

Conclusions

In this sense sporting interventions are believed to work because they are seen to provide relief from a criminogenic environment. A romantic fiction of modernist sporting certainties is reproduced which is associated with the conventional functionalist interpretation of sports as inculcating a sense of self-discipline, routine and personal responsibility (Crabbe, 2000), now enhanced by the seductive glamour and performativity of the celebrity version. Football is a metaphor for the positively imbued social values that the 'healthy' majority claim as their own and which are wheeled out to the 'seriously wild' zones of exclusion in an effort to alter the behaviour and consciousness of 'risky' populations. In this fashion, community sport operates at the intercedes of the seductive and repressive regimes of social control; providing a means of educating the 'flawed' or 'illegitimate' consumers in 'our way of doing things', emphasising the legitimate rules of consumer society which have often proven beyond the community youth worker, probation officer and educational welfare officer without resort to the cache of social and cultural capital that goes with contemporary sport.

What this kind of social intervention represents for the mainstream is an extension of the seductive appeal of its own consumer society. For as we saw in Chapter 6, football can be identified as a powerful consumerist force and it is through its appeal that 'Bob', 'Paulo', 'Frank', 'Reuben', 'Barry' and the others are drawn to its presence on their estate. 'Paulo' remains the star, performatively cruising the streets on one of his brother's motorbikes with 'Bob' eulogising over these iconic symbols of consumerism, relating every detail of their power and acceleratory capacity, because of 'Paulo's' period in the 'big time' with Bristol Rovers and despite his ultimate failure to stick it out away from the more familiar surroundings of the Gascoigne.

In this sense, whilst empathetic and non-judgemental of the social outcasts they engage, part of the attraction of these forms of community sports work to the mainstream is their lack of any ideological critique of the consumerism which contributes to the ghettoisation, just as the hierarchical authority of physical education reinforced the solidity of social relations under industrial capitalism. The offer of a 'passport' or gateway out is premised upon the mediated appeal of one of the most rabidly commercialised industries on the planet, whose appeal is tied up with the newer forms of consumptive 'deviance' discussed earlier as much as in sporting glory and Olympian ideals.

In this respect, 'safely' packaged forms of 'deviance' in the wider sporting domain remain, to be contingently consumed, copied and performatively condemned as 'sport' and all that goes with it is legitimised by the mainstream as long as the headline crime rate falls. As such, despite the diversity and differential social norms and values that go with liquid modernity, sport's continued association with modernist assumptions can, in the context of interventions which are predominantly focused on young men, lead to the predominance of an exclusionary masculinist perspective (Hargreaves, 1994).

Whilst encouraging the integration of women into the core staff team and its wider inclusionary philosophy, the 'tougher' estate-based work of LOCSP and other similar organisations often remains colonised as 'men's' or 'geezers' work, where women are welcome but sexist language remains ubiquitous and largely unchallenged. In some respects the street vernacular among young men in such neighbourhoods often exemplifies Mark Simpson's illustration of the heavily eroticised masculinist discourse of football through his quotation from Tony Gould's novel *Inside Outsider*:

> What you must do, son, is become a fucker and not become a fucked. It's as simple as that. Boys or girls, up the pussy or the arse, whichever you prefer, but you've got to remember there's a cock between your legs and you're a man.
> (Gould, 1983: 89, in Simpson, 1994: 69)

Through 'wind ups' and 'cussing' by young men and young women (Back, 1996) demonstrations of effeminacy or weakness are widely derided through the use of the term 'pussy'. Regardless of its authorial voice the metaphoric implication of this form of denigration is clear, that to be a 'pussy', a woman, fit for fucking, is to be 'deviant', to be inferior.

The extent to which contemporary community sports coaches are complicit, through their silence, in these expressions of masculine dominance is in marked departure from the conventional restrictions, imposed or otherwise, on 'inappropriate' language which are associated with mainstream forms of youth work (Frosh *et al.*, 2002; Tett, 1996). Yet they are entirely consistent with the non-judgemental frameworks and ability to read and adapt to local discursive formations through which the coaches operate. This pragmatism, which acknowledges the alternative social realities of participants, is emblematic of the liquid modern condition and what marks these forms of practice apart from the singular authorial voice of solid modernity with its imposition of order on to subservient subjects.

It would be easy to dismiss this departure from the conventions of contemporary youth work, which are themselves to be found in practice on the Gascoigne estate, as idle or a product of a shared 'male' outlook, but to do so would be an injustice to the complexities of this approach. The work described here is not delivered by a youth work organisation and does not embrace building-based educational programmes in this context. Equally, the coaches were not invited on to the estates by those they work with. Rather, they made their own introductions and, as pilots of an engagement strategy, must navigate their own pathways into participants' lives. Whilst we are not naïve enough to assume that such approaches will necessarily transform social outlooks grounded within the wider discursive restraints of sexist social arrangements in sport and further beyond, it is through their engagement with participants' lives that the opportunity arises to have more meaningful discussions concerning respect for partners, sexual behaviour and responsibility; in turn influencing behaviour in a way that would not be possible through moralistic challenges to the vernacular use of sexist language by participants with whom relationships have not yet developed.

The pragmatism associated with 'knowing' what is appropriate and what is not, when and where, is the key to such liquid modern social control strategies. It is this which underpins the community sports workers' own commitment to addressing the deleterious effects of the circumstances in which some of their participants live, deriving as it does from an intimate knowing of the bewildering complexity of that existence. Yet it is also this approach which generates the 'access' and proximity denied to the state's conventional agents of control and repression, and which offers an alternative dimension with which to address its desire to reduce crime and its threat to the promise of consumer society.

It is this individual reflexive skill and capacity, the embodied cultural intermediary, alongside the allure of sport, that opens up the seductive potential of that consumer society and which compels restraint in the face of the more excessive potential of the market-place. Whilst 'Billy Casper's' 'deviance' emerged out of the need for conformity to the limited horizons of solid modernity, today, the aspirational qualities associated with the endless possibilities of a consumer society, even if they remain merely a wishful enterprise tortuously pursued, leaves sport as a powerful seductive force in drawing individuals beyond those circumstances rather than ensuring submission to them.

9 Conclusion
They call it 'roasting'

As our project draws to a conclusion the sports pages and indeed much of the news reporting of Britain's newspapers are engulfed by a universal sense of crisis in the 'national game', prompted by an outbreak of 'deviance', 'lawlessness' and 'shameful' behaviour among football's young stars. In many respects the events seemed to bring together many of the issues we have attempted to address in our book. There was no single incident which prompted the outpouring but rather a conflation of unrelated events including: the arrest and suspension of a Leeds United first team player in relation to accusations of serious sexual assault; the fining of Newcastle United and Wales international Craig Bellamy for abusive behaviour towards a young female student outside a nightclub; Manchester United and England centre-back Rio Ferdinand missing a compulsory random drugs test; England players discussing the possibility of a strike following Ferdinand's subsequent omission from the national squad for a crunch Euro 2004 qualifying match against Turkey; and a young Liverpool player being shot in a bar in the city at 1:30 in the morning. All of this came in the fortnight after a group of Premiership players were accused of raping a 17-year-old woman at the Grosvenor House Hotel on London's Park Lane. An incident which brought the term 'roasting' into the public consciousness as Britain's largest circulation newspaper, the *News of the World* reported on 5 October 2003 how:

> The soccer-rape allegations have exposed an appalling new sex culture among young football stars called 'roasting'.
> It is based on seducing girls with huge shows of wealth then taking them back to hotel rooms and degrading them with group sex and partner swapping.
> 'Roast, like a chicken,' said party organiser Nicholas Meikle, distastefully describing a girl as a piece of meat. 'It gets stuffed.'
> ... Meikle insisted that many of the players he knew would regard it as 'normal' to share or 'roast' a girl.
> Asked how often he had been on roasting expeditions this year, he added offhandedly: 'Probably at least seven, eight this year, maybe nine times ... definitely.' And claiming that girls make all the running, he went on: 'I've noticed a change in the last three or four years. Girls are more up for it nowadays than ever before. Orgies are definitely happening.'

. . . A 'roasting' night usually starts with a group of young players and their friends taking over the best possible table in a club or bar – ideally in the VIP area.

'Footballers are like pop stars. Girls know they've got money and are so attracted to wealth and celebrity it's unbelievable,' said Meikle.

. . . 'Before, I didn't get involved in sharing girls. But the more I've moved around with footballers, the more I've seen they just share their girls around.' Meikle insists that roasting is mainly the preserve of the new, young stars – flash, rich and directionless. 'There's a generation of young players coming up now who are all doing it, white guys just as much as black guys,' he said . . .

But despite his experience of roasting, Meikle insisted that on the night of the rape allegation he had taken the girl to his room to sleep with her alone . . . and did not realise that he was about to share her.

'Still, that sort of thing happens,' he shrugged. 'My door gets opened up and they just walk in.'

'But they're used to that – they do it all the time, they're in each other's rooms all the time.'

'The night was nothing special until the rape allegation – by far was it not unusual . . . by far.'

(*News of the World*, 5 October 2003: 4–5)

The reporting style, blanket coverage of the incidents and associated reflections on a wider malaise within 'society' seemed to suggest not the death of 'deviance', but the pertinence of Stan Cohen's classic theorisation of it through the concept of the 'moral panic' (1972). As we suggested earlier in the construction of a 'moral panic', Cohen and others (especially Jock Young in his *The Drugtakers* (1971)) showed how agents of social control, 'amplified' 'deviance'. They also demonstrated the media role in this process and thus started to draw attention to the ideological role of the media in actively constructing meanings, rather than merely 'reflecting' some supposedly shared reality. The model also argued that not only do the media generate a ready-made history for these events, but they also engage in predicting that reported 'deviant' activities will be followed by similar events with the likelihood of even worse consequences requiring an institutional response; in this case revealed by the subsequent efforts to catalogue further 'victims' of footballer 'roastings' and the call for tighter controls on players (see *News of the World*, 12 October 2003: 6–7). Finally, the publicity given to the events is seen to entail a form of symbolisation in which key symbols are stripped of favourable or neutral connotations. Put simply, in this instance, the category, 'footballer', becomes synonymous with 'deviant' behaviour manifest in the 'deviant' practice of 'roasting', and emerges as a new 'folk devil'. By focusing our attention on the supposedly 'deviant' behaviour of outsider groups, such as footballers, it was claimed that the media helps to create and underpin the social consensus around our society's core values.

We are by now of course familiar with the key criticisms of this approach which relate to Angela McRobbie's assertion that in a media-saturated age the increasingly ubiquitous moral panic is 'no longer about social control but rather about the fear of being out of control' (McRobbie 1994: 199). Without naming it as such, McRobbie's critique alerts us to the performativity of moral crusades of this type which provide the platform for the assertion of a multitude of perspectives by active agents rather than the generation of consensus against a universally identified symbolic 'deviant'. She also makes the postmodern point that 'we do not exist in social unreality while we watch television or read the newspaper, nor are we transported back to reality when we turn the TV off to wash the dishes or discard the paper to go to bed' (McRobbie, 1994: 217). As such, McRobbie acknowledges the meaninglessness of speaking of any kind of social reality outside the world of 'amplified' representation, since any account of reality which is not sensationalised and exaggerated is, like any other account, partial and selective.

Our concern in this book, however, has been to offer something more than a critique of classical and more progressive deviancy theories. At the outset we suggested that we preferred to reinvent the sociology of 'deviance' as a beginning enterprise. Our motivation for doing so was our fierce determination to refuse the more comfortable role of bystander in our commitment to take active responsibility for engaging in unearthing and understanding the contested sense of what does or does not constitute 'deviance' in sport today. For as the assertion of morality associated with the current crop of sensational sporting headlines suggests, the characterisation of 'deviant' practice lives on in the popular imagination as much as it does within the discipline of sociology. In this light the challenge is not to lay the ghost of 'deviance', following Sumner's obituary (1994) which we reviewed at the outset, nor to retrieve more conventional approaches in the manner of Rojek's (2000) invocation of Durkheim in his discussion of 'abnormal' leisure which we considered in Chapter 3. Rather, what we hope to have achieved is, however modestly, to have constituted some beginnings, some starting points for a theory of 'deviance' made to the measure of our times.

This beginning enterprise calls for more than critique, in the manner of McRobbie, for whilst insightful and progressive in its own right, such an approach does not address our concern to take *responsibility* for the 'deviance' that surrounds us within the mediated social realities that constitute our lives. Reflecting on the current media fascination with 'misbehaviour' in English professional football it is clear that the principle limitation of conventional deviance theory is not its focus on 'deviance' *per se* but rather its concern with the desire to bring it under control, to the neglect of the performativity of the 'deviance' we see and our own ready consumption of it. Since, to our eyes, the 'crisis' enveloping English professional football at the time of writing reveals not the horrors of rape or any genuine, universal moral repugnance but rather the presentation of rape and sexual deviance as a titillating performance for widespread public consumption. There is no 'moral panic' only a soap opera scandal. We are faced with a staged presentation of morality, with its own twists and turns, subplots and spin, to which we are all party and which gives us license to 'safely' consume the 'deviance' of others.

Having been paid £10,000 for the privilege, Nicholas Meikle was invited by the *News of the World* to tell 'the men's side of events' from the night of Friday

26 September which led to the rape allegation against eight Premiership football players (5 October, 2003). The 'exclusive' was printed despite the continuing police investigation that was underway and threats of legal action against anyone naming the individuals rumoured to be involved, not because it would aid any future trial or deter other potential transgressors, but because the public's fascination demanded a story be told. Pictured tantalisingly at the 'scene of the crime' in one of the bedrooms of the Grosvenor House Hotel, wearing a designer vest and ski hat, Meikle was in performative mood. Cast as a 'party organiser' who is 'a familiar face in clubland' he revels in the image and his connections to the celebrity circuit through an account which celebrates the glammed up, pseudo pornographic 'deviance' of his celebrity friends:

> At Browns, Meikle invited the girl back to his hotel. He said they started kissing in the mini cab and continued in his hotel room. Then they both undressed for full sex . . .
>
> It was after some minutes of sex, that his pal walked in. 'Usually when we go out people always try and get in each other's room', he said. 'They say things to staff like, "I'm locked out of my room, can I have the key"?'
>
> His pal walked around the bedroom, clearly visible to the girl, said Meikle.
>
> 'Even so, she carried on having sex with me,' he insisted. 'She didn't tell him to get out. So I thought, "Oh she doesn't mind, I don't really care".'
>
> The man left the bedroom, but Meikle did not hear the outer door close. He added: 'I thought, "You're seeing if you can get involved".'
>
> 'So I finished and found he was in the corridor by my bathroom. He asks me, "What's she saying?" And I go, "Why? Do you reckon you can get involved?" And he told me that in the club he asked her if she liked any one of us and she said, "I like all of you". So I said, "Try your luck".'
>
> Meikle watched as his pal went into the bedroom where the girl was sitting naked on the edge of the bed. The man sat beside her and they chatted. Meikle then went into the bathroom and, shortly after he returned, the Chelsea player entered the bedroom.
>
> 'By the time I looked around my mate is kissing the girl,' Meikle went on. 'Then she lays back and he starts having sex with her.'
>
> With that the other Premiership player arrived as well – now there were four men.
>
> 'They were stood having a look,' Meikle went on. 'Then the Chelsea player says to my pal, "Go on boy". She didn't stop. She knew there was other guys in the room now. So then the other player goes, "I wanna get involved".'
>
> The player, he said, exposed himself, and moved in close enough so the girl could perform a sex act on him . . .
>
> When the other Premiership player stopped, said Meikle, the Chelsea player also had sex with her. His friend moved to one side so the girl could perform a sex act on him while the Chelsea player had full sex with her. Shortly after, said Meikle, the girl had sex with the Chelsea player and his friend.

Then Meikle and the other Premiership player left the suite and went to the star's room where he had a naked blonde 'aged about 24–25' waiting.

Meikle added: 'He must have guessed there was gonna be a girl back at my room.'

'It's not unnatural for everyone in our crowd to have sex with a girl for 15 or 20 minutes and then get up and wonder what the other boys are doing. I tried with the blonde but she wasn't having it so I went back to my room.'

The two men and the girl were still having sex, claimed Meikle . . .

(*News of the World*, 5 October, 2003: 2–3)

Framed by the language of moral rectitude and shame, the newspaper *sells* a form of 'deviance' which is eagerly performed in its revelation of the performativity of young celebrity footballers very own sexual 'deviance'. The term 'roasting', an abbreviation of 'spit roasting', used to describe the practice of having someone perform oral sex on one partner while a second has full sexual intercourse with them, popularising new terminology within the lexicon of sexual practice; playing with consumerist fantasies for the limitless potential of a celebrity life style, where everything 'comes' easily. Condemnation mobilised through the performativity of the revelation of every detail of how many times sex acts were performed in what positions, with how many participants, in what clubs and hotels, in how many cities, on how many occasions, all under the front page banner headline 'SOCCER RAPE CONFESSION'. Here, rape is for sale.

In the framework of the performativity of consumptive deviance, whether the rape 'happened' or whether it did not is unimportant and, indeed, is quite consciously left ambiguous. The audience invited to speculate on the 'victim's' motives as her silhouette is depicted on the front page above the caption 'GIRL: "Agreed to it all"' whilst the young woman herself is reported to have consulted the country's leading publicist, Max Clifford, in her efforts to secure justice. In the manner of living soaps and reality TV it is through the performativity of the presentation and the central actors, that 'rape' secures the *News of the World*'s status as the most read paper in Britain, reaching an audience of over 10 million people. In the sideshows of popular culture the broadsheet press plays to the same tune reprocessing the story within an alternative discourse while playing to the same fascinations and desires.

It is here that we may be able to draw a line from this celebrity 'deviance', put up for mass consumption, to our own accounts of the overt display of sexist and misogynist language in the masculinist performative arena of 'cruising' and on the housing estates of East London. For while our claims to take responsibility may be challenged by those who consider our accounts to have failed to fully consider the consequences of this behaviour, we caution against the focus on over-essentialised 'deviant' acts, bodies and categories. Since performativity is characteristic of these settings also, whether it be in the staged professionalism and 'cool respect' of the community sports coach or the contingent, fleeting assertion of presence of a 'modded' Fiat Punto owner. Our concern is not to search for assignable 'deviant', 'sexist', individuals, who would be better understood with regard to their contingency, but rather to theorise the contexts in which their 'deviance' is made 'real' and celebrated in the contemporary quotidian through its performativity and consumption.

For sport is precisely the sort of setting which gives license to the performance of the 'deviant' life style celebrated in our fascination with celebrity. At all its levels sport is a locus for excess, the breaking of boundaries, doing what has not been done before. It provides the means to make a mark, to be seen, to be desired. In this fashion it demands and is defined by 'deviance'. The more of it the better in a consumer society that demands excesses that in turn commodify and normalise yesterday's transgressions. But if this consensualising of 'deviance' might be seen to reaffirm Sumner's argument that 'deviance' is a redundant concept, to abandon it would seem to us to be to resign ourselves to the celebration of sporting excess and its performative license to misogyny, racism and violence.

As what is still dressed as 'deviance' – the transgressive, the abnormal, the wild, the outlandish, the extreme, the forbidden – is performed more and more freely, in front of bigger and bigger, increasingly restless audiences, to declare the 'end of deviance' is to refuse to take responsibility for the consequences it implies. In our reassertion of the sociology of deviance as a beginning enterprise, through the notions of performative and consumptive 'deviance' we take responsibility by seeking to highlight the perniciousness and dangers associated with the vacuous pursuit and 'safe' consumption of the ever more filthy, dirty and bizarre. For excess inevitably implies potential casualties and victims in the shadows, away from the consumerist gaze: battered Asian students; raped groupies; personal lives wrecked by kiss and tell fortune and celebrity seekers; pedestrians knocked down and residents 'terrorised' by the fear and noise of cruisers' cars; lives wrecked by childhood sexual abuse and coaches afraid to interact for fear of charges of abuse; the health and financial pain of conformity to the designer celebrity body; the isolation and frustration of the 'flawed consumers'.

As such, rather than focus on the categorisation of 'deviance' as an 'act', 'person' or 'group', if we are to use the concept of 'deviance' to engender social progress and relieve suffering, it might be appropriate to turn our condemnatory judgements away from the performative 'deviance' of cruisers and the like. Since we might ask what kind of morality is at work when the performances of 'deviant' others are projected on screen or where they are forced to 'confess' their 'deviant' life styles before a disapproving audience. Such images and accounts are, we would suggest, only comforting in as much as they depict the 'deviance' of others as something remote from the consumer's experience. In this fashion the 'deviance' of working-class men at cruises in Wakefield and on the streets of London, just as much as that of the pampered young celebrities cast as a disgrace to the game of football, can be imagined as the product of their social environs, which lie outside of respectable society.

It is our contention though that what we have characterised as consumptive 'deviance' is just that. It has no essential existence in an act, body or place. It is not to be found in the racism of Mathew Simmons, nor in the injuries suffered by Sarfraz Najeib, nor in the bedrooms of the Beckhams or even the Grosvenor House Hotel since it is a version of 'deviance' that has been produced *for* the screen, for consumption by those who would be cast as respectable society. It is not the amplified reporting of the 'deviance' of the outsiders that generates the fear of more 'deviance' with increasingly disastrous consequences for conventional social values unless repressive action is taken as suggested by Stan Cohen's model. Rather, the tales of 'deviance' reproduce themselves in an orgiastic interplay between the consumerist desires of 'respectable' society and the moral entrepreneurship of the mass media. The assertion of social control represents a secondary storyline which sustains and legitimates the reproduction and gorging on fantasy spectacles of sexual deviance, corruption and violence. For in this scheme of things, the respectability of the mainstream is confirmed through their consumption and their capacity for consumption. It is the excluded minorities, who through their 'flawed' consumption are depicted as the social 'deviant's' in need of restorative action, to be imparted in some cases through the supposed responsibility and moral values of participation in sport.

This is categorically not to deny that rape physically takes place with all its inescapable horrors, nor that Sarfraz Najeib was not similarly the victim of a vicious and unrelenting assault which deserves justice. Our somewhat depressing point is that in the age of consumer capitalism, when those experiences come into contact with celebrity, they become commodity forms which are presented performatively, glamorised and, like the prospect of weapons of mass destruction, 'sexed up' for our consumption. For we would contend that it is through our participation in this process that we are all encouraged to reflect on the possibility that Sarfraz Najeib and his friends were just an arrogant bunch of 'Pakis' who asked for it, that the fight was just another night-club brawl or that 'rape' is just an economically motivated cry of convenience, after the fact. This is where we take our responsibility. Not in siding against the performative misogyny of the male cruisers in Wakefield for the sake of it, nor indeed the moral entrepreneurs at the production end of the associated morality plays, but against ourselves, all of us, and the consumerism of which we are a part and which makes a spectacle of horror and suffering, which reduces that suffering to titillation, entertainment, performativity.

In this respect this very book might be regarded as being not far behind in the disingenuiness stakes in its brazen usage of populist narratives and sexy, filthy, dirty storylines in order to convey our arguments. But we would suggest that it could not conceivably be any other way, since to convey performativity, requires performativity. We did not adopt the tactics we did merely for the sake of populism but rather to demonstrate the performativity of the Beckhams' sexuality, of the cruisers' 'edgework' and the coach's 'easiness'. We could of course have adopted a more conventional ethnographic reportage on the basis of the recurring themes from the testimonies of informants and participant observation, but if we are honest, in terms of a contribution to the theorisation of 'deviance', this would have revealed little more than the surface construction of cruising as being a 'top laugh'. It would certainly not have got to the inner 'truth' of the Beckhams' sex life, nor would it have unearthed much more about the activities of Lee Bowyer and

Jonathon Woodgate on the night of the attack on Sarfraz Najeib than was identified during two court cases and countless journalistic accounts.

Our point is that there is no need to go beyond the surface representation of such celebrities or indeed, in the fleeting moments of retail park and council estate fame, everyday folk, since they are constituted and consumed through their contingent performativity, which is deployed in the face of the researcher just as readily as the television camera. Rather, we hope that through our own interpretive accounts we have revealed something of the verisimilitude of the performativity of the 'deviance' that we have encountered in sport and the complicity of all of us in its consumption.

In our articulation of the sociology of 'deviance' reconsidered as a beginning enterprise we are acutely aware of the partiality and limitations of the suggestive theoretical reorientations we have presented. However, it is our hope that the concepts we have outlined here will provide a basis for critical debate and for refreshing sociological enquiry in this area, both within the sociology of sport and 'deviance' and the wider discipline of sociology.

Notes

Preface

1 This is more than a little surprising, because for a while now a reappraisal of the 'nature' of the world of sport has been going on in more imaginative ways. Indeed, the major journals associated with the sociology of sport are replete with works which provide myriad understandings of the contemporary world of sport and many of these analyses have uncovered new and exciting insights and perspectives about how we go about thinking about sport in these 'new' times.

2 Our only comfort being that 'deviancy's' enduring legacy as a ubiquitous cultural force in sport reassures us that a modicum of disturbance from the 'norm' is both desirable and inevitable.

4 Understanding sport and 'deviance' in liquid modernity

1 For a discussion, see Downes and Rock, 1998.

5 Talking 'tactics': representing 'deviance' in sport

1 Funded by the Football Foundation and the Sir John Cass Foundation.

6 *The Premiership*: sporting soap opera and consumptive 'deviance'

1 This interview was conducted in relation to the Cultures of Racism in Football project conducted jointly with Les Back and John Solomos and supported by the ESRC (R 000235639).

2 We are nevertheless conscious of the contingency of such assertions in the context of the explosion of news media interest in David Beckham's alleged infidelities following tabloid revelations in April 2004, as this book went to press. Following the exposé in the *News of the World* (4 April 2004), the tabloid and broadsheet press as well as the broadcast media in the UK focused for several weeks on the most intimate details of the couples 'private' relations.

7 Cruising and the performativity of consumptive 'deviance'

1 O'Hagan (2003: 5) argues that Britain has the highest density of surveillance equipment in the world. He also notes that since 1994, 'British Governments have spent more than £205 million on CCTV installation in towns and cities, supporting 1,400 projects, far more than any other country in Europe'. That Britain is the most watched place on earth is not in question, but what is as interesting to us in the context of this discussion is not so much the mundane and all-pervasive use of CCTV, but the extent

to which liquid modern surveillance develops its own spectacular performativity through police car chases with high-powered cars, motor cycles, boats and helicopters.

2   We acknowledge that there is a long tradition in cultural studies that has theorised the 'performativity' of 'youth' culture (see, for example, Hall and Jefferson (1976); Clarke *et al.* (1976); McRobbie (1982, 1991) and Hebdidge (1979, 1988). Yet we agree with Hebdidge (1988) that the majority of these analyses merely tended to 'shine their own political light' on the 'youth' cultures in question, to the extent that, in the main, they uncritically equated much of what they observed as structural resistance.

3   Both the research strategy and the analysis which underpin the following discussion reject essentialist feminist approaches and follow those which adopt a social construc-tionist position, such as that found in the work of Judith Butler. As a result our findings are partial rather than conclusive – it would be pretentious to suggest otherwise – but they deal with women's issues by putting an emphasis on our observations of their lived experiences in the 'male-dominated gender order' (Stacey, 1988) that is cruising culture.

8 'Jumpers for goalposts': the community sports agenda and the search for effective social control

1   Names have been changed.

2   Following the commencement of the organisation's work on the estate crime began to fall, according to local police figures by more than 50 per cent (LBBD, 2001a).

3   Whilst 'Terry's' approach to engaging with young people is very much characterised by this casual, easy-going and confident approach, the coaching sessions that he organises are nothing of the sort. Indeed, much of the respect that he and his staff have built up among participants in their schemes is derived from the organisational and coaching skills they possess and their ability to make participants work hard and emulate their own commitment and sense of responsibility. The point of departure with 'Sugden' is that the young people recognise 'Terry' as one of their own and worthy of emulation.

4   The community programme described here is a registered charity, which since 1997 has been wholly independent of the football club from which it takes its name, although it continues to have its offices at the stadium under one of the new stands.

5   The estate-based social inclusion interventions invoked here were the subject of a 3-year detailed empirical ethnographic study funded by the Football Foundation and the Sir John Cass Foundation, conducted by Tim Crabbe and Pat Slaughter (2004), which sought to establish a more complete picture of the relationships between the interventions and the young people they encountered. This passage is based upon observations made by Pat Slaughter.

Bibliography

Abercrombie, N. (1996) *Television and Society*, Cambridge: Polity Press.

Adorno, T. and Horkheimer, M. (1979) 'Culture Industry: The Enlightenment of Mass Deception', in T. Adorno and M. Horkheimer (eds) *Dialectic of Enlightenment*, London: Verso.

Allen, R. (1983) 'On Reading Soaps: A Semiotic Primer' from E. Kaplan (ed.) *Regarding Television*, Frederick, MD: University Publication of America, in L. Harrington and D. Bielby (eds) (2001) *Popular Culture: Production and Consumption*, Oxford: Blackwell.

Allen, R. (2001) 'On Reading Soaps: A Semiotic Primer', in L. Harrington and D. Bielby (eds) *Popular Culture: Production and Consumption*, Oxford: Blackwell.

Althusser, L. (1971) *Lenin and Philosophy and Other Essays*, London: New Left Books.

Andrews, D. (2000) 'Posting up: French Post-structuralism and the Critical Analysis of Contemporary Sporting Culture', in J. Coakley and E. Dunning (eds) *Handbook of Sports Studies*, London: Sage.

Ang, I. (1985) *Watching Dallas: Soap Opera and the Melodramatic Imagination*, London: Methuen.

Armstrong, G. (1998) *Football Hooligans: Knowing the Score*, Oxford: Berg.

Armstrong, G. and Harris, M. (1991) 'Football Hooligans: Theory and Evidence', *Sociological Review*, 39, 3: 427–58.

Augé, M. (1995) *Non-Places: Introduction to an Anthropology of Supermodernity*, London: Verso.

Austin, J. L. (1975) *How to Do Things with Words*, edited by J. O. Urmson and M. Sbisa, Cambridge, MA: Harvard University Press.

Back, L. (1996) *New Ethnicities and Urban Culture: Racisms and Multiculture in Young Lives*, London: UCL Press.

Back, L., Crabbe, T. and Solomos, J. (2001) *The Changing Face of Football: Racism, Identity and Multiculture in the English Game*, Oxford: Berg.

Baker, A. and Boyd, T. (1997) *Out of Bounds: Sports, Media and the Politics of Identity*, Bloomington, IN: Indiana University Press.

Bakhtin, M. (1981) 'Discourse in the Novel', in M. Holquist (ed.) *The Dialogic Imagination*, Austin: University of Texas Press.

Bakhtin, M. (1984) *Rabelais and His World*, Bloomington: University of Indiana Press.

Bale, J. (1994) *Landscapes of Modern Sport*, London: Leicester University Press.

Ball, D. and Loy, J. (eds) (1975) *Sport and Social Order: Contributions to the Sociology of Sport*, Reading, MA: Addison-Wesley.

Barnes, B. (1995) *The Elements of Social Theory*, London: UCL Press.

Barthes, R. (1957) *Mythologies*, London: Paladin.

Barthes, R. (1968) 'Death of the Author', in *Image-Music-Text: Essays Selected and Translated by Stephen Heath* (1977), New York: Hill and Wang.

Bateson, G. (1978) 'A Theory of Play and Fantasy', in *Steps to an Ecology of Mind*, London: Paladin.

Baudrillard, J. (1983) *Simulations*, New York: Semiotext(e).

Baudrillard, J. (1989) *America*, London: Verso.

Baudrillard, J. (1991) *The Gulf War Did Not Take Place*, Sydney: Power Publications.

Baudrillard, J. (1993) *The Transparency of Evil: Essays on Extreme Phenomena*, London: Verso.

Baudrillard, J. (2001) *Impossible Exchange*, London: Verso.

Bauman, Z. (1987) *Legislators and Interpreters: On Modernity, Postmodernity and Intellectuals*, Cambridge: Polity Press.

Bauman, Z. (1990) *Thinking Sociologically*, Oxford: Blackwell.

Bauman, Z. (1991) *Modernity and Ambivalence*, Cambridge: Polity Press.

Bauman, Z. (1992a) *Intimations of Postmodernity*, London: Routledge.

Bauman, Z. (1992b) *Mortality, Immortality and Other Life Strategies*, Cambridge: Polity Press.

Bauman. Z. (1994) 'Desert Spectacular', in K. Tester (ed.) *The Flâneur*, London: Routledge.

Bauman, Z. (1995) *Life in Fragments: Essays in Postmodern Morality*, Oxford: Blackwell.

Bauman, Z. (1997) *Postmodernity and its Discontents*, Cambridge: Polity Press in association with Blackwell.

Bauman, Z. (1998a) *Globalization: The Human Consequences*, Cambridge: Polity Press in association with Blackwell.

Bauman, Z. (1998b) *Work, Consumerism and the New Poor*, Buckingham: Open University Press.

Bauman, Z. (1999) *In Search of Politics*, Cambridge: Polity Press.

Bauman, Z. (2000) *Liquid Modernity*, Cambridge: Polity Press.

Bauman (2001) *The Individualized Society*, Cambridge: Polity Press in association with Blackwell.

Bauman, Z. (2002a) *Society Under Siege*, Cambridge: Polity Press.

Bauman, Z. (2002b) 'Cultural Variety or Variety of Cultures?' in S. Malešević and M. Haugaard (eds) *Making Sense of Collectivity: Ethnicity, Nationalism and Globalization*, London: Pluto Press.

Bauman, Z. (2002c) 'Interview with Zygmunt Bauman', in *Network: Newsletter of the British Sociological Association*, 83: October.

Bauman, Z. (2003) *Liquid Love*, Cambridge: Polity Press.

Beal, B. (1995) 'Disqualifying the Official: An Exploration of Social Resistance Through the Subculture of Skateboarding', *Sociology of Sport Journal*, 12: 252–67.

Beck, U. (1992) *Risk Society: Towards a New Modernity*, London: Sage.

Beck, U. (1994) 'The Re-invention of Politics: Towards a Theory of Reflexive Modernization', in U. Beck, A. Giddens and S. Lash, *Reflexive Modernization: Politics, Tradition and Aesthetics in the Modern Social Order*, Cambridge: Polity Press.

Beck, U. (2002) 'Zombie Categories: Interview with Ulrich Beck', in U. Beck and E. Beck-Gernsheim, *Individualization*, London: Sage.

Beck, U., Giddens, A. and Lash, S. (1994) *Reflexive Modernization: Politics, Tradition and Aesthetics in the Modern Social Order*, Cambridge: Polity Press.

Becker, H. (1963) *Outsiders: Studies in the Sociology of Deviance*, London: The Free Press.

Bégout, B. (2003) 'I Put My Head in the Maw of the Leviathan – Las Vegas', *The Times Higher Education Supplement*, 15 August.

Beilharz, P. (2000) *Zygmunt Bauman: Dialectic of Modernity*, London: Sage.

Bell, V. (1999) 'Performativity and Belonging: An Introduction', in V. Bell (ed.) *Performativity and Belonging*, TNS, London: Sage.

Bhabha, H. (1994) *Location of Culture*, London: Routledge.

Birrell, S. and Richter, D. (1987) 'Is a Diamond Forever? Feminist Transformation of Sport', *Women's Studies International Forum*, 10: 395–409.

Blackshaw, T. (2002) 'The Sociology of Sport Re-assessed in the Light of the Phenomenon of Zygmunt Bauman', *International Review for the Sociology of Sport*, 37, 2: 199–217.

Blackshaw, T. (2003) *Leisure Life: Myth, Masculinity and Modernity*, London: Routledge.

Bolin, A. (1992) 'Vandalized Vanity: Feminine Physiques Betrayed and Portrayed', in F. Mascia-Lees and P. Sharpe (eds) *Tattoo, Torture, Mutilation and Adornment*, Albany, NY: State University of New York Press.

Bourdieu, P. (1984) *Distinction: A Social Critique of the Judgement of Taste*, Cambridge, MA: Harvard University Press.

Bourdieu, P. (1999) 'Understanding', in Bourdieu, P. (ed.) *The Weight of the World: Social Suffering in Contemporary Society*, Cambridge: Polity Press.

Bourdieu, P. (2000) *Pascalian Meditations*, Cambridge: Polity Press.

Bourdieu, P. with Wacquant, L. (1992) *An Invitation to Reflexive Sociology*, Oxford: Polity Press.

Bower, T. (2003) *Broken Dreams*, London: Simon & Schuster.

Box, S. (1971) *Deviance, Reality and Society*, London: Holt, Rinehart and Winston.

Box, S. (1986) *Deviance, Reality and Society*, 2nd edition, London: Cassell.

Brackenridge, C. (1999) 'Call for Clampdown on Abusive Sports Coaches', *BBC Online Network*, August 9.

Brackenridge, C. (2001) *Spoilsports: Understanding and Preventing Sexual Exploitation in Sport*, London: Routledge.

Bramham, P. (2002) 'Rojek, the Sociological Imagination and Leisure', *Leisure Studies*, 21: 221–34.

Brohm, J.M. (1978) *Sport: A Prison of Measured Time*, trans. Ian Fraser, London: Ink Links.

Brown, A. (1993) 'Football Fans and Civil Liberties: The Case of Istanbul '93', *Working Papers in Law*, MIPC, Manchester Metropolitan University.

Brunsdon, C. (1981) 'Crossroads: Notes on Soap Opera', *Screen*, 22, 4: 32–7.

Buhrmann, H. (1977) 'Athletics and Deviance: An Examination of the Relationship Between Athletic Participation and Deviant Behaviour of High School Girls', *Review of Sport and Leisure*, 2: 17–35.

Butler, J. (1990) *Gender Trouble: Feminism and the Subversion of Identity*, London: Routledge.

Butler, J. (1991) 'Contingent Foundations: Feminism and the Question of "Postmodernism"', in Butler, J. and Scott, J. (eds) *Feminists Theorize the Political*, London: Routledge.

Butler, J. (1993) *Bodies That Matter: On the Discursive Limits of Sex*, London: Routledge.

Butler, J. (1994) 'Gender as Performance: An Interview with Judith Butler', *Radical Philosophy*, 67 Summer.

Butler, J. (1997) *The Psychic Life of Power: Theories in Subjection*, Stanford, CA: Stanford University Press.

Byrne, D. (1995) 'Deindustrialisation and Dispossession: An Examination of Social Division in the Industrial City', *Sociology*, 29, 1: 95–115.

Cassell (not dated) *Cassell's Book of Sports and Pastimes*, London: Cassell & Co.

Castells, M. (1996) *The Information Age, Volume 1: The Rise of the Network Society*, Oxford: Blackwell.

Castoriadis, C. (1987) *The Imaginary Institution of Society*, Cambridge: Polity Press.

Channel 4 (2003) 'Black like Beckham', *Channel 4*, 25 April 2003.

Cicourel, A. (1964) *Method and Measurement in Sociology*, New York: Free Press.

Clarke, J. (1973) 'Football and the Skinheads', *Occasional Paper, Centre for Contemporary Cultural Studies*, University of Birmingham.

Clarke, J. (1976) 'The Skinheads and the Magical Recovery of Community', in S. Hall and T. Jefferson (eds) *Resistance Through Rituals: Youth Subcultures in Post-War Britain*, London: Hutchinson.

Clarke, J. (1978) 'Football and Working Class Fans: Tradition and Change', in R. Ingham (ed.) *Football Hooliganism: The Wider Context*, London: Inter-Action Imprint.

Clarke, J. and Critcher, C. (1985) *The Devil Makes Work: Leisure in Capitalist Britain*, Basingstoke: Macmillan Press.

Clarke, J., Hall, S., Jefferson, T. and Roberts, B. (1976) 'Subcultures and Class', in S. Hall and T. Jefferson (eds) *Resistance Through Rituals: Youth Subcultures in Post-war Britain*, London: Hutchinson.

Clément, J. (1995) 'Contributions of the Sociology of Pierre Bourdieu to the Sociology of Sport', *Sociology of Sport Journal*, 12, 2: 147–58.

Coakley, J. (1998) *Sport in Society: Issues and Controversies*, 6th edition, Boston: McGraw-Hill.

Coakley, J. and Dunning, E. (2002) *Handbook of Sport Studies*, London: Sage.

Coalter, F. (1989) *Sport and Anti-social Behaviour: A Literature Review*, Edinburgh: Scottish Sports Council.

Cohen, A. (1955) *Delinquent Boys*, Chicago: Free Press.

Cohen, S. (ed.) (1971) *Images of Deviance*, Harmondsworth: Penguin.

Cohen, S. (1972) *Folk Devils and Moral Panics: The Creation of the Mods and Rockers*, London: MacGibbon & Kee.

Cole, C. (1996) 'American Jordan: P.L.A.Y., Consensus, and Punishment', *Sociology of Sport Journal*, 13: 366–97.

Cole, C. (1998) 'Addiction, Exercise, and Cyborgs: Technologies of Deviant Bodies', in G. Rail (ed.) *Sport in Postmodern Times*, Albany, NY: State University of New York Press.

Cole, C. (2000) 'Body Studies in the Sociology of Sport: A Review of the Field', in J. Coakley and E. Dunning (eds) *Handbook of Sport Studies*, London: Sage.

Cole, C. and Denny, H. (1994) 'Visualizing Deviance in (post)Reagan America: Magic Johnson, AIDS and the Promiscuous World of Professional Sport', *Critical Sociology*, 20: 123–47.

Collins, M., Henry, I. and Houlihan, B. (1999) *Sport and Social Exclusion Report to Policy Action Team 10*, London: DCMS.

Connerton, P. (1989) *How Societies Remember*, Cambridge: Cambridge University Press.

Connor, S. (1989) *Postmodernist Culture*, Oxford: Blackwell.

Connor, S. (2003) 'Maybe a Banana Is Just a Banana', *The Times Higher Education Supplement*, 23 May.

Conrad, P. (2003) 'Blend it Like Beckham', *The Observer*, 25 May.

Crabbe, T. (2000) 'A Sporting Chance?: Using Sport to Tackle Drug Use and Crime', *Drugs: Education, Prevention and Policy*, 7, 4: 381–91.

Crabbe, T. (2003) 'The Public Gets What the Public Wants': England Football Fans, "Truth" Claims and Mediated Realities', *International Review for the Sociology of Sport*, 38, 4: 413–25.

Crabbe, T. and Slaughter, P. (2004) 'On the Eastside: Research Report into the

Estate Based Social Inclusion Interventions of Leyton Orient Community Sports Programme', London: The Football Foundation.

Crabbe, T. and Wagg, S. (2000) '"A Carnival of Cricket?": The Cricket World Cup, "Race" and the Politics of Carnival', *Culture, Sport Society*, 3, 2: 70–88.

Critcher, C. (1971) 'Football and Cultural Values', *Working Papers in Cultural Studies*, 1, (spring): 103–19, Birmingham: CCCS.

Critcher, C. (1979) 'Football Since the War', in J. Clarke, C. Critcher and R. Johnson (eds) *Working Class Culture: Studies in History and Theory*, London: Macmillan.

Croall, H. (1992) *White Collar Crime: Criminal Justice and Criminology*, Buckingham: Open University Press.

Crosset, T. and Beal, B. (1997) 'The Use of Subculture and Subworld in Ethnographic Works On Sport: A Discussion of Definitional Distinctions', *Sociology of Sport Journal*, 14: 73–85.

Csikszentmihalyi, M. (1975) *Beyond Boredom and Anxiety: The Experience of Play in Work and Games*, San Francisco: Jossey-Bass Publishers.

Delanty, G. (1999) *Social Theory in a Changing World*, Cambridge: Polity Press.

Deleuze, G. and Guattari, F. (1983) *Anti-Oedipus: Capitalism and Schizophrenia*, Minneapolis: University of Minnesota Press.

Derrida, J. (1973) *Speech and Phenomena, and Other Essays on Husserl's Theory of Signs*, Evanston, IL: North Western University Press.

Derrida, J. (1978) *Writing and Difference*, London: Routledge & Kegan Paul.

Diamond, E. (1997) *Unmaking Mimesis*, London: Routledge.

Donnelly, P. (1985) 'Sport Subcultures', in R. Terjung (ed.) *Exercise and Sport Sciences Reviews*, Volume 13, New York: Macmillan.

Donnelly, P. (1993) 'Subcultures in Sport: Resilience and Transformation', in A. Ingham and J. Loy (eds) *Sport in Social Development: Traditions, Transitions, and Transformations*, Champaign, IL: Human Kinetics.

Donnelly, P. (2002) 'Interpretive Approaches to the Sociology of Sport', in J. Coakley and E. Dunning (eds) *Handbook of Sport Studies*, London: Sage.

Douglas, J. (1976) *Investigative Social Research: Individual and Team Field Research*, Beverley Hills: Sage.

Douglas, M. (1986) *How Institutions Think*, Syracruse: Syracruse University Press.

Downes, D. and Rock, P. (1998) *Understanding Deviance: A Guide to the Sociology of Crime and Rule Breaking*, Oxford: Oxford University Press.

Dreyfus, H. and Rabinow, P. (1982) *Beyond Structuralism and Hermeneutics*, Chicago: Chicago University Press.

Dube, J. (2000) Wrestling with Death, ABCNews.com http: //abcnews.go.com/sections/living/DailyNews/wrestlingdanger991007.html.

Dunn, R. G. (2000) 'Identity, Commodification and Consumer Culture', in J. E. Savis (ed.) *Identity and Social Change*, London: Transaction Publishers.

Dunning, E. (1999) *Sport Matters: Sociological Studies of Sport, Violence and Civilization*, London: Routledge.

Dunning, E., and Rojek, C. (eds) (1992) *Sport and Leisure in the Civilizing Process: Critique and Counter Critique*, Basingstoke: Macmillan.

Dunning, E., Murphy, P. and Williams, J. (1988) *The Roots of Football Hooliganism: An Historical and Sociological Study*, London: Routledge.

Durkheim, E. (1938 [1893]) *The Division of Labour in Society*, Glencoe, IL: Free Press.

Durkheim, E. (1952 [1897]) *Suicide: A Study in Sociology*, London: Routledge.

Durkheim, E. (1964 [1895]) *The Rules of Sociological Method*, Glencoe, IL: Free Press.

Düttman, A. G. (2002) *The Memory of Thought: An Essay on Heidegger and Adorno*, London: Continuum.

Eco, U. (1986) *Travels in Hyperreality*, San Diego: Harcourt.

Elias, N. (1994) *The Civilizing Process*, Oxford: Basil Blackwell.

Elias, N. and Dunning, E. (1986) *Quest for Excitement: Sport and Leisure in the Civilizing Process*, Oxford: Basil Blackwell.

Evans, M. (2003) *Love: An Unromantic Discussion*, Cambridge: Polity Press.

Ewald, K. and Jiobu, R. (1985) 'Explaining Positive Deviance: Becker's Model and the Case of Runners and Bodybuilders', *Sociology of Sport Journal*, 2: 144–56.

Featherstone, M. (1991) *Consumer Culture and Postmodernism*, Nottingham: Theory, Culture and Society.

Feeley, M. and Simon, J. (1992) 'The New Penology: Notes on the Emerging Strategy of Corrections and its Implications', *Criminology*, 30, 4: 449–74.

Ferrell, J. (1995) *Cultural Criminology*, Boston, MA: Northeastern University Press.

Fiske, J. (1990) *Understanding Popular Culture*, London: Routledge.

Flynn, T. (1994) 'Foucault's Mapping of History', in G. Gutting (ed.) *The Cambridge Companion to Foucault*, Cambridge: Cambridge University Press.

Foucault, M. (1967) *Madness and Civilisation*, London: Tavistock.

Foucault, M. (1972) *The Archaeology of Knowledge*, London: Tavistock.

Foucault, M. (1973) *The Order of Things: the Archaeology of the Human Sciences*, New York: Vintage.

Foucault, M. (1975) *The Birth of the Clinic*, New York: Vintage.

Foucault, M. (1977) *Discipline and Punish: the Birth of the Prison*, Harmondsworth: Penguin.

Foucault, M. (1980a) 'Two Lectures', in C. Gordon (ed.) *Michel Foucault: Power/Knowledge*, Hemel Hempstead: Harvester.

Foucault, M. (1980b) 'Truth and Power', in C. Gordon (ed.) *Michel Foucault: Power/Knowledge*, Hemel Hempstead: Harvester.

Foucault, M. (1981) *The History of Sexuality: Volume 1: An Introduction*, Harmondsworth: Pelican.

Foucault, M. (1983) 'Preface', in G. Deleuze and F. Guattari, *Anti-Oedipus: Capitalism and Schizophrenia*, Minneapolis: University of Minnesota Press.

Foucault, M. (1986) *The History of Sexuality: Volume 3: The Care of the Self*, New York: Pantheon.

Foucault, M. (1987) *The History of Sexuality: Volume 2: The Use of Pleasure*, London: Peregrine.

Foucault, M. (1988) 'The Dangerous Individual' in L. D. Kritzman (ed.) *Politics, Philosophy, Culture: Interviews and Other Writings 1977–1984*, London: Routledge.

Foucault, M. (1998) 'Different Spaces' in J. Faubion (ed.) *Michel Foucault: Aesthetics, Method and Epistemology*, London: Penguin.

Franklin, S. (1996) 'Postmodern Body Techniques: Some Anthropological Considerations on Natural and Post Natural Bodies', *Journal of Sport and Exercise Psychology*, 18, 95–106.

Franseen, L. and McCann, S. (1996) 'Causes of Eating Disorders in Elite Female Athletes', *Olympic Coach*, 6, 3: 15–17.

Freud, S. (1920) *Beyond the Pleasure Principle*, London: The Hogarth Press.

Frosh, F., Phoenix, A. and Pattman, R. (2002) *Young Masculinities: Understanding Boys in Contemporary Society*, Basingstoke: Palgrave.

Fukuyama, F. (1992) *The End of History and the Last Man*, London: Hamish Hamilton.

Fulgham, R. (1995) *From Beginning to End*, New York: Ballantine Books.

Gane, (2001) 'Zygmunt Bauman: Liquid Modernity and Beyond', *Acta Sociologica*, 44, 3: 267–75.

Garfield, S. (2003) 'Out of Time: Why is Sport the Last Bastion of Homophobia?', *The Observer Sport Monthly*, 39 May.

Garfinkel, H. (1967) *Studies in Ethnomethodology*, Englewood Cliffs, NJ: Prentice-Hall.

Garland, D. (1990) *Punishment in Modern Society: A Study in Social Theory*, Oxford: Oxford University Press.

Garland, D. (2000) *The Culture of Control: Crime and Social Order in Late Modernity*, Oxford: Oxford University Press.

Garland, D. and Sparks, R. (2000) 'Criminology, Social Theory, and the Challenge of Our Times', in D. Garland and R. Sparks, *Criminology and Social Theory*, Oxford: Oxford University Press.

Geertz, C. (1973) 'Deep Play: Notes on the Balinese Cockfight pt 2', http: //webhome. idirect.com/~boweevil/BaliCockGeertz2.html.

Gelder, K. and Thornton, S. (1997) *The Subcultures Reader*, London: Routledge.

Gelsthorpe, L. and Morris, A. (1988) 'Feminism and Criminology in Britain', *British Journal of Criminology*, 28.

Geraghty, C. (1991) *Women and Soap Opera*, Cambridge: Polity Press.

Gibson, J. (2000) 'Comics Find Ali G Is an Alibi for Racism', *The Guardian*, 11 January, 2000, http: //www.guardian.co.uk/ali/article/0,2763,195448,00.html.

Giddens, A. (1990) *The Consequences of Modernity*, Cambridge: Polity Press.

Giddens, A. (1991) *Modernity and Self-Identity: Self and Society in the Late Modern Age*, Cambridge: Polity Press.

Giddens, A. (1992) *The Transformation of Intimacy: Sexuality, Love and Eroticism in Modern Societies*, Cambridge, Polity Press.

Giddens, A. (1994) 'Living in Post-Traditional Society', in U. Beck, A. Giddens and S. Lash, *Reflexive Modernization: Politics, Tradition and Aesthetics in the Modern Social Order*, Cambridge: Polity Press.

Giulianotti, R. (1991) 'Scotland's Tartan Army in Italy: The Case for the Carnivalesque', *Sociological Review*, 39, 3: 503–27.

Giulianotti, R. (1995) 'Football and the Politics of Carnival: An Ethnographic Study of Scottish Fans in Sweden', *International Review for the Sociology of Sport*, 30, 2: 191–224.

Giulianotti, R. (1999) *Football: A Sociology of the Global Game*, Cambridge: Polity Press.

Goffman, E. (1959) *Asylums*, Harmondsworth: Penguin.

Goffman, E. (1961) *The Presentation of the Self in Everyday Life*, Harmondsworth: Penguin.

Golder, A. (2003) 'Crime Rates Fall, but Fear is Still Rife', *The Recorder*, 1 October, 2003 http: //www.recorderonline.co.uk/archived/2003/wk28/ilfbark/barkdagnews/crime.asp.

Gould, T. (1983) *Inside Outsider: The Life and Times of Colin MacInnes*, London: Chatto and Windus.

Gramsci, A. (1971) *Selections from the Prison Notebooks*, ed. Q. Hoare and G. Nowell-Smith, London: Lawrence & Wishart.

Greenfield, S. and Osborne, G. (2001) *Regulating Football Commodification Consumption and the Law*, London: Pluto Press.

Griffin, P. (1998) *Strong Women, Deep Closets: Lesbians and Homophobia in Sport*, Champaign, IL: Human Kinetics.

Gruneau, R. (1983) *Class, Sports and Social Development*, Amherst, MA: University of Massachusetts Press.

Gubrium, J. F. and Holstein, J. A. (1994) 'Grounding the Postmodern Self', *The Sociological Quarterly*, 35, 4: 685–703.

Haber, H. (1996) 'Foucault Pumped: Body Politics and the Muscled Woman', in S. Hekman (ed.) *Feminist Interpretations of Michel Foucault*, University Park: Pennsylvania State University Press.

Habermas, J. (1976) *Legitimation Crisis*, London: Heinemann Educational Books.

Hall, S. (1978) 'The Treatment of Football Hooliganism in the Press', in R. Ingham (ed.) *Football Hooliganism: The Wider Context*, London: Inter-Action Imprint.

Hall, S. (1981) 'The Whites of Their Eyes: Racist Ideologies and the Media', in G. Bridges and R. Brunt (eds) *Silver Linings: Some Strategies for the Eighties*, London: Lawrence & Wishart.

Hall, S. (1996) *Race, the Floating Signifier*, London: Media Education Foundation.

Hall, S. and Jefferson, T. (eds) (1976) *Resistance Through Rituals: Youth Subcultures in Post-war Britain*, London: Hutchinson.

Hall, S., Critcher, C., Jefferson, T., Clarke, J. and Roberts, B. (1978) *Policing the Crisis: Mugging, the State and Law and Order*, London: Macmillan.

Hamil, S., Michie, J., Oughton, C. and Warby, S. (2000) *Football in the Digitial Age: Whose Game is it Anyway?*, Edinburgh: Mainstream.

Hammersley, M. and Atkinson, P. (1995) *Ethnography: Principles in Practice*, 2nd edn, London: Routledge.

Hargreaves, John (1986) *Sport, Power and Culture*, Cambridge: Polity Press.

Hargreaves, Jennifer (1994) *Sporting Females: Critical Issues in the History and Sociology of Women's Sports*, London: Routledge.

Hargreaves, J. and Tomlinson, A. (1992) 'Getting There: Cultural Theory and the Sociological Analysis of Sport in Britain', *Sociology of Sport Journal*, 9, 2.

Harland, R. (1987) *Superstructuralism: the Philosophy of Structuralism and Post-Structuralism*, London: Routledge.

Harraway, D. (1991) *Simians, Cyborgs and Women: The Reinvention of Nature*, London: Routledge.

Hartsock, N. (1993) 'Foucault on Power: A Theory for Women?', in C. Lemert (ed.) *Social Theory: The Multicultural and Classic Readings*, Boulder, CO: Westview Press.

Hastad, D., Segrave, J., Pangrazi, R. and Peterson, G. (1984) 'Youth Sport Participation and Deviant Behaviour', *Sociology of Sport Journal*, 1: 366–73.

Hebdidge, D. (1979) *Subculture: The Meaning of Style*, London: Methuen.

Hebdidge, D. (1988) *Hiding in the Light: On Images and Things*, London: Routledge.

Heinila, K. (1969) 'Football at the Crossroads', *International Review of Sport Sociology*, 4: 5–30.

Hill, J. (2002) *Sport, Leisure and Culture in Twentieth Century Britain*, Basingstoke: Palgrave.

Hines, B. (1968) *A Kestral for a Knave*, London: Penguin.

Hobbs, D. (1988) *Doing the Business: Entrepreneurship, The Working Class and Detectives in the East End of London*, Oxford: Oxford University Press.

Hoberman, J. (1992) *Mortal Engines: The Science of Performance and the Dehumanization of Sport*, New York: The Free Press.

Hoberman, J. (1997) *Darwin's Athletes: How Sport Damaged Black America and Preserved the Myth of Race*, Boston: Houghton Mifflin Company.

Hobson, D. (1982) *Crossroads: The Drama of a Soap Opera*, London: Methuen.

Horkheimer, M. and Adorno, T. (1976) *Dialectic of Enlightenment*, trans. J. Cumming, Continuum.

Horne, J. and Jary, D. (1987) 'The Figurational Sociology of Sport and Leisure of Elias and Dunning: An Exposition and Critique', in J. Horne, D. Jarry and A. Tomlinson (eds) *Sport, Leisure and Social Relations (Sociological Review Monograph 33)*, London: Routledge.

Horrocks, C. (1999) *Baudrillard and the Millennium*, New York: Icon Books.

Hughes, R. and Coakley, J. (1991) 'Positive Deviance among Athletes', *Sociology of Sport Journal*, 8: 307–25.

Irigaray, L. (1985) 'Any Theory of the Subject Has Already Been Appropriated By the Masculine', in L. Irigaray, *Speculum of the Other Woman*, Ithaca, NY: Cornell University Press.

Jackson, S. and Csikszentmihalyi, M. (1999) *Flow in Sports: The Keys to Optimal Experiences and Performances*, Champaign, IL: Human Kinetics.

Jarvie, G. and Maguire, J. (1994) *Sport and Leisure in Social Thought*, London: Routledge.

Jarvis, S. (2003) 'Thinking-Cum-Knowing: A Book Review', *Radical Philosophy*, 117: 43–5.

Jenkins, K. (1995) *What is History': From Carr and Elton to Rorty and White*, London: Routledge.

Jennings, A. (1996) *The New Lords of the Rings*, London: Pocket Books.

Jones, A. and Stephenson, A. (1997) 'Introduction', in A. Jones and A. Stephenson (eds) *Performing the Body: Performing the Text*, London: Routledge.

Jones, D. (2003) 'Give a dog a bad name . . .', *The Observer Sport Monthly*, 35: January.

Kaskisaari, M. (1994) 'The Rhythmbody', *International Review for the Sociology of Sport*, 29, 1: 15–21.

Katz, J. (1988) *Seductions of Crime*, New York: Basic Books.

Kenyon, G. (1986) 'The Significance of Social Theory in the Development of Sport Sociology', in C. Rees and A. Miracle (eds) *Sport and Social Theory*, Champaign, IL: Human Kinetics.

Kristeva, J. (1986) *The Kristeva Reader*, ed. T. Moi, New York: Columbia Press.

Lacan, J. (1977) *Ecrits: A Selection*, London: Tavistock.

Lash. S. (1994) 'Reflexivity and its Doubles: Structure, Aesthetics, Community', in U. Beck, A. Giddens and S. Lash, *Reflexive Modernization: Politics, Tradition and Aesthetics in the Modern Social Order*, Cambridge: Polity Press.

Lash, S. (2002) *Critique of Information*, London: Sage.

Lawrence, E. (1982) 'Just Plain Common Sense: the "Roots" of Racism', in Birmingham Centre for Contemporary Cultural Studies, *Empire Strikes Back*, London: Hutchinson.

Layder, D. (1986) 'Social Reality as Figuration: A Critique of Elias's Conception of Sociological Analysis', *Sociology*, 20, 3: 367–86.

LBBD (London Borough of Barking and Dagenham) (2001a) 'Youth Project Leads to Biggest Reduction in Youth Crime in the Country, http: //www.lbbd.gov.uk/2-press-release/press-release-item.asp?item_code=515.

LBBD (London Borough of Barking and Dagenham) (2001b) *Barking and Dagenham Audit of Crime and Disorder*, Community Safety Team, London Borough of Barking and Dagenham.

Lenskyj, H. (1986) *Women, Sport and Sexuality*, Toronto: Women's Press.

Lianos, M. (2000) 'Dangerization and the End of Deviance', *British Journal of Criminology*, 40: 261–78.

Lianos, M. with Douglas, M. (2000) 'Dangerization and the End of Deviance: The Institutional Environment', in D. Garland and R. Sparks (eds) *Criminology and Social Theory*, Oxford: Oxford University Press.

Lloyd, M. (1999) 'Performativity, Parody, Politics', in V. Bell (ed.) *Performativity and Belonging*, London: Sage.

Long, J. and Sanderson, I. (2001) 'The Social Benefits of Sport: Where's the Proof?', in C. Gratton and I. Henry (eds) *Sport in the City: The Role of Sport in Economic and Social Regeneration*, London: Routledge.

Loy, J. (1969) 'Game Forms, Social Structure, and Anomie', in R. Brown and B. Cratty (eds) *New Perspectives of Man in Action*, Englewood Cliffs, NJ: Prentice Hall.

Loy, J. and Booth, D. (2000) 'Functionalism, Sport and Society', in J. Coakley and E. Dunning (eds) *Handbook of Sport Studies*, London: Sage.

Luke, T. (1995) 'New World Order or Neo-World Orders: Power, Politics and Ideology in the Informationalising Global Order', in M. Featherstone, S. Lash and R. Robertson (eds) *Global Modernities*, London: Sage.

Luschen, G. (1969) 'Small Group Research and the Group in Sport', in G. Kenyon (ed.) *Aspects of Contemporary Sport Sociology*, Chicago: The Athletic Institute.

Luschen, G. (1971) 'Delinquency', in L. Larson and D. Hermann (eds) *Encyclopedia of Sport Sciences and Medicine*, New York: Macmillan.

Luschen, G. (1976) 'Cheating in Sport', in D. Landers (ed.) *Social Problems in Athletics: Essays in the Sociology of Sport*, Urbana, IL: University of Illinois Press.

Luschen, G. (1984) 'Before and After Caracas: Drug Abuse and Doping as Deviant Behaviour in Sport', in K. Olin (ed.) *Contribution of Sociology to the Study of Sport*, Jyvaskyla: University of Jyvaskyla.

Lushchen, G. and Sage, G. (eds) (1981) *Handbook of Social Science of Sport*, Champaign, IL: Stipes.

Lyng, S. (1990) 'Edgework: A Social Psychological Analysis of Voluntary Risk Taking', *American Journal of Sociology*, 95, 4: 851–86.

Lyng, S. and Snow, D. (1986) 'Vocabularies of Motive and High risk Behaviour: The Case of Skydiving', in E. Lawler (ed.) *Advances in Group Processes*, vol. 3, Greenwich, CT: JAI.

Lyotard, J.-F. (1984) *The Postmodern Condition: A Report on Knowledge*, Minneapolis: University of Minesota Press.

Lyotard, J.-F. (1988) *Peregrinations: Law, Form, Event*, New York: Columbia University Press.

McCall, M. and Becker, H. (1990) 'Introduction', in H. Becker and M. McCall (eds) *Symbolic Interaction and Cultural Studies*, Chicago: University of Chicago Press.

MacCannell, D. (1992) *Empty Meeting Grounds: The Tourist Papers*, London: Routledge.

McKeganey, N. and Barnard, M. (1996) *Sex Work on the Streets: Prostitutes and their Clients*, Milton Keynes: Open University Press.

McNay, L. (1994) *Foucault: A Critical Introduction*, Cambridge: Polity Press.

MacNeill, M. (1998) 'Sex, Lies and Videotape: The Political and Cultural Economies of Celebrity Fitness Videos', in G. Rail (ed.) *Sport and Postmodern Times*, New York: State University of New York Press.

McRae, D. (1996) *Dark Trade: Lost in Boxing*, Edinburgh: Mainstream.

McRobbie, A. (1982) 'Jackie: An Ideology of Adolescent Feminity', in B. Waites, T. Bennett and G. Martin (eds) *Popular Culture: Past and Present*, London: Croom Helm.

McRobbie, A (1991) *Feminism and Youth Culture: From Jackie to Just Seventeen*, London: Macmillan.

McRobbie, A. (1994) *Postmodernism and Popular Culture*, London: Routledge.

Maffesoli, M. (1996) *The Time of the Tribes: The Decline of Individualism in a Mass Society*, London: Sage.

Maguire, J. (1999) *Global Sport*, Cambridge: Polity Press.

Mansfield, A. and McGinn, B. (1993) 'Pumping Irony: The Muscular and the Feminine', in S. Scott and D. Morgan (eds) *Body Matters*, London: Falmer Press.

Markula, P. (1995) 'Firm but Shapely, Fit but Sexy, Strong but Thin: The Postmodern Aerobicizing Female Bodies', *Sociology of Sport Journal*, 12, 4: 424–53.

Marsh, P., Rosser, E. and Harre, R. (1978) *The Rules of Disorder*, London: Routledge.

Mathiesen, T. (1997) 'The Viewer Society: Michel Foucault's "Panopticon" Revisited', *Theoretical Criminology*, 215–34.

Mead, G. (1918) 'The Psychology of Punitive Justice', *American Journal of Sociology*, 23.

Merton, R. (1938) 'Social Structure and Anomie', *American Sociological Review*, 3.

Messner, M. (1992) *Power at Play: Sport and the Problem of Masculinity*, Boston, MA: Beacon Press.

Messner, M. and Sabo, D. (1990) *Sport, Men and the Gender Order: Critical Feminist Perspectives*, Champaign, IL: Human Kinetics.

Mestrovic, S. (1998) *Anthony Giddens: The Last Modernist*, London: Routledge.

Midol, N. and Broyer, G. (1995) 'Toward an Anthropological Analysis of New Sport Cultures: The Case of Whiz Sports in France', *Sociology of Sport Journal*, 12: 204–212.

Miller, J. (1993) *The Passion of Michel Foucault*, London: Harper Collins.

Mills, C. W. (1959) *The Sociological Imagination*, Harmondsworth: Penguin.

Money, T. (1997) *Manly and Muscular Diversions: Public Schools and the Nineteenth Century Sporting Revival*, London: Duckworth.

Morgan, W. (1994) *Leftist Theories of Sport*, Urbana, IL: University of Illinois Press.

Mumford, L. (1995) *Love and Ideology in the Afternoon*, Bloomington, IN: Indiana University Press.

Naffine, N. (1997) *Feminism and Criminology*, Cambridge: Polity Press.

Nash, H. (1987) 'Do Compulsive Runners and Anorectic Patients Share Common Bonds?' *The Physician and Sportsmedicine*, 15, 12: 162–7.

National Playing Fields Association (2003) 'Playgrounds Continue to Slide into Decline', http://www.npfa.co.uk/content/newsarticle/66/.

National Statistics (2003) *Statistics about Gascoigne*, http://neighbourhood.statistics.gov.uk/area.

Natoli, J. (1997) *A Primer to Postmodernity*, Oxford: Blackwell.

Nixon, H. (1993) 'Accepting the Risks and Pain of Injury in Sport: Mediated Cultural Influences on Playing Hurt', *Sociology of Sport Journal*, 10, 2: 183–96.

Nixon, H. (1996) 'Explaining Pain and Injury Attitudes and Experiences in Sport in Terms of Gender, Race and Sports Status Factors', *Journal of Sport and Social Issues*, 20, 1: 33–44.

O'Connor, B. and Boyle, B. (1993) 'Dallas with Balls: Televised Sport, Soap Opera and Male and Female Pleasures', *Leisure Studies*, 12: 107–19.

O'Hagan, A. (2003) 'Watching Me Watching Them Watching You', *London Review of Books*, 25,19: 3–9.

Orwell, G. (1979) *Nineteen Eighty-Four*, Harmondsworth: Penguin.

PA (2003) 'Gang-rape Claim Footballers' Names still on Internet', 1 October, *Guardian Unlimited*, http://football.guardian.co.uk/News_Story/0,1583,1053364,00.html.

Park, R., Burgess, E. and McKenzie, R. (eds) (1925) *The City*, Chicago: University of Chicago Press.

Parsons, T. (1966) *Societies: Evolutionary and Comparative Practices*, Englewood Cliffs, NJ: Prentice-Hall.

Patton, C. (2000) 'Rock Hard', in C. Cole, J. Loy and M. Messner (eds) *Exercising Power: The Making and Re-making of the Body*, Albany, NY: State University of New York Press.

Pearce, F. (1976) *Crimes of the Powerful: Marxism, Crime and Deviance*, London: Pluto Press.

Phillips, A. (2003) 'Bored With Sex', *London Review of Books*, 25, 5: 6 March.

Pike, K. (1967) *Language in Relation to a Unified Theory of the Structure of Human Behaviour*, pt 1, Preliminary edn, Glendale, CA: Glendale Summer Institute of Linguistics.

Pilz, G.(1996) 'Social Factors Influencing Sport and Violence: On the "Problem" of Football Violence in Germany', *International Review for the Sociology of Sport*, 31: 49–65.

Presdee, M. (2000) *Cultural Criminology and the Carnival of Crime*, London: Routledge.

Prokop, U. (1971) *Soziologie der Olympishchen Spiel. Sport und Kapitalismus*, Munich: Hanser.

Pronger, B. (1990) *The Arena of Masculinity: Sports, Homosexuality and the Meaning of Sex*, New York: St Martin's Press.

Pronger, B. (1995) 'Rendering the Body: The Implicit Lessons of Gross Anatomy', *Quest*, 47: 427–46.

Pronger, B. (2002) *Body Fascism: Salvation in the Technology of Physical Fitness*, Toronto: University of Toronto Press.

Rail, G. and Harvey, J. (1995) 'Body at Work: Michel Foucault and the Sociology of Sport', *Sociology of Sport Journal*, 12, 2: 164–79.

Redhead, S. (1990) *The End-of-the-Century Party: Youth and Pop Towards 2000*, Manchester: Manchester University Press.

Ricoeur, P. (1991) *From Text to Action: Essays in Hermeneutics*, ll, Evanston, IL: Northwest University Press.

Ricoeur, P. (1992) *Oneself as Another*, Chicago: Chicago University Press.

Rigauer, B. (1969) *Sport und Arbeit. Soziologische Zusammenhänge und ideologische Implikationen*, Frankfurt am Main: Suhrkamp (*Sport and Work*, trans. by A. Guttmann, New York, 1981, Columbia University Press).

Rinehart, R. (1998a) 'Fictional Methods in Ethnography: Believability, Specks of Glass and Chekhov', *Qualitative Inquiry*, 4, 2: 200–24.

Rinehart, R. (1998b) 'Born-again Sport: Ethics in Biographical Research', in G. Rail (ed.) *Sport and Postmodern Times*, Albany, NY: SUNY.

Rinehart, R. (1998c) *Players All: Performances in Contemporary Sport*, Bloomington, IN: Indiana University Press.

Ritzer, G. (1997) *Postmodern Social Theory*, London: McGraw Hill.

Ritzer, G. (2003) *Contemporary Social theory and Its Classical Roots: The Basics*, New York: McGraw Hill.

Ritzer, G. (2004) *The Globalization of Nothing*. London: Pine Forge Press.

Robins, D. (1984) *We Hate Humans*, Harmondsworth: Penguin.

Robins, D. (1990) *Sport as Prevention, the Role of Sport in Crime Prevention Programmes Aimed at Young People*, Centre for Criminological Research, Oxford University.

Robinson, K. (2003) 'The Passion and the Pleasure: Foucault's Art of Not Being Oneself', *Theory Culture and Society*, 20, 2: 119–44.

Robson, G. (2000) *'No One Likes Us, We Don't Care': The Myth and Reality of Millwall Fandom*, Oxford: Berg.

Robson, T. and Zalcock, B. (1995) 'Looking at Pumping Iron II: The Women', in T. Wilton (ed.) *Immortal, Invisible Lesbians and the Moving Image*, London: Routledge.

Rock, P. (1985) 'Deviance', in A. Kuper and J. Kuper (eds) *The Social Science Encyclopaedia*, London: Routledge Kegan Paul.

Rojek, C. (1985) *Capitalism and Leisure Theory*, London: Tavistock.

Rojek, C. (1986) 'The Problems of Involvement and Detachment in the Writings of Norbert Elias', *The British Journal of Sociology*, 37, 4: 584–96.

Rojek, C. (1990) 'Baudrillard and Leisure', *Leisure Studies*, 9, 1: 7–20.

Rojek, C. (1992) 'The Field of Play in Sport and Leisure Studies', in E. Dunning and C. Rojek (eds) *Sport and Leisure in the Civilizing Process: Critique and Counter-Critique*, London: Macmillan.

Rojek, C. (1995) *Decentring Leisure: Rethinking Leisure Theory*, London: Sage.

Rojek, C. (2000) *Leisure and Culture*, Basingstoke: Macmillan.

Rojek, C. (2001) *Celebrity*, London: Reaktion.

Rorty, R. (1979) *Philosophy and the Mirror of Nature*, Princeton, NJ: Princeton University Press.

Rorty, R. (1982) *Consequences of Pragmatism*, Minneapolis: University of Minnesota Press.

Rorty, R. (1986) 'The Contingency of Community', *The London Review of Books*, 24 July.

Rorty, R. (1989) *Contingency, Irony and Solidarity*, Cambridge, MA: Cambridge University Press.

Rorty, R. (1991) *Essays on Heidegger and Others: Philosophical Papers, Volume 2*, Cambridge: Cambridge University Press.

Rose, A. and Friedman, J. (1997) 'Television Sports as Mas(s)culine Cult of Distraction', in A. Baker and T. Boyd (eds) *Out of Bounds: Sports, Media and the Politics of Identity*, Bloomington, IN: Indiana University Press.

Ruggiero, V. (1996) *Organized and Corporate Crime in Europe: Offers that Can't Be Refused*, Dartmouth: Aldershot.

Said, E. (1975) *Beginnings: Intention and Method*, New York: Basic Books.

Sato, I. (1991) *Kamikaze Biker*, Chicago: University of Chicago Press.

Sawacki, J. (1994) 'Foucault, Feminism and Questions of Identity', in G. Gutting (ed.) *The Cambridge Companion to Foucault*, Cambridge: Cambridge University Press.

Schafer, W. (1969) 'Some Sources and Consequences of Interscholastic Athletics: The Case of Participation and Delinquency', *International Review of Sport Sociology*, 4: 63–79.

Scheff, T. J. (1997) 'Unpacking the Civilizing Process: Shame and Integration in Elias's Work', at http: //shop.usyd.ed.au/su/social/elias/confpap/scheff2.htm 17 February 2000.

Schwartz, M. and DeKeseredy, W. (1991) 'Left Realist Criminology: Strengths, Weaknesses and the Feminist Critique', *Crime, Law and Social Change*, 15: 51–72.

Scraton, S. (1995) ' "Boys Muscle in Where Angels Fear to Tread" – Girls' Sub-cultures and Physical Activities', in C. Criticher, P. Bramham and A. Tomlinson (eds) *Sociology of Leisure – A Reader*, London: E & FN Spon.

Scull, A. (1983) 'Community Corrections: Panacea, Progress or Pretence' in J. Garland and J. Young (eds) *The Power to Punish*, London: Heinemann Educational Books.

Sedgwick, E. (1992) 'Epidemics of the Will', in J. Crarry and S. Kwinter (eds), *Incorporations*, New York: Zone Books.

Sennett, R. (2003) *Respect: The Formation of Character in an Age of Inequality*, London: Allen Lane.

Shields, R. (ed.) (1992) *Lifestyle Shopping*, London: Routledge.

Simpson, M. (1994) *Male Impersonators: Men Performing Masculinity*, New York: Routledge.

Sloop, J. (1997) 'Mike Tyson and the Perils of Discursive Constraints: Boxing, Race and the Assumption of Guilt', in A. Baker and T. Boyd (eds) *Out of Bounds: Sports, Media and the Politics of Identity*, Bloomington, IN: Indiana University Press.

Smart, C. (1977) *Women, Crime and Criminology*, London: Routledge.

Smith, D. (1999) *Zygmunt Bauman: Prophet of Postmodernity*, Cambridge: Polity Press.

Smith, M. (1983) *Violence and sport*, Toronto: Butterworths.

Snow, T. (2003) 'Black like Beckham', *Channel4.com*, http: //www.channel4.com/history/microsites/B/blackhistorymap/articles_02.html.

Snyder, E. (1994) 'Interpretations and Explanations of Deviance Among College Athletes: A Case Study', *Sociology of Sport Journal*, 11: 231–48.

Spencer, H. (1861) *Education: Intellectual, Moral and Physical*, New York: D. Appleton.

Stacey, M. (1988) *The Sociology of Health and Healing*, London: Unwin.

Stallybrass, P. and White, A. (1986) *The Politics and Poetics of Transgression*, London: Methuen.

Stebbins, R. (1992) *Amateurs, Professionals and Serious Leisure*, Montreal: McGill University Press.

Stebbins, R. (1997) 'Casual Leisure: A Conceptual Statement', *Leisure Studies*, 16, 1: 17–26.

Stebbins, R. (1999) 'Serious Leisure', in T. L. Burton and E. L. Jackson (eds) *Leisure Studies: Prospects for the Twenty-First Century*, State College, PA: Venture Publishing.

Stephenson, C. (1975) 'Socialization Effects of Participation in Sport: A Critical Review of the Research', *Research Quarterly*, 47: 1–8.

Stone, G. (1955) 'American Sports: Play and Display', *Chicago Review*, 9, 3: 83–100.

Stone, G. (1957) 'Some Meanings of American Sport', *Proceedings of the National College Physical Education Association for Men*, Washington, DC: 6–29.

Stott, C.J., Hutchison, P. and Drury, J. (2001) 'Hooligans Abroad? Intergroup Dynamics, Social Identity and Participation in Collective "Disorder" at the 1998 World Cup Finals', *British Journal of Social Psychology*, 40: 359–84.

Sugden, J. and Tomlinson, A. (1999a) *Great Balls of Fire: How Big Money is Hijacking World Football*, Edinburgh: Mainstream.

Sugden, J. and Tomlinson, A. (1999b) 'Digging the Dirt and Staying Clean', *International Review for the Sociology of Sport*, 34, 4: 385–97.

Sugden, J. and Tomlinson, A. (2003) *Badfellas: FIFA Family at War*, Edinburgh: Mainstream.

Sumner, C. (1994) *The Sociology of Deviance: An Obituary*, Milton Keynes: Open University Press.

Sumner, C. (2001) 'Social Deviance', in E. McLaughlin and J. Muncie *The Sage Dictionary of Criminology*, London: Sage.

Sutherland E. (1983) [1940] *White Collar Crime*, New Haven, CT: Yale University Press.

Suttles, G. (1968) *The Social Order of the Slum: Ethnicity and Territory in the Inner City*, Chicago: University of Chicago Press.

Sydnor, S. (2000) Sport, Celebrity and Liminality, in N. Dyck (ed.) *Games, Sports and Cultures*, Oxford: Berg.

Taylor, I. (1971) 'Soccer Consciousness and Soccer Hooliganism', in S. Cohen (ed.) *Images of Deviance*, Harmondsworth: Penguin.

Taylor, I. (1982) 'On the Sports Violence Question: Soccer Hooliganism Revisited', in J. Hargreaves (ed.) *Sport, Culture and Ideology*, London: Routledge.

Taylor, I., Walton, P. and Young, J. (1973) *The New Criminology: For a Social Theory of Deviance*, London: Routledge.

Tett, L. (1996) 'Changing Masculinities: Single-sex Work with Boys and Young Men', *Youth and Policy*, 55: 14–27.

Thompson, E. P. (1963) *The Making of the English Working Class*, London: Victor Gollancz.

Thompson H. S. (1971) *Fear and Loathing in Las Vegas: A Savage Journey to the Heart of the American Dream*, New York: Warner.

Thompson H. S. (1979) *The Great Shark Hunt: Strange Tales from a Strange Time*, New York: Warner.

Thompson, K. (1998) *Moral Panics*, London: Routledge.

Tomlinson, A. (2002) 'Theorising Spectacle: Beyond Debord', in J. Sugden and A. Tomlinson (eds) *Power Games: A Critical Sociology of Sport*, London: Routledge.

Trifonas, P. (2001) *Post-modern Encounters: Umberto Eco and Football*, Cambridge: Icon Books.

Turner, B. (1984) *The Body and Society: Explorations in Social Theory*, Oxford: Blackwell.

Turner, V. W. (1973) 'The Center Out There: Pilgrim's Goal', *History of Religions*, 12, 3: 191–230.

Vinnai, G. (1970) *Fußballsport als Ideologie*, Frankfurt am Main: Europäische Verlagsanstalt.

Virillio, P. (1997) *Open Sky*, London: Verso.

Wacquant L. (1992) 'The Social Logic of Boxing in Black Chicago: Toward a Sociology of Pugilism', *Sociology of Sport Journal*, 9, 3: 221–54.

Walklate, S. (1992) 'Appreciating the Victim: Conventional, Realist or Critical Victimology?', in R. Matthews and J. Young (eds) *Issues in Realist Criminology*, London: Sage.

Ward, S. (1997) 'Being Objective about Objectivity: The Ironies of Standpoint Epistemological Critiques of Science', *Sociology* 31, 4: 773–91.

Watkins, L. (2002) 'More than Spectacular . . . Football and the Society of the Soap Opera', unpublished undergraduate dissertation, Sheffield Hallam University.

Webb, J. Schirato, T. and Danaher, G. (2002) *Understanding Bourdieu*, London: Sage.

Weber, M. (1930) *The Protestant Ethic and the Spirit of Capitalism*, London: Unwin Hyman.

Weber, M. (1947) *The Theory of Social and Economic Organisation*, New York: The Free Press.

Wellman, B., Carrington, P. and Hall, A. (1988) 'Networks as Personal Communities', in B. Wellman and S. Berkowitz (eds) *Social Structures: A Network Approach*, Cambridge: Cambridge University Press.

Welsh, I. (1993) *Trainspotting*, London: Minerva.

Whannel, G. (1979) 'Football, Crowd Behaviour and the Press', *Media, Culture and Society*, 1: 327–42.

Wheatley, E. (1994) 'Subcultural Subversions: Comparing Discourses on Sexuality in Men's and Women's Rugby Songs', in S. Birrell and C. Cole (eds) *Women, Sport and Culture*, Champaign, IL: Human Kinetics.

Whyte, W. F. (1943) *Street Corner Society: The Social Structure of an Italian Slum*, Chicago: University of Chicago Press.

Williams, A. and Smith, S. (1999) *When You Walk Through the Storm: The Hillsborough Disaster and One Mother's Quest for Justice*, Edinburgh: Mainstream.

Willis, P. (1977) *Learning to Labour: How Working Class Kids Get Working Class Jobs*, London: Saxon House.

Young, A. (1991) 'Feminism and the Body of Criminology', unpublished paper cited in D. Downes and P. Rock, *Understanding Deviance: A Guide to the Sociology of Crime and Rule Breaking*, 3rd edn, Oxford: Oxford University Press.

Young, A. and Rush, P. (1994) 'The Law of Victimage in Urban Realism: Thinking Through Inscriptions of Violence', in D. Nelken (ed.) *The Futures of Criminology*, London: Sage.

Young, J. (1971) *The Drugtakers*, London: Paladin.

Young, J. (1988) 'Radical Criminology in Britain', *British Journal of Criminology*, 28: 159–313.

Young, J. (1999) *The Exclusive Society: Social Exclusion, Crime and Difference in Late Modernity*, London: Sage.

Young, K. (2000) 'Sport and Violence', in J. Coakley and E. Dunning (eds) *Handbook of Sport Studies*, London: Sage.

Young, K. and White, P. (1995) 'Sport, Physical Danger and Injury: The Experiences of Elite Women Athletes', *Journal of Sport and Social Issues*, 19, 1: 45–61.

Young, M. and Willmott, P. (1957) *Family and Kinship in East London*, London: Routledge Kegan Paul.

Younge, G. (2000) 'Is it cos I is black', *The Guardian*, 12 January 2000, http: //www.guardian.co.uk/ali/article/0,2763,195449,00.html.

Index

Abercrombie, N. 111, 112
abnormality 59; *see also* deviance
Adam, T. 85
Adorno, T. 73, 113
agency 24, 93
alcohol abuse 57
Ali, M. 77
Ali G 129–32
alienation 31–2, 57, 166
Allen, R. 112
Althusser, L. 31
Andrews, D. 45
anomie 20, 21, 22
anthropoemia 56
anthropophagia 56
Armstrong, G. 27–8, 44
athletes 31–2, 67, 72, 166
athletics 18, 26
Atkinson, P. 46
Atlanta Olympics 72
Augé, M. 134–5
Austin, J. L. 80
authenticity: community sports coach
    168–9; consumer culture 69, 75;
    experience 114; subculture 33
authority figures 35

Back, L. 122, 125–6
Bailey, R. 124
Baker, A. 113
Bakhtin, M. 146, 148
Bale, J. 44
Balinese cockfight 26
Barker, D. 124
Barnes, J. 115
Barthes, R. 3, 6, 53, 122–3
base-jumping 86
Batty, P. 124
Baudelaire, C. 9

Baudrillard, J.: body 69–72; consumption
    72; dice-life 67–8; double life 75–6;
    ecstatic experience 54; freedom 114;
    Gulf War 123; individualism 69; 'into'
    culture 70, 76; performativity 77;
    real/illusion 113; violence/media 57
Bauman, Z.: abnormality 59;
    anthropoemia 56; anthropophagia 56;
    celebrity 83; community 160;
    consumption 82, 85, 167; cruising 140,
    145; deviance 65; and Foucault 49;
    hermeneutics xi, 15, 91; idealizations
    65–6; identity 68, 159; idiaphorisation
    82–3, 167–8; individualism 26;
    Legislators and Interpreters 44, 166;
    liquid modernity x, 7, 63–4, 65, 66–7,
    72–3, 158; *nowhereville* 134–5;
    reality/pleasure principle 8; social
    control 153; space 85; status 158
Beal, B. 24, 33
Beck, U. 14, 26, 39, 54, 66
Becker, H. 23, 26
Beckham, D.: celebrity 128–9, 181; as
    floating signifier 75, 132; gay icon
    128–9; infidelity alleged 184[6]n2;
    irony 132; McGowan on 126–9;
    sexuality 129–31, 182
Beckham, V. (née Adams) 127, 128,
    129–32
Bégout, B. 140
behaviour: crowds 57; identity 10; social
    31, 157
Bell, V. 49
Bellamy, C. 176
Bentham, J. 43
Bhabha, H. 53
bio-power 47
Birmingham Centre for Contemporary
    Cultural Studies 23, 32, 35

Black like Beckham 132
Blackshaw, T. 28, 89, 102, 105
Blades hooligans 28
body: alienation 31–2; athletes 31–2, 166;
    Baudrillard 69–72; commodification
    69; hedonism 70; pleasure 70; self-
    loathing 56–7; surface 75, 80
body-building 38, 48, 69–70
body-cultivation 71
Bolin, A. 48
borderline work 54
boundary-breaking 181
Bourdieu, P.: cultural capital 157–8;
    Distinction 171; ethnography 102–3;
    habitus 34; *illusio/lusiones* 7; unified
    sociological theory 33–4
Bowyer, L. 4, 119, 120–1, 122, 123, 182
Box, S. 22, 29–30
boxing 34, 49
Boyd, T. 113
Boyle, B. 131
Brackenridge, C. 38, 39
Bramham, P. 58–9
Brighton School 100
Brohm, J.-M. 31–2, 44, 166
bungs 30
Butler, J. 48, 78–9, 80, 150

Cantona, E. 109–10, 113, 114–15, 116
career/structure 24
carnivalesque 53, 80, 146, 147, 151–2
cars, modified 134–5, 136
Cartesian duality 56, 69
Cassell's Book of Sports and Pastimes 18, 21
Castells, M. 67, 159
Castoriadis, C. 99, 149–50, 152
CCTV evidence 124, 125, 184–5 [7]n1
celebrity: Bauman 83; Beckham 128–9,
    181; confession 85; consumer
    capitalism 182; consumption 75, 128;
    deviance 8–9; footballers 177, 179–80;
    media 115–16; poststructuralism 128;
    solicitor 133; sportspeople 58; strain 22
censure 6–7, 8, 9
characters, absolutes 121
Charlton, B. 158
cheating 32
Chelsea football club 122
Chicago school 23, 32, 89
Christianity, muscular 21, 157
Clarke, J. 31, 32, 33, 160
class: criminality 29–30; locality 27; race
    124, 125; stereotypes 126; *see also*
    working-class

Clifford, M. 180
Coakley, J. 11–12, 24–5, 35, 48
cockfight, Balinese 26
Cohen, P. 33
Cohen, S. 4, 23, 177, 182
Cohen, S. B. 129–32, 131–2
Cole, C. 48–9
comedy 131–2
commercialisation of sport 31, 32, 33
commodification 69, 144
communitarianism 37
community 12–13, 140–1, 160
community sport 106, 165
community sports coach 106; authenticity
    168–9; Gascoigne estate 160–5, 170–2,
    185[8]n3; intuition 162; male
    dominance 174
community welfare 161
competition 137–9
confessional: celebrity 85; deviance 8–9;
    Foucault 45–9; liquid modernity 85;
    sexual 47–8; surveillance 87
conformity 21, 60
Connor, S. 73
Conrad, P. 75, 129
consumer capitalism 64, 182
consumer culture: authenticity 69, 75;
    deviance 64; Foucault 87; meritocracy
    159; modernity 72–5; narcissism 74–5
consumption: Baudrillard 72; Bauman 82,
    85, 167; celebrity 75, 128; deviance 9,
    77, 132–3, 144, 183; flawed 82, 168,
    173; media 182; performativity xi, 181
Crabbe, T. 53, 173, 185[8]n5
crime: carnivalesque 80; community 160;
    deviance 19, 25, 30; fear of 161;
    Gascoigne Estate 161; modernity, late
    63–4; normalcy 20
criminality 21, 29–30, 31, 125
criminology: administrative 38; cultural
    55; feminist 36; masculinist 37; radical
    23, 31, 36
Critcher, C. 31, 32, 160
Croall, H. 30
Crosset, T. 33
crowd behaviour 57
Croydon Advertiser 114–15
cruising: audience 144; Bauman 140, 145;
    commodification 144; community
    140–1; competition 137–9; difference
    143–4; ephemeral 140–1; excess 147;
    flow 146; gender 147–8; life-world 151;
    masculinities 147–8; modified cars
    134–5, 136; performativity 104–6, 136,

140–2, 152, 180; ritual 148; sexism
143–4; social interactions 139; street
racing 146–7; surface 105, 139, 151;
transformations 145, 148; tyre
shredding 134; young women 139,
148–9, 151
Crystal Palace 103, 110, 114–15, 116
Csikszentmihalyi, M. 26, 54
cultural capital 157–8
cultural studies 32–3
cyborgs 137, 138

Daily Mirror 118, 119
dangerisation 39, 71
death 85
Debord, G. 58, 133
decarceration 160
Deleuze, G. 68
depth/surface 89, 94–7, 101, 142
Derrida, J. 68, 81, 95, 124
desires 47, 84
detachment 93
determinism: biological 36; political 33;
structural 157
deviance ix–xii; Bauman 65; celebrity 8–9;
confessional 8–9; conformity 21, 60;
consumer culture 64; consumption 9,
77, 132–3, 144, 183; crime 19, 25, 30;
ethics 13, 15; exoticism 101; Foucault
42; institutional corruption 30; as label
24; marxian interpretations 5, 7;
named 10–11; non-conformity 157,
167, 175; normalcy 8; performativity
78–81, 183; positive/negative 25–6;
reality 12; relativism 11–13; social
order 20; social progress 181; sociology
3–4, 5, 178; sociology of sport 63;
vicarious 133
The Devil Makes Work (Clarke and
Critcher) 159–60
Diamond, E. 81
dice-life 67–8
difference 143–4
discipline 18, 44
distancing 83, 105
domination; *see also* patriarchy
domination, male 149, 174, 185[7]n3
Donnelly, P. 24
doping 32
double life 75–6
Douglas, M. 20–1, 39, 89
Downes, D.: criminology 36, 38; deviance
11; good/evil 21; sociology of deviance
5; *Understanding Deviance* 18–19, 42

drag 48, 80–1
Dreyfus, H. 47
drug abuse 57, 72
Dunning, E. 27, 28
Durkheim, E.: anomie 21; crime/deviance
19, 25; *The Division of Labour in Society*
19; elementary forms 141; labour
divisions 20; suicide 22; *Suicide* 20
Düttman, A. G. 10–11, 14

Eco, U. 112, 114, 115
edgework 26, 27, 53–5, 57, 182
Elias, N. 26–7, 28–9, 93, 150
empiricism 37, 97
ephemera 140–1
ethics 13, 15, 101
ethnography: Bourdieu 102–3; gonzo
journalism 97–100, 102; hermeneutics
100–1, 102; sociology of sport 88;
surface/depth 89, 94–7, 101
ethnomethodology 78
Evans, M. 80
excess 147
excitement quest 26
exclusion from school 163, 164; *see also*
social exclusion
exercise addiction 48–9
exoticism 101
experience: authenticity 114; ecstatic 54;
individual 78–9; limit-experience 55,
57; lived 20, 113–14
extreme sports 22
extremes 22, 71–2
eye lust 144–5

The Face 128
fans 114
Fashanu, J. 47–8
Featherstone, M. 171
Feeley, M. 40, 82
feminism: Foucault 44–5;
poststructuralism 149; sport 37
Ferdinand, R. 176
Ferguson, A. 110
figurational sociology 26–7, 28, 93
Fiske, J. 53
flow concept 26, 135, 146
Flynn, T. 43–4
football: chants 121; Crystal Palace 103,
110, 114–15, 116; gossip 103–4; media
123; Millwall 34, 169; soap opera 104,
109–16; social exclusion 173; ticket
touting 89, 98–9; World Cup 30, 77,
128; *see also* community sports

football fans 53, 122
football hooligans: English 27, 122; folk
    devil 35; German 54; resistance 33;
    Taylor 36–7
football tournament 169–71
footballers: celebrity 177, 179–80; gay
    47–8; media 47, 116–17; misbehaviour
    178; nightclubs 116–17; racism 115,
    121; rape accusations 49, 176–80;
    transfers 30, 67–8; trial 119–20;
    violence 57, 123, 128
Foreman, G. 77
Formula 1 racing 64
Foucault, M.: agency 93; *The Archaeology
    of Knowledge* 96; *Birth of the Clinic*
    42–3; confessional 45–9; consumer
    culture 87; deviance 42; *Discipline and
    Punish* 42, 43, 157; feminist critics
    44–5; functionalism 45; genealogy 46,
    95; heterotopia 42, 52; *History of
    Sexuality* 46–7; individuality 96;
    knowledge 38, 96; *Madness and
    Civilisation* 42; panopticon 6, 43–4;
    power 96; risk 55; self-government 87;
    sexuality 46–7; social enquiry 46;
    surveillance 42–3, 49, 82, 166
Frankfurt school 31
Franklin, S. 48–9
freedom 114
Freud, S.: death 85; performativity 148;
    pleasure principle 84; reality principle
    9, 84; self 69
Fulghum, R. 52
functionalism 19, 20–1, 45, 50–1

games 142
gangs 37
gangsta rapper 129–32
Garfield, S. 47
Garland, D. 45, 63–4, 66–7, 157, 159
Gascoigne estate: crime 161; social
    exclusion 168; sports coach 160–5,
    170–2, 185[8]n3
gay and lesbian studies 9–10, 37–8
gay footballers 47–8
Gay Games 22
gay icon 128–9, 130
gaze: bio-medical 42; clinical 43; male
    149; mortification 72; normalising 47,
    60, 81–2; panopticon 84;
    performativity 49; regulatory 166;
    scopophilic 83, 149–50; sexual 131;
    synopticon 84
Geertz, C. xi, 24, 26

Gelsthorpe, L. 36
gender: cruising 147–8; performativity 81,
    149, 150; resistance 37
gender-bending 10
genealogy 46, 95
Gibson, J. 131
Giddens, A. 26, 66, 67, 82, 89, 93
Giulianotti, R. 28, 44, 53
Goffman, E. 54, 78–9
gonzo journalism: ethnography 97–100,
    102; rhetoric 99; Sugden and
    Tomlinson 89–90, 93
Gould, T. 174
Gowan, A. 127–8
GQ 129
Gramsci, A. 32
gratification, instant 84
Gruneau, R. 31, 32, 157
The Guardian 124, 126
Guattari, F. 68
Gubrium, J. F. 125, 147–8
Gulf War 123

Haber, H. 48
Habermas, J. 82
habitus 34, 79, 142
Hall, S. 35, 125, 132
Hammersley, M. 46
Harding, T. 113
Hargreaves, John 32, 44, 157
Harland, R. 46
Harraway, D. 137, 138
Harris, M. 27–8
Hawkes, G. 48
hedonism 70, 139
hermeneutics: Bauman xi, 15, 91;
    ethnography 100–1, 102; interpretive
    sociology 23; media 24
heteroglossia 148
heterotopia 42, 52
Heysel Stadium 57
Hill, J. 52
Hillsborough stadium 30–1
Hines, B. 153–6, 157, 166–7
Hobbs, D. 89
Hoberman, J. 31–2, 125
Holstein, J. A. 125, 147–8
Home Office Positive Futures initiative
    106
homophobia 131
Horkheimer, M. 73, 113
Horrocks, C. 71
hyper-femininity 139, 149
hyper-reality 76, 113, 123

idealism/realism 101
idealizations 65–6
identity: Bauman 68, 159; behaviour 10; fluid 162; performativity 81, 122, 145; poststructuralism 68; racial 170; self 56, 68–9
idiaphorisation 82–3, 167–8
illusio 7, 67
illusion/reality 14, 113
imaginary 99, 152
incorporation/resistance 149
individualisation: social inequality 67, 159; sport 86
individualism: abnormal leisure 55–6; Baudrillard 69; Bauman 26; experience 78–9; Foucault 96; meta-discourse 145; socialisation 22
industrial capitalism 65, 66, 173
innovation 22, 25
Insider Outsider (Gould) 174
institutional corruption 30
interactionism 23
International Review For the Sociology of Sport 88–9
interpreters/legislators 44, 166
interpretive sociology 23
intertextuality 113–14
'into' culture 70, 76
intuition 96–7, 97, 142, 162
involvement 93
Irigaray, L. 149
irony 13, 94, 132

Jackson, S. 54
Jenkins, K. 12
jogging 69, 70–1
Jones, A. 151
Jones, D. 4
journalism 100; *see also* gonzo journalism; media
joy-riding 55, 83, 147

Kerrigan, N. 113
Kes 156
A Kestrel for a Knave (Hines) 106, 153–6, 166–7
King, R. 49
knowledge: Foucault 38, 96; intuition 96–7; postmodernism 79–80; power 11, 95, 96; situated 92
Kristeva, J. 149

labelling theories 22
labour 19–20

Lacan, J. 149
Las Vegas 140
Lash, S. 66, 140–2, 146
Law, D. 158
Lawrence, E. 125
Layder, D. 29
League Weekly 124, 126
Leeds Rhinos 124–6
Leeds United 109, 119, 122, 176
legislators 166, 167
Leicester school 27, 28
leisure: abnormal 51–2, 55–60, 178; deviant 52; functionalism 50–1; invasive 56–7; mephitic 57; normal 58–9; serious/casual 50–1; wild 27, 57, 133; work 49–50
Leisure Studies 58
Lévi-Strauss, C. 56
Lianos, M. 39
life-world 151
liminality 52–3, 54
limit-experience 55, 57
locality factor 27, 169–71
LOCSP 173
Luke, T. 146
Lushchen, G. 21, 32
lusiones 7
Lyng, S. 26, 27, 53–5
Lyotard, F. 79, 145, 148

McCall, M. 26
McCannell, D. 68–9
McGinn, B. 48
McGowan, A. 126–8, 129
McGuiness, E. 126
McRobbie, A. 177–8
Maffesoli, M. 140, 141, 142
Manchester United 110
Mansfield, A. 48
Marcuse, H. 149
marketisation 8–9
Marsh, P. 27
marxian interpretations 5, 7, 31
masculinities 147–8
Massachusetts, University of 24
Mathieson, T. 83
Mead, G. 20, 54, 55
media: celebrity 115–16; consumption 182; football violence 57, 123, 128; footballers 47, 116–17; gays 47–8; hermeneutics 24; local 124; marketisation 8–9; moral panic 35, 177–8; sport 4, 113
Meikle, N. 176–7, 178–9

men, domination 174, 185[7]n3; *see also*
    gender; masculinities
meritocracy 159
Merton, R. 21–2
metanarratives 79
metaphor 13
Mills, C. W. 89–90, 91
Millwall football club 34, 169
mind/body duality 69
misbehaviour 178
misogyny 131, 143, 148, 182
modernity 72–5
modernity, late 63–4
modernity, liquid: Bauman x, 7, 63–4, 65,
    66–7, 72–3, 158; confession 85; ethics
    101; Rojek 68; social control 106, 165
modernity, solid 65, 66, 67, 106, 141–2,
    166
Moore, B. 77
moral panic 35, 177–8
morality 21, 84, 157
Morgan, W. 32
Morris, A. 36
mugging 35
Mumford, L. 112
Murdoch, R. 109

Naffine, N. 37
Najeib, S. 117–18, 119, 123, 181, 182,
    183
narcissism 74–5
National Front 37
Natoli, J. 74, 94
neo-capitalism 79–80
neo-functionalism 24
neo-marxism 31, 32
News of the World 109, 120, 132, 176–7,
    178–80
nightclubs 116–18
non-conformity 157, 167, 175
non-places 134–5
non-responsibility 64–5
normalcy 8, 20
nowhereville 134–5, 143–4

The Observer 116
O'Connor, B. 131
O'Leary, D. 120
Olympic Games 30
Orwell, G. 43
otherness x, 171
overtraining 25
Owen, P. 124
Oxford joy-riding 83

paedophilia 40
panopticon 6, 43–4, 83, 84, 86, 167
Parsons, T. 21
passion 114
patriarchy 149, 150, 151
Patton, C. 48
performativity xi–xii; Baudrillard 77;
    consumption xi, 181; cruising 104–6,
    136, 140–2, 152, 180; deviance 78–81,
    183; drag 48, 80–1; Freud 148; gaze 49;
    gender 81, 149, 150; identity 81, 122,
    145; patriarchy 151; sublime 80; truth
    79–80; youth culture 185[7]n2
Phillips, A. 69
physical education 157, 158–60, 166
Pilz, G. 54
players 57, 142; *see also* footballers
pleasure 47, 70, 139
pleasure principle 8, 84–6
police 161
polysemy 74
Positive Futures initiative 106
positivism 20
postmodernism x, 46, 56, 79–80
poststructuralism 46, 68, 94, 128, 149
power 11, 26–7, 95, 96
The Premiership 109, 110
Presdee, M. 53, 55, 64–5, 76, 80, 83,
    146–7
Probation Officers 168
Prokop, U. 31, 157
Pronger, B. 44, 48
Protestant ethic 66
Pryce, L. 126
public domain 146–7
publicity 104
Pumping Iron films 48

queer theory 9–10, 48, 69

Rabinow, P. 47
race: class 124, 125; identity 170;
    stereotyping 162–3
racism: comedy 131–2; football
    tournament 169–71; footballers 115,
    121; gangs 37; stereotypes 125, 162–3;
    violence 116–19
rape 182
rape accusations 49, 176–80
Real Madrid 127
The Real McCoy 131
realism 36, 92, 101
reality 12, 14, 113, 135; *see also*
    hyper-reality

reality principle 8, 9, 84–6
rebellion 22
Redhead, S. 33
reflexivity 5, 67
relativism xi, 11–13, 91–2
repression 82, 167, 168
research process 88; poststructuralism 94; social enquiry 93; subjectivity 96–7; *see also* ethnography
resistance: functionalism 33; gender 37; incorporation 149; sport 157; subculture 24
responsibility xi, 8, 15, 102, 178, 180
retreatism 22, 25
rhetoric 99, 101
Ricoeur, P. xi, 151
Rigauer, B. 31, 157
Rinehart, R. 44, 97–8, 100, 101
risk 55, 64, 71–2
risk society 39, 54
ritual 22, 122, 148
Ritzer, G. 78, 112–13, 135
roasting 176–7, 180
Robins, D. 37
Robson, G. 34, 169
Rochdale Hornets 124
Rock, P.: criminology 36, 38; deviance 11; good/evil 21; sociology of deviance 5; *Understanding Deviance* 18–19, 42
Rodman, D. 10
Rojek, C.: abnormal leisure 51–2, 55–60, 59, 178; abnormal work 20; Baudrillard 113; critiqued 58–60; liquid modernity 68; morality 84; normal leisure 58–9; self/identity 56; serious leisure 50–1; wild leisure 27, 57, 133
Rorty, R. 3; deviant other x; irony 94; relativism 91–2; sociology of deviance 15; truth 102; unnoticed people 12–13, 88
rugby league press 124
rugby players 124–6
rugby songs 38
rule-breaking activities 4, 8, 15, 76–7
Rush, P. 37

sadomasochism 86
Sage, G. 21
scopophilia 83, 149–50
Scottish fans 53
Scull, A. 160
Sedgwick, E. 48
seduction 82
self: decentred 68; Freud 69; identity 56,

68–9; polysemy 74; social construction 78
self-government 87
self-injury 25, 71
self-loathing 56–7
self-reflexivity 46
Sennett, R. 171
sexism 143–4, 148, 173–4
sexual abuse 39–40, 77
sexual difference 48
sexual exploitation 38
sexuality 46–7, 129–31, 182
shame 84
Shaw, R. 110
Shaw, T. 132
Sheffield 28
Shergar 77
Simeone, D. 128
Simmel, G. 141
Simmons, M. 111, 113, 115–16, 181
Simon, J. 40, 82
Simpson, M. 173–4
Simpson, O. J. 113
skateboarding 24, 69–70
skinhead culture 33, 37
skydiving 53
Slaughter, P. 185[8]n5
Sloop, J. 49
Smart, C. 36
Smith, D. 68
Snow, D. 53
snowboarding 86
Snyder, E. 26
soap opera/football 104, 109–16
social behaviour 31, 157
social construction 78
social control 39; Bauman 153; community sport 106; liquid modernity 106, 165; moral panic 178; physical education 158–60; repression 82; working-class 158–60
social enquiry 46, 93
social exclusion 168, 171–2, 173
social inclusion 165, 173–4, 185[8]n5
social inequality 67, 159
social interactions 92, 139, 173
social psychological ethogenic approach 27
socialisation 21, 22
sociation 141
society: discipline 44; mechanical/organic 19; norms 21
sociological imagination xi, 40–1, 90–2, 102

sociology: censures 8, 9; deviance 5, 178; figurational 26–7, 28, 93; interpretive 23; realism 92; reflexivity 5; rhetoric 101
sociology of deviance 15; death of 3, 5, 50, 63, 178
sociology of sport 21, 63, 88, 90–1
solidarity 26
solvent abuse 57
space 85
space-time 145
Sparks, R. 63–4, 66–7, 159
spectacle 57–8, 133
spectators 33; *see also* fans
Spencer, H. 21
sport ix–xii; cartels 30; celebrity 58; commercialisation 31, 32; dangers 39, 71; ethic 25–6; feminism 37; functionalism 19, 21; gay and lesbian studies 37–8; health 18; individualisation 86; media 4, 113; morality 21, 157; passion 114; resistance 157; romanticised 156–7; rule-breaking activities 4, 76–7; sexual abuse 39–40; sexual exploitation 38; social behaviour 31, 157; socialisation 21, 22; surveillance 44; television 133; transgressive 48
sports geography 44
status 158
Stebbins, R. 50–1
Stephens, M. 133
Stephenson, A. 151
stereotypes: class 126; race 125, 162–3
Stone, G. 24
strain theory 22, 25
street racing 146–7
structural-functionalism 21
students 117–18
subculture: authenticity 33; cultural studies 32–3; female 37–8; resistance 24; skateboarding 24; violence 27
subjectivity 96–7
subversion 38; *see also* resistance
Sugden, J. 88–92, 93, 94–100
suicide 22
Sumner, C.: censures 6–8; death of sociology of deviance 35, 50, 63, 178; illusory concretion 14; relativism xi
Sunday Mirror 119
Sunday People 120
surface: body 75, 80; cruising 105, 139, 151; depth 89, 94–7, 101, 142
surveillance: confession 87; Foucault 42–3,

49, 82, 166; repression 82, 168; sport 44; *see also* panopticon; synopticon
Sutcliffe, P. 122
Sutherland, E. 29
Suttles, G. 27
swimming 40
symbolic interactionism 78
synopticon 75, 83–4, 86

Taylor, I. 36–7
Taylor, P. 103
Taylor, R. 124
televised sport 133
thick description 24
Thompson, E. P. 32
Thompson, H. S. 53–5, 89, 91
ticket distribution systems 30
ticket touting 89, 98–9
Tomlinson, A. 89–92, 93, 94–100, 133
Trainspotting 51
transformations 145, 148
Trifonas, P. 115
truth: CCTV 124, 125; journalism 100; performativity 79–80; Rorty 102
Turner, B. 51–2
Turner, V. 52
tyre shredding 134
Tyson, M. 4, 49, 58, 64, 113

underclass 37, 83

Valéry, P. 134
Venables, T. 109
videos 133
Vinnai, G. 31, 157
violence: crowd behaviour 57; figurational sociology 26; football 57, 123, 128; media 57; racism 116–19; rugby players 124–6; social psychological ethogenic approach 27; spectacle 57–8; spectators 33
Virillio, P. 138, 144–5
voyeurism 64, 131

Wacquant, L. 34, 92
Wagg, S. 53
Wakefield 134–5, 181, 182
Walker, C. 124
Ward, S. 89
Watkins, L. 112–13
Webb, J. 7
Weber, M.: bureaucracy 43; industrial capitalism 65; interpretive sociology 23; Protestant ethic 66

welfare services 167
Wellman, B. 140
Welsh, I. 51
Westwood, T. 131
Whannel, G. 35–6
Whyte, W. F. 97
Willis, P. 89, 158
Willmot, P. 161
Wittgenstein, L. 13
women 173–4; *see also* gender; young
    women
Woodgate, J. 119, 121, 183
work/leisure 49–50
working-class: communitarianism 37;
    social control 158–60; young men 32

World Cup 30, 77, 128
wrestling 53, 123

Yorkshire Post 124, 125
Young, A. 37
Young, J. 23, 36, 38–9, 177
Young, M. 161
young men 32
young women/cruising 139, 148–9, 151
Younge, G. 131–2
youth cultures 32, 185[7]n2
Youth Justice Board 165
Youth Offending Teams 168

zones, wild/tame 146